C000079054

Solidarity with...

Reading Gramsci

General Editors:

Peter Ives, Professor of Politics, University of Winnipeg
and
Adam David Morton, Professor of Political Economy,
University of Sydney

Also available

Gramsci, Culture and Anthropology
An Introductory Text
Kate Crehan

Language and Hegemony in Gramsci
Peter Ives

Unravelling Gramsci:
Hegemony and Passive Revolution in
the Global Political Economy
Adam David Morton

Subalternity, Antagonism, Autonomy:
Constructing the Political Subject
Massimo Modonesi

Translated by
Adriana V. Rendón Garrido and Philip Roberts

Gramsci on Tahrir
Revolution and Counter-Revolution in Egypt
Brecht De Smet

Solidarity without Borders

Gramscian Perspectives on Migration
and Civil Society Alliances

Edited by
Óscar García Agustín and Martin Bak Jørgensen

www.plutobooks.com

First published 2016 by Pluto Press
345 Archway Road, London N6 5AA

www.plutobooks.com

British Library Cataloguing in Publication Data
A catalogue record for this book is available from the British Library

ISBN   978 0 7453 3626 8   Hardback
ISBN   978 0 7453 3631 2   Paperback
ISBN   978 1 7837 1761 3   PDF eBook
ISBN   978 1 7837 1763 7   Kindle eBook
ISBN   978 1 7837 1762 0   EPUB eBook

This book is printed on paper suitable for recycling and made from fully managed and sustained forest sources. Logging, pulping and manufacturing processes are expected to conform to the environmental standards of the country of origin.

Typeset by Stanford DTP Services, Northampton, England

Simultaneously printed in the European Union and United States of America

Contents

PART IV: SPACES OF RESISTANCE

CONCLUSION

Series Preface

Antonio Gramsci (1891–1937) is one of the most frequently referenced political theorists and cultural critics of the twentieth century. His pre-disciplinary ideas and especially his articulation of hegemony are commonly referred to in international relations, social and political theory, political economy, historical sociology, critical geography, postcolonial studies, cultural studies, literary criticism, feminism, new social movements, critical anthropology, education studies, media studies and a host of other fields. And yet, his actual writings are steeped in the complex details of history, politics, philosophy, and culture that shaped Italy's formation as a nation-state as well as in the wider turmoil of twentieth-century world history.

Gramsci began his practical and intellectual odyssey when he moved to Turin University (1911). This move to mainland industrial Italy raised cultural and political contradictions for the young Sardinian, whose identity had been deeply formed by the conditions of uneven development in the 'South'. These issues were pursued by Gramsci whilst he devoted his energy to journalism (between 1914 and 1918) in the newspapers *Il Grido del Popolo*, *Avanti!* and *La Città Futura*. His activity centred on the Factory Council movement in Turin – a radical labour mobilisation – and editorship of the journal *L'Ordine Nuovo* (1919–20). Exasperated by the Italian Socialist Party's lack of leadership and effective action during the *Biennio Rosso*, Gramsci turned his attention to the founding and eventual leadership of the Italian Communist Party (PCd'I) as well as the organisation of the workers' newspaper *L'Unità* until 1926. Gramsci spent from May 1922 to December 1923 in the Soviet Union actively involved in organisational issues within the Communist International (Comintern). This included functioning on the Executive Committee of the Comintern in Moscow as the representative of the PCd'I and as a member of various commissions examining organisational, political, and procedural problems that linked the various national communist parties. During this period, Gramsci had direct contact with Leon Trotsky and led discussions on the 'Italian Question', including the united front tactics to tackle Fascism, the trade union relationship, and the limits of party centralism. These issues were developed by Gramsci through the work of ideological hegemony carried out by the PCd'I and, following his Moscow period, as a central author and architect of 'The Lyon Theses' –

a collection of positional statements on the tactics and strategies needed in response to Fascism. The theses are regarded as a major survey of the conditions of uneven development confronting social forces within Italy and the European states-system at the time.

By 1926, after drafting his famous essay 'Some Aspects of the Southern Question', Gramsci was arrested as a Communist Party deputy by the Fascist authorities and was incarcerated until a few days before his death in 1937. Gramsci wrote almost 500 letters in prison; over half were to his sister-in-law, Tatiana Schucht, who was living in Rome and became his key supporter and his most frequent visitor. She also conveyed Gramsci's ideas to another significant patron, Piero Sraffa, the Italian economist then at Cambridge. These letters constitute a rich mixture of intellectual, cultural, and political analysis as well as representing the daily struggle of prison life including Gramsci's increasingly severe health problems. But the most enduring and influential component of his legacy is the 33 notebooks penned between 1929 and 1936 that together constitute the *Quaderni del carcere* (*Prison Notebooks*). Tatiana Schucht hid these notebooks in a vault at the *Banca Commerciale Italiana* while she arranged for their transportation to Moscow. Publication of the *Prison Notebooks* in Italian ensued from the late 1940s onwards and has continued in various languages ever since.

The breadth of the above political and intellectual journey is perhaps matched by the depth of detail and coverage contained within Gramsci's pre-prison and prison writings. The study of intellectuals in Italy, their origins and grouping according to cultural currents; his engagement with, and critique of, Italy's most important intellectual of the time, Benedetto Croce; the study of comparative linguistics and the Italian language question; analysis of the Sicilian writer Luigi Pirandello and the potential his plays offered for transforming Italian culture and society; and discussion of the role of the serialised novel and popular taste in literature would be later expanded into a wider plan. This chiefly focused on Italian history in the nineteenth century, with special attention being directed to Italy's faltering entrance into capitalist modernity under conditions of 'passive revolution', including the imposition of a 'standard' Italian language; the theory of history and historiography; and the expansion of the capitalist labour process through assembly plant production techniques beyond the United States under the rubric of 'Americanism and Fordism'. In summary, issues of hegemony, consciousness, and the revolutionary process are at the centre of Gramsci's attention. It is for such reasons that Antonio Gramsci can be regarded as one of the most significant Marxists of the twentieth century, who merits inclusion in any register of classical social theorists.

Reading Gramsci, however, is no easy task. He plunges into the complexities of debates of his time that are now obscure to many readers and engages in an enormous range of topics that at first seem unrelated. Moreover, the prison conditions and his own method yield a set of open-ended, fragmented, and intricately layered *Prison Notebooks* whose connections and argumentation do not lead linearly from one note to the next, but seem to ripple and weave in many directions. This has sometimes led to aggravation on the part of Gramsci scholars when they see how often his name is invoked by those with quite partial or superficial understanding of these complexities. It has also generated frustration on the part of those who want to use Gramsci's ideas to illuminate their own studies, analyses, and political acumen. After all, while Gramsci himself was a meticulous researcher with a rigorous philological method, he was deeply committed to people understanding their own political and cultural contexts in order to engage and change them. These points, about the necessity of deploying an openness of reading Gramsci to capture the branching out of his thought *and* the necessity of deploying a practical interest in understanding the here and now of contemporary events, were central to Joseph Buttigieg's original idea for initiating this 'Reading Gramsci' series. Buttigieg's contributions to Gramscian scholarship extend also to his monumental and superbly edited and translated English critical edition of the *Prison Notebooks* (Columbia University Press), the final volumes of which are still in process. In keeping with Buttigieg's initial goals, this series aims to provide expert guides to key features and themes in Gramsci's writings in combination with the pressing political, social, and cultural struggles of our time. Rather than 'applying' Gramsci, the point of the series is to provide monographs that think through and internalise Gramsci's method of thinking about alternative historical and contemporary social conditions. Given that no single study can encapsulate the above political and intellectual depth and breadth, each volume in the 'Reading Gramsci' series is focused in such a way as to open readers to specific aspects of his work as well as raise new questions about our contemporary history.

Peter Ives
Adam David Morton

Preface and Acknowledgements

The story of this book begins in early 2013. The Arab Spring and the popular mobilisations in Europe and especially in countries like Greece and Spain created a rupture in the political order. The mobilisations gained our interest for several reasons. First of all they carried a social and political message we could identify with. Secondly, they implied some analytical aspects which we were intrigued by. The mobilisations constructed new civil society alliances and constituted new political subjectivities. We did not find it adequate to understand these movements within a conventional social movement framework. Something else was at stake. Later that year we visited colleagues in Norrköping in Sweden and started discussing the relevance of taking up a Gramscian perspective to develop an empirical, conceptual and political understanding of the contemporary forms of protest and mobilisation.

Getting back to Denmark the idea of working on an edited volume emerged. Our intention was to include both experts in Gramsci and experts in the relations between migration and civil society who were developing relevant and interesting work. Pluto Press went along with our idea; the editors of the 'Reading Gramsci' series, Adam David Morton and Peter Ives, have given us motivation and continuous support for the project. Likewise commissioning editor David Castle has been very supportive and made our cooperation with Pluto Press easy and fruitful. We are grateful for all the constructive suggestions we have received from all of them. We also thank the contributing authors of this book for their effort and contribution to enrich the perspectives on Gramsci and alliances between migration and civil society. We would also like to thank the three external readers who read the initial proposal and gave us constructive feedback. Our hope for the book is that it will inspire academics, activists, practitioners and those who are, in general, interested in the topic. We hope that it will be read as a tale of practices aiming at transforming the social and political order towards more solidary and inclusive societies. Gramsci was first and foremost a thinker of political practice and he deserves to be read in this way.

We would like to thank the Department of Culture and Global Studies, Aalborg University, for supporting us financially. Special thanks go to Annette Bruun Andersen for help with the English language. We are especially grateful for the support and patience of our families. Martin finished his part of the edited volume while he was in Andalucia with his wife Nienke and daughters Thilde, Sigga and Nellie. It was not easy bringing an infant to a mountain in Spain with no regular electricity after a 7,500 kilometre road trip – and not easy spending so much time in front of a laptop. He owes his family a great deal. Óscar thanks Lise, Kira, Linus and Marcos for helping him throughout the project by forging new and enjoyable forms of solidarity. Finally we would like to dedicate this book to the thousands of people struggling to change society and to expand a solidarity that goes beyond borders. These changes are needed.

Óscar García Agustín and Martin Bak Jørgensen
Aalborg, October 2015

Introduction

1

Solidarity without Borders: Gramscian Perspectives on Migration and Civil Society Alliances

Óscar García Agustín and Martin Bak Jørgensen

12 September 2015 marked an important day for an emerging solidarity movement. In more than 85 cities in 30 countries across Europe hundreds of thousands of protesters marched under banners of 'Refugees Welcome' and 'Europe Says Welcome'. Citizens participated in marches, demonstrations and other events during the day of action. The message was very clear: refugees are welcome here. In London the newly elected leader of the Labour Party, Jeremy Corbyn, spoke to more than 100,000 people joining the Refugees Welcome Here event. This can be read as an act of solidarity; but support for the message goes beyond participating in a single march and reflects the need for a new politics of migration in which civil society speaks out and opens new spaces of cooperation and of rethinking social identities.

During the months following the refugee crisis in Europe, we witnessed a popular mobilisation. The solidarity actions included a wide range of participants, from veteran activists and leftist militants to people who approached the issue from a humanitarian perspective. All of them agreed on the need for elaborating new migration policies, very different from the existing ones, which were considered inhumane and restrictive. In different countries initiatives have sprung up developing new forms of everyday politics and acts of solidarity. In Austria 2,200 drivers joined a campaign to pick up refugees stranded in Budapest. In Germany, Denmark and Sweden locals have organised support for arriving refugees, donating food, water, clothes and other supplies to those in need, sometimes using civil disobedience by smuggling refugees to neighbouring countries or sheltering refugees privately. In Iceland more than 11,000 Icelanders (out of a total population of approximately 323,000 people) offered to accommodate Syrian refugees in their private homes and pay their costs as a response to the government suggesting that it would accept 50 Syrian refugees. These are citizens' initiatives which all express a solidarity that is more than a symbolic support, but that constitutes a genuine attempt to spur social and political change and to demonstrate solidarity beyond borders in practice.

The emerging solidarity manifests itself not just from below however; cracks are also opening up in the established political system. In Barcelona the newly elected mayor Ada Colau challenged the Spanish government and proposed creating a network of refugee cities, following up the proposal with the suggestion that 10 million euros of surplus funds from 2015 be allocated for this purpose. In the United Kingdom the prime minister, David Cameron, arguably bowed to the pressure from the popular mobilisations taking place over the previous months and agreed that Britain should take in another 100,000 refugees. On an even larger scale, German chancellor Angela Merkel took the decision on 4 September to suspend European asylum rules and allow tens of thousands of refugees stranded in Hungary to enter Germany via Austria. The consequences of this decision are enormous, both in terms of the numbers of refugees involved and, even more significantly, for the future of the European asylum system.

How can these emerging solidarities between civil society and refugees be explained? It would clearly be insufficient to reduce them (as well as the social and political power they imply) to the political moment. Without denying the importance of that moment and its strong impact on European public opinion, the different kinds of solidarity that have been forged during the years prior to the refugee crisis must not be ignored. The actions of solidarity, many of them developed under unfavourable circumstances, have been carried out in different manners as a rejection of hegemonic migration politics. In this regard, we find it necessary to consider all those alliances and shaping of spaces of resistance which have enhanced a different way of understanding migration politics, produced within the civil society sphere. To account for those solidarities and their effects we find it intriguing to return to the ideas expressed by Antonio Gramsci and place them in dialogue with the current political and social context. The main reason for this choice is that 90 years ago Gramsci was already reflecting upon the potential of such popular mobilisations and the power of alliance building in expanding a conflict and bringing about social and political transformation.

GRAMSCIAN PERSPECTIVES

In 'Some Aspects of the Southern Question' (1926), Antonio Gramsci traces a geographical model (Said 1995) to explain the division of Italy into two regions, North and South, intertwined in a relation of exploitation between the industrialising North and the dependent South with its economy based on agriculture. The bourgeois democracy strengthened this asymmetry and the dominance of the North, using state power to reinforce the industrial development of the North and increasing the South's dependence. The bourgeoisie in the North and landowners in the South took advantage of this division and the lack of a common response by proletariat and peasants.

Indeed, Gramsci's main message in the 'Southern Question' is that proletariat and peasants should form a new alliance to change the hegemonic order. Solidarity between the subaltern groups (here subjects on the margins of history, immersed in the autonomous space of their own historicity; see Mellino in this volume) should be beneficial for both proletariat and peasants and enable them to transform social and economic relations and eliminate exploitation and dependence. Gramsci assigns to the proletariat the role of the leading class against capitalism that might attract other popular classes and incorporate the claims of the peasants into a unified struggle.

Today, Gramsci's reflections on the 'Southern Question' (and his work in general) are as relevant as they were then. The economic crisis which began in 2008 revealed a structural crisis of capitalism which was not limited to the financial or economic arenas. It turned into an *organic crisis* (i.e. a rupturing of the structure and superstructure) as political consensus dissolved and the ruling class was incapable of leading society forward. Especially in 2011, citizens mobilised, became politically active and rebelled against the capitalist system in the name of democracy. In 2015 we have seen citizens mobilising under paroles of humanitarian obligations and solidarity. However, it is unclear if these contestations will be constituted as a new *historical bloc* (i.e. a unity of structure and superstructure) with an alternative hegemonic system (i.e. hegemony obtained by a fundamental class exercising the intellectual, political and moral role of leadership as well as monopolising the 'common sense' within the system) (Mouffe 2014). Gramsci proposed an alliance between proletariat and peasants to form a new historical bloc. Nowadays it is still unclear who the social and political actors involved should be. In Gramsci's words, 'the old is dying but the new cannot [yet] be born' (Gramsci 1971: 275–6, Q3§34).[1] However, it is certain that the terrain of civil society has become the terrain for hegemonic struggles in which political society can only use coercion and not persuasion. We add the 'yet' in Gramsci's famous statement and investigate, in the contributions of this book, civil society alliances in historical and especially contemporary perspectives, reflecting on their potential to challenge the hegemonic system.

In recent years, there has been a growing literature on what can be characterised as Gramscian and neo-Gramscian perspectives on transnational solidarities in the era of neoliberalism (e.g. Bieler 2014; Bieler and Morton 2004; Featherstone 2012; Morton 2007). Approaches in this literature include case studies on the (transnational) labour movement, alliances between unions and social movements, subaltern class struggles, the global justice movement, anti-colonial struggles and lately anti-austerity struggles. They underline the fact that exploitation and resistance to exploitation cannot be reduced to material aspects, but include amongst others ethnic, nationalist, religious and gender-based identities, which are all engaged in struggles (Bieler and Morton 2004; Cox 1987). Despite a theoretical openness to diversifying struggles, there has been little focus on migrants. Our objective with this book is to analyse alliances in civil society comprising immigrants and non-immigrant actors that challenge the hegemonic order and undo the political closure which, in the form of consensus, has allowed the implementation of restrictive and exclusionary immigration and integration policies. The contributions offer long historical perspectives as well as case studies on contemporary issues. Their common focus is that they analyse alliances in civil society through Gramscian and neo-Gramscian perspectives.

The category of the migrant is characterised by heterogeneity. The same can be said for the analysis of migrants as political subjects. The chapters conceptualise migrant subjects from four angles: labour mobility, migration (both economic and political), colonialism and transnational relations. We here understand processes of subjectivisation as being produced by mechanisms of social and cultural exclusion, division of labour and ethnicisation in a context of global capitalism. Figures such as the numbers of precarious workers, refugees, undocumented migrants and labour migrants are analysed. Furthermore, we consider the multidimensional conception of migration in the dynamics of global capitalism necessary to understand how new alliances and relations of solidarity, with other members of civil society who are exposed to similar processes of precarisation, can emerge. In our opinion, this scenario makes it particularly relevant to rethink Gramsci in relation to migration.

Following Edward Said's and later Adam David Morton's (2013) approach, we read Gramsci's framework as a 'travelling theory'. Solidarity struggles are situated in place and space and on a hierarchy of scales. Gramsci's 'Some Aspects of the Southern Question' establishes the framework for understanding how new alliances are composed and their potential to change the capitalist system by different degrees and at different levels. We thus speak against more recent contributions like that of Richard Day (2005), who claims that 'Gramsci is dead' because he does not capture the demands of the latest social movements. We argue that Gramsci's analysis of alliances and solidarities is very much alive in the dynamics of subaltern political activism and the generative character of political struggle (Featherstone 2013). Consider for instance the emerging refugee solidarity movement *Venligboerne* (literally 'friendly inhabitants') in Denmark: its membership now numbers thousands of people across the country. This is not primarily an urban phenomenon; it started in the countryside and spread from there. Its activities include legal aid, practical help, medical support, language training, job-seeking assistance and everyday donations as well as engagement in political protest against what is believed to be a xenophobic policy. Rethinking 'Some Aspects of the Southern Question' entails addressing four important topics in order to understand the relation between immigration and civil society as resistance against the current hegemonic policies and political consensus:

1. The heterogeneity of political actors
2. Solidarity and alliances across and around borders
3. Avoiding misplaced alliances
4. Spaces of resistance

We consider these four dimensions, which correspond to the four parts of this book, useful for explaining the potential (as well as the limits) of civil society as spaces of resistance offering alternatives to the political closure on migration and integration policies.

THE HETEROGENEITY OF POLITICAL ACTORS

Gramsci supports the idea of the proletariat as the class that would propose and lead a new hegemony and defeat capitalism. He explains how Turin communists furthered their cause by including the Southern question on the agenda. Despite their vanguard role, workers could not lead social change without establishing new alliances, especially with the peasants in the South, in order to mobilise the working population. One social class cannot challenge the hegemonic order without opening up to other social actors. This conclusion does not derive from a general reflection about working classes but from a historical and situated reflection that makes every development unique. We have to contextualise social struggles if we want to understand why specific alliances are formed and what possibilities they represent.

The proletariat can no longer be the only class leading a process of social change. Other popular classes must be taken into account as well.

As Hall (1986) points out, we cannot expect a homogenous class to be decisive when an organic crisis occurs. It is more reasonable to think that the class composition will be complex. Furthermore, 'though such a political and social force has its roots in the fundamental class division of society, the actual forms of the political struggle will have a *wider* social character' (Hall 1986). For instance, the Occupy Wall Street movement has tried to change the terms of social conflict by distinguishing between the 99 per cent (the people) and the 1 per cent (the representatives of the interests of capital). This reflects the effort of rethinking a more inclusive conception of class composition which is open to other groups, and not only the proletariat. In this sense, it is possible to move beyond the interests of those particular groups and identify common goals. Gramsci talked already about the need to overcome particularism as the only way to include different kinds of workers and peasants:

> [I]t is necessary – in order to win the trust and consent of the peasants and of some semiproletarian urban categories – to overcome certain prejudices and conquer certain forms of egoism which can and do subsist within the working class as such, even when craft particularism has disappeared. The metalworker, the joiner, the building-worker, etc., must not only think as proletarians, and no longer as metalworker, joiner, building-worker, etc.; they must also take a further step. They must think as workers who are members of a class which aims to lead the peasants and intellectuals. (Gramsci 1978: 448)

The heterogeneity of the political actors has to be included in and reflected by categories such as 'multitude' (Hardt and Negri 2004; Virno 2004) or 'depolarised pluralities' (de Sousa Santos 2006). However, it is not easy to account for the composition of this complex heterogeneity. Ernesto Laclau and Chantal Mouffe (1985) refer to the 'logic of difference and equivalence' to depict how a coalition of plural, quite diverse actors could lead to a new form of hegemony. The economic crisis has intensified the plurality of political subjectivities (Hardt and Negri 2012) and made the economic dimension of social inequalities, which are not necessarily linked only to the division of labour, more evident. All these elements must be taken into consideration to understand how the 'subaltern' becomes a subject of history in the constant shaping and reshaping of power relations (Capuzzo and Mezzadra 2012).

The plurality of subjectivities includes workers, the unemployed, different categories of immigrants (political and economic refugees, undocumented and documented immigrants, expatriates, etc.) and less obvious groups such as the indebted (Lazzarato 2012) or what has been labelled as the 'precariat' (Standing 2011) and reflects the new economic and social divisions caused by capitalism. The configuration of the plurality of subjectivities should be reflected in a moment of organic crisis and solidarity must be constituted based on such a diversity in which it is difficult to imagine the working class playing a leading role, although it must clearly be included and be an active part of it.

Part I of the book includes three contributions on this topic. Ursula Apitzsch argues, in a historiographical reading of Gramsci, that his thoughts regarding the so-called 'subaltern social strata' supply a wealth of ideas relating to precisely the connection between migration and the Southern question: as a hegemonic framework in which dominated and subordinated cultures encounter each other. She further claims that it is necessary to reflect on the process by which the entire complex develops not only in the framework of the Italian nation state but also in the context of new European challenges. In the chapter by Nazlı Şenses and Kıvanç Özcan they employ a neo-Gramscian framework to challenge the now commonly accepted claim that the Gezi protests in Istanbul can be read as a middle-class phenomenon. They emphasise that the heterogeneity of the social composition of the protesters was a conjunction of diverse antagonisms in which different classes, ethnic and religious groups coalesced against the government. They focus on the role of internal migrants and minorities within Turkey and show how especially the Kurdish and Alevi minorities, who reside in migrant neighbourhoods, disturb the idea of homogeneous middle-class participation in the Gezi protests. Miguel Mellino offers a theoretical perspective from cultural and postcolonial studies. He argues that focusing on the anomalies of postcolonial translations of Gramsci's toolbox reveals the economic and political configuration of the contemporary world and of global (postcolonial) capitalism. He links the postcolonial reading of Gramsci to migration and citizenship struggles in Europe and argues that they constitute a privileged arena from which to regard the current neoliberal capitalism as postcolonial capitalism.

SOLIDARITY AND ALLIANCES

It is made very clear in 'Some Aspects of the Southern Question' that the two main social forces, the proletariat and the peasants, must create an alliance in opposition to the hegemonic bloc. It is important to recognise that the resulting unity is not automatic and dependent on the position of the political actors in the mode of economic production but rather emerges due to a system of alliances (Hall 1986). The conformation of alliances among civil society actors opposed to the hegemonic forces raises the question of solidarity:

> The Northern bourgeoisie has subjugated the South of Italy and the Islands, and reduced them to exploitable colonies; by emancipating itself from capitalist slavery, the Northern proletariat will emancipate the Southern peasant masses enslaved to the banks and the parasitic industry of the North. The economic and political regeneration of the peasants should not be sought in a division of uncultivated or poorly cultivated lands, but in the solidarity of the industrial proletariat. This in turn needs the solidarity of the peasantry and has an 'interest' in ensuring that capitalism is not reborn economically from landed property; that Southern Italy and the Islands do not become a military base for capitalist counterrevolution. (Gramsci 1978: 442)

Class alliances are necessary to fight the hegemonic system and they imply an understanding of how inequalities affect different classes and the responsibility of the ruling classes therein. The heterogeneity of political actors can only converge in a complex social composition if they manage to identify the diverse oppressive effects of the dominant order. This plurality generates a relation of solidarity that benefits all parties as the possibility of challenging the system is enhanced. Thus, solidarity becomes essential in promoting social change from civil society.

Solidarity cannot precede political actors nor can political actors impose their identities or interest upon others. The only way to ensure that solidarity is going to be in the 'interest' of all involved actors is that their positions are mutually constitutive, as in the case of peasants and industrial workers (Featherstone 2012). The practices that construct solidarity are transformative and allow us to focus on the importance of political organisation and interaction with other political actors. In other words, as emphasised by Featherstone (2012), solidarity as practice means that it is not only a matter of well-defined identities and ideas, but also an active process in which different political struggles are connected.

In Gramsci's words, ideas that 'organise human masses, and create the terrain on which men move, acquire consciousness of their position, struggle' are organic (Gramsci 1971: 376–7, Q7§19). Practices of solidarity revolve around such ideas: they can shatter the common sense and develop alternatives. Studies of the cooperation between the unions and social movements have shown how such alternatives can be developed (Bieler 2014; Bieler and Morton 2004; Munck 2002). Such studies entail focusing on the political formations – alliances – which the subaltern activists constitute and the way in which they set forward claims or assert their autonomy of action within the prevailing hegemony (Morton 2007: 174). This coming-into-being as groups and as political subjects draws parallels with Sylvère Lotringer's analysis of autonomous struggles among the Italian working class in a setting of post-industrial social conflicts. In 'The Return of Politics', he captures some basic characteristics of autonomous struggles. Autonomy is a 'body without organs of politics, anti-hierarchic, anti-dialectic, anti-representative. It is not only a political project ..., it is a project for existence' (in Lotringer and Marazzi 1980: 8). Autonomous formations do not develop in a vacuum. They develop in a structural context, but the structures do not determine agency in the present. They can, as Bieler argues, 'prevent, constrain or enable agency' and may 'be changed by collective agency' (Bieler 2014: 116).

Concerning the new alliances between civil society and immigrants, the question is not an identitarian one but rather it is about how different political actors converge in ongoing social struggles in order to undo the political closure. As mentioned above, the plurality of actors involved in the fight for fairer immigration and integration policies must find a way to include this diversity and avoid the dominance of certain forms of particularism. This entails, among other things, equating ethnic struggles with class struggles, which implies combining the fight for emancipation with claims of economic redistribution. Immigrant struggles for rights can and must be connected to the anti-austerity struggles. The *International Coalition of Sans-Papiers and Migrants* organising alongside the European precarity movement is one such example. The Refugees Welcome campaign is another. Here it is evident that the way in which refugees and immigrants are treated can become a proxy for the rest of society. If immigrants can do without social benefits or rights so can native unemployed. If refugees are paid less for comparable work done by others, wages can be lowered in the future. Solidarities from below (Featherstone 2012), as practised in different settings and on different levels – from the local to the global – ensure the conformation and redefinition of political identities in defence of the common, but also as constituting a shared understanding of what the common is. In this sense, it is relevant to explore the relations among actors working with migrants, such as trade unions, NGOs, social movements, immigrants' organisations, local communities, etc., as well as the alliances they constitute through their practices.

Part II contains three chapters. Derek Boothman, like Apitzsch, takes a historiographical approach in outlining the importance of alliances in Gramsci's writings and for contemporary migration issues. More specifically, Boothman argues that possible lines of reconstructing

Gramsci's approach to alliances are expressed in both the prison and the pre-prison period and draws on this approach to reflect on how Gramsci's ideas may or should be rethought now by connecting them to aspects of the United Kingdom and immigration there. Mary Hyland and Ronald Munck investigate solidarity and alliances by looking at relations between workers, migrants and trade unions. They argue that the movement of labour is inseparable from the generation of a labour movement. In a Gramscian perspective, a relationship between workers and migrants is a contingent process of political articulation in an open ensemble whose elements are always relational. Hyland and Munck analyse the roles of trade unions in regard to workers, migrants and the new figure of the precarious worker migrant and show how the trade unions forged a hegemonic alliance against any xenophobic reactions and created a new 'common sense' through which migrants became the 'new Irish'. Laurence Cox offers a different perspective on civil society. He draws on Gramsci to tackle some of the problems involved in giving an adequate account of the specificities of Irish social movements, with particular reference to migration *out of* Ireland, the role of 'outsiders' to the local community within Irish activism, and the recent upsurge in international migration to Ireland. In this chapter he seeks to translate Gramsci's analysis of Italy to an Irish context.

AVOIDING MISPLACED ALLIANCES

The fight against misplaced alliances (Mayo 2008) is as important as solidarity in building a new system of alliances within civil society. Underlining the geographical (and economic and political) distinction between the North and South of Italy, Gramsci reveals how the bourgeoisie of the North produce a simplified and negative picture of the Southerners. Besides the identitarian essentialism, it is worrying that the economic causes of inequality remain hidden and only cultural reasons are put forward. This sort of argumentation (which Gramsci calls propaganda) makes it impossible to create ties of solidarity between North and South and it strengthens the exclusionary understanding of the cultural community, in this case the North, which is defined as the positive side of the lack of qualities attributed to the South.

> It is well known what kind of ideology has been disseminated in myriad ways among the masses in the North, by the propagandists of the bourgeoisie: the South is the ball and chain which prevents the social development of Italy from progressing more rapidly; the Southerners are biologically inferior beings, semi-barbarians or total

barbarians, by natural destiny; if the South is backward, the fault does not lie with the capitalist system or with any other historical cause, but with Nature, which has made the Southerners lazy, incapable, criminal and barbaric – only tempering this harsh fate with the purely individual explosion of a few great geniuses, like isolated palm-trees in an arid and barren desert. (Gramsci 1978: 444)

The financial crisis has reinforced the division between North and South in the European Union (with Germany and Greece as the most obvious representatives), and it has likewise reinforced the ideologies, myths and prejudices contained in cultural explanations of the crisis, for example, that the Greeks are lazy and abuse state benefits. As a wider phenomenon, and yet quite recognisable in Greece, the emergence of populist right-wing movements and parties complicates the solidarity between civil society and immigrants because it creates a misplaced alliance within national communities.

Instead of constructing solidarity with other groups in similar states of precariousness, for example immigrants, the working class is attracted to the neo-fascist discourse (Mayo 2008). Misplaced alliances hinder the recognition of a subaltern, albeit heterogeneous, class and set the agenda for homogeneity as the main goal, ignoring the consequences of the capitalist system. Furthermore, trade unions, as representatives of the working class, sometimes prioritise misplaced alliances that are prejudicial to immigrants' rights. Referring to the Southern syndicalism and the role of intellectuals, Gramsci warned about the 'gradual passage of syndicalist leaders into the bourgeois camp' assuming the ideas of the latter especially regarding two topics, namely emigration and free trade.

In sum, solidarity must enhance civil society alliances and, at the same time, fight against misplaced alliances that would explain the emergence of the populist right wing and the occasional division between working class and immigrants. If the shaping of new alliances fails, the hegemonic system remains unquestioned and the lack of awareness of expansive precariousness allows for the reproduction of social and economic inequalities.

Part III offers two chapters on this topic. In his reading of Gramsci's analysis of the Italian migratory contexts of his time and the strange alliances forged, Peter Mayo argues that these are relevant in the contemporary context of migration across the Mediterranean and the risk that misplaced alliances between capital/business and labour form against projected 'enemies', such as 'foreign competition' and migrant labour power. He argues that without an educational strategy, work-ing-class people, living in a state of precariousness, are likely to be attracted to the populist right-wing parties that are gaining strength across Europe, which might ultimately increase segmentation among workers along ethnic lines. Óscar García Agustín and Martin Bak Jørgensen likewise tackle the issue of misplaced alliances. Using the same diagnosis as Mayo, they argue that the neoliberal restructuring of economy, labour markets and welfare states has had pronounced effects on life conditions for people living in different states of precariousness. Taking up Gramsci's emphasis in the 'Southern Question' on the danger of misplaced alliances and his reflections on how to generate solidarity, their chapter examines the construction and dynamics of misplaced alliances in a Danish context. It analyses how relations amongst migration, the nation state, the welfare state, the EU and protectionism constitute a misplaced alliance which reinforces divisions in society and thereby processes of marginalisation, segregation and xenophobia.

SPACES OF RESISTANCE

The alliance between proletariat and peasants represents a geography of solidarity between the North and the South. However, this is not merely a geographic distinction; it is also grounded historically and constituted economically and politically. 'Some Aspects of the Southern Question' is primarily concerned with the national sphere, but it does comment briefly on internationalisation using other scales such as the regional and the local. Indeed, Gramsci is capable of comprehending the interaction between different spatial scales and relating them to economic and social conditions. To explain why the peasants did not succeed in creating a centralised expression of their interests, Gramsci appeals to the intertwined geographic and economic causes:

> The South can be defined as a great social disintegration. The peasants, who make up the great majority of its population, have no cohesion among themselves (of course, some exceptions must be made: Apulia, Sardinia, Sicily, where there exist special characteristics within the great canvas of the South's structure). Southern society is a great agrarian bloc, made up of three social layers: the great amorphous, disintegrated mass of the peasantry; the intellectuals of the petty and medium rural bourgeoisie; and the big landowners and great intellectuals. (Gramsci 1978: 458)

The approach to the formation of civil society alliances must begin with the understanding of the geographies of resistance, that is, how alliances and practices of solidarity are constituted at different scales, ranging from the local to the global. Following Gramsci, Bob Jessop (2007) argues that the analysis of social forces and their alliances must be spatialised. The alliance between the proletariat and the peasants responds to the diversity of political, economic and social conditions in the North and in the South. There is no universal formula for constituting alliances. Gramsci was against generalisations that are not rooted in spatial conditions and against nationalism as methodology (Jessop 2007), not because of the predominance of the global logic (Beck 1999) but because of the interconnection between all scales: local, regional, national, international and transnational.

As Bieler and Morton (2004) have argued, hegemony is never static. It is constantly constructed and contested through combinations of structural and agential processes. Global resistance is given meaning through local responses (Morton 2007). Solidarities and connections are ongoing, productive and contested and must be analysed through relations of power. They are not generated and constructed as static objects with fixed interests, but carve out new common grounds. Formations of alliances are situated in history and space and must be analysed with respect to the multi-scalar forms of organising. The spaces of resistance are important for understanding civil society alliances. The 2011 protests appropriated space through encampments in order to give visibility to alternative ways of conceiving and practising democracy. According to Gramsci, space does not exist in itself, 'independently of the specific social relations that construct it, reproduce it, and occur within it' (Jessop 2007: 105). Herein lies the relevance of looking at how diverse political actors interact. Combining spaces and scales makes it possible to account for social struggles within and amongst contemporary civil societies and how these struggles challenge the hegemonic order (at different levels) with reference to migrants, migration, integration and diversity.

The three chapters in Part IV of the book scrutinise different spaces of resistance. David Featherstone underlines Gramsci's claim in 'Some Aspects of the Southern Question' that connections and solidarities are generative as particularly relevant for the contemporary conjuncture of crisis and austerity. He uses Stuart Hall's argument that race is a 'key' to interpreting crises to analyse how different struggles in the past have sought to engage with solidaristic alternatives in contexts of crisis and austerity and in opposition to racist articulations of migration. He argues that 'subalternised mobilities can be important to shaping political alternatives which might offer alternatives to the divisive geographies of austerity and crisis'. Lisa Kings, Aleksandra Ålund and Nazem Tahvilzadeh outline a neo-Gramscian perspective on ideological hegemony of the state and its institutional apparatus – both including and subordinating civil society – to analyse the contemporary rise of the Swedish urban justice movement in relation to political and ideological production of contemporary urban politics in Sweden. They argue that the urban justice movement with its focus on space, 'orten' (neighbour-hoods), has been part of bringing forward and merging local solidarities, thus grounding a social space of resistance in Sweden. It has positioned itself as a public voice against polarised development of contemporary urban, social landscape and, in sum, has become a base for solidarity and a potential space of resistance. In the final chapter, Susi Meret and Elisabetta Della Corte analyse the collective resistance undertaken by a formation of sub-Saharan African migrants in Hamburg – the Lampedusa in Hamburg group. Employing Gramsci's concepts of hegemony, dominant relationships of (economic, social, political) power and subalternity, they analyse migrants' resistance today. They argue that this particular space of resistance harbours 'architects' of new political subjectivities and collective identities. It is in these spaces that migrants start to organise, mobilise and to verbalise their right to live, work, move freely and stay like the majority of the population. They link this analysis to the forging of alliances and solidarity between migrant organic intellectuality and advocacy groups, as well as a civil society that can understand the common sense of their claims.

SOLIDARITIES WITHOUT BORDERS

'The categories of "refugees", "migrants", and "citizens" ... create borders between people. The division of people and countries by borders kills human beings daily. Abolish all borders! Stop the killing!' (March for Freedom 2014; translated from French). This rallying cry was used in the transnational solidarity march 'Freedom Not Frontex', which originated in cities all over Europe (especially Germany) and ended in Brussels in May 2014. The subsequent Action Week in Brussels in conjunction with the European Council meeting was supported by Blockupy but it was self-organised and directed by refugee actors. This event strengthened the link between struggles of migrants and refugees with anti-austerity politics and thereby broadened the conflict and expanded the political space for struggle. Referring to the commonalities in the precarious conditions of immigrant and non-immigrant actors might create a new unity. The national precarity movements (uniting sans-papiers) from different European countries (France, Belgium, Italy) were among the central organisers in Brussels. The struggles illustrate what Néstor Rodríguez (1996) in a US setting has termed 'the battle for the border'.

He shows how borders on the one hand are contested by autonomous (immigrant) actors who challenge the established stratified socio-spatial global order, and on the other hand are defended and reified by the authorities in an attempt to halt irregular migration and curtail regular migration.

Will such events change the conditions for migrants, regular and irregular, living in European countries? Is this an example of what 'is not yet born'? The event embodies a focal point in this book: alliances must be analysed beyond borders – 'real' (that is, geographical) borders as well as categorical borders. Both must be transgressed to understand the new modes of contestation and resistance we currently identify in Europe.

Reading Gramsci as a spatial thinker, as Jessop, Morton and Said do, allows us also to think analytically beyond the constraints of borders. This approach demonstrates that Gramsci recognised that the national was 'nodal' rather than 'dominant' (Jessop 2007; Morton 2007). Gramsci went beyond spatial metaphors and deployed a programmatic and politically strategic terminology to write about the social contestation over territory and space (Morton 2013: 51). Using Gramsci's framework as a travelling theory, we follow the same approach in this book to examine where a historical bloc can be founded. Can 'counter' hegemony develop outside the nation state? This book cannot answer that question fully, but the chapters offer different directions on how this might develop.

Thinking beyond categorical borders requires, on the one hand, that we do not subordinate relations of race, ethnicity, gender, nationality, etc. to those of class struggle and, on the other hand, that we do not let these categories cause division and fragmentation. This is a difficult task. We can pursue this by identifying practices. In the age of austerity, experiences from Greece show how resistance to austerity includes diverse forms of solidarity and initiatives to create alternatives (Bieler 2014). Similar practices can be identified in Spain. The challenge here is to understand how social divisions of interests can be overcome. Analytically, we draw on Featherstone's understanding of solidarity (Featherstone 2012: 4–7). Solidarities can develop across borders since they are transformative relations and forged from below. Since political activism and alliances refuse to stay within the container of the nation state, they are constructed through uneven power relations and geographies (in interactions between different spaces and scales). Finally, solidarities are 'inventive', they produce new configurations of political relations, political subjectivities and spaces. Solidarity is not a given. This position opens up the possibility for reading the diversity of struggles and for analysing the formation of alliances in civil society as constitutive, productive and basically as politics. Gramsci's analyses in

'Some Aspects of the Southern Question' and in his other works underpin all these understandings and show a potency and vitality for analysing national and transnational social struggles and a new collective political will in the twenty-first century. The chapters in this book take up this challenge and investigate how this might be identified in practice.

NOTE

1. Here we follow the standard convention associated with citing the *Prison Notebooks* (Morton 2007). In addition to giving the reference to the selected anthologies, the notebook number (Q) and section (§) accompanies all citations, to enable the reader to trace their specific collocations. The concordance table used is that compiled by Marcus E. Green and is available at the website of the International Gramsci Society (www.internationalgramscisociety.org/resources/concordance_table/anthologies.html).

REFERENCES

Beck, U. 1999. *What Is Globalization?* Cambridge: Polity Press.

Bieler, A. 2014. 'Transnational Labour Solidarity in (the) Crisis'. *Global Labour Journal* 5(2): 114–33.

—— and Morton, A.D. 2004. '"Another Europe is Possible"? Labour and Social Movements at the European Social Forum'. *Globalizations* 1/2: 303–25.

Capuzzo, P. and Mezzadra, S. 2012. 'Provincializing the Italian Reading of Gramsci'. In *The Postcolonial Gramsci*. London: Routledge: 34–54.

Cox, R. 1987. *Production, Power, and World Order: Social Forces in the Making of History*, vol.i. Columbia University Press.

Day, R. 2005. *Gramsci is Dead*. London: Pluto Press.

Featherstone, D. 2012. *Solidarity: Hidden Histories and Geographies of Internationalism*. London: Zed Books.

—— 2013. 'Gramsci in Action'. In M. Ekers et al. (eds). *Gramsci: Space, Nature, Politics*. Oxford: Wiley-Blackwell.

Gramsci, A. 1971. *Selections from the Prison Notebooks*, ed. and trans. Q. Hoare and G. Nowell-Smith. London: Lawrence and Wishart.

—— 1978. *Selections from Political Writings, 1921–1926*, ed. and trans. Q. Hoare. New York: International.

Hall, S. 1986. 'Gramsci's Relevance for the Study of Race and Ethnicity'. *Journal of Communication Inquiry* 10: 5–27.

Hardt, M. and Negri, A. 2004. *Multitude: War and Democracy in the Age of Empire*. London: Penguin Books.

—— —— 2012. *Declaration*. Ebook: Kindle.

Jessop, B. 2007. *State Power: A Strategic–Relational Approach*. Cambridge: Polity Press.

Laclau, E. and Mouffe, C. 1985. *Hegemony and Socialist Strategy: Towards a Radical Democratic Politics*. London: Verso.

Lazzarato, M. 2012. *The Making of the Indebted Man*. New York: Semiotext(e).

Lotringer, S. and Marazzi, C. 1980. 'The Return of Politics'. In S. Lotringer and C. Marazzi (eds). *Autonomia: Post-Political Politics*. Los Angeles: Semiotext(e).

March for Freedom. 2014. *Contre Accords de Schengen*. http://freedomnotfrontex.noblogs.org/files/2014/06/anti-schengen-front-french_merged1.pdf

Mayo, P. 2008. 'Antonio Gramsci and his Relevance for the Education of Adults'. *Educational Philosophy and Theory* 40 (3): 418–35.

Morton, A.D. 2007. *Unravelling Gramsci: Hegemony and Passive Revolution in the Global Economy*. London: Pluto Press.

—— 2013. 'Travelling with Gramsci'. In M. Ekers et al. (eds). *Gramsci: Space, Nature, Politics*. Oxford: Wiley-Blackwell.

Mouffe, C. (2014 [1979]). *Gramsci and Marxist Theory*. London: Routledge.

Munck, R. 2002. *Globalization and Labour: The New 'Great Transformation'*. London: Zed Books.

Rodríguez, N. 1996. 'Immigration: A Civil Rights Issue for the Americas in the 21st Century'. *Social Justice* 23(3)(65): 21–37.

Said, E. 1995. *Orientalism*. London: Penguin.

Sousa Santos, B. de 2006. *The Rise of the Global Left: The World Social Forum and Beyond*. London and New York: Zed Books.

Standing, G. 2011. *The Precariat: The New Dangerous Class*. London: Bloomsbury Academic.

Virno, P. 2004. *A Grammar of the Multitude: For an Analysis of Contemporary Forms of Life*. New York: Semiotext(e).

Part I

The Heterogeneity of Political Actors

2

Gramsci's 'Philosophy of Praxis' and the Topic of Migration

Ursula Apitzsch

The theme of 'emigration' is one of the *'argomenti principali'* (principle topics) listed by Antonio Gramsci on 8 February 1929 in his first prison notebook. His concern is very clearly to criticise culturalist analyses of emigration from the Italian South and to counter these with an approach derived from his 'philosophy of praxis' and the understanding of subalternity. Can his categories and empirical analyses still be useful for the study of recent migration processes from the global South to Europe?

Some thoughts and categories developed by Gramsci from the workers' council's 'Ordine Nuovo' period to the *Prison Notebooks* seem particularly relevant in that:

- he views emigration processes from the South and immigration processes in the North as social phenomena of one and the same dynamics of a specific (hegemonic) type of political and social development;
- he sees migration as a global phenomenon, bearing in mind the spread of Italian labour over the whole world;
- he wants to understand the culturally particular, in its marginalised and folklorised subaltern form, as well as its role in a new form of *civiltà*.

In order to elaborate and evaluate those hypotheses, however, we have (1) to look more closely at the relationships between what he describes as the 'Southern question' and his critique of the common categories of the analysis of migration processes; (2) to understand in detail what he describes as 'subalternity' in the context of the Southern question and the role of intellectuals; and (3), in conclusion, to evaluate what his categories can mean to us today for the question of disparities and possible alliances in migration processes.

GRAMSCI'S CRITIQUE OF THE
CULTURALIST VIEW ON MIGRATION

Gramsci makes particular reference to the fact that the society which loses emigrants is very reluctant to reflect on the phenomenon of migration. Nor does migration comply with the notion of human worth inherent in popular consciousness in the North. It provokes images of the terrible and reluctantly discussed side of the Italian Risorgimento, the unresolved issue of the economic and social 'backwardness' of the South. In response to an article printed in the *Pegaso* magazine in September 1930, which dealt with the curious phenomenon that while Italian labour is distributed over the entire planet, there is hardly any literature in Italy which deals with the subject, Gramsci writes:

> That writers concern themselves little with the emigrant abroad is less surprising than the fact that they do not deal with the life he leads before actual emigration, in other words with the conditions that compel him to emigrate; ... which are bound up with the inner process of emigration, long before the actual journey to a foreign country. (Gramsci 1975b: 2254, Q23)

One of the few literary works about migration from Italy known at Gramsci's time (besides those portraying the 'American Myth', such as De Amici's) was Francesco Perri's novel *The Emigrants*. This story deals with the historical conflict that gave rise to emigration from Calabria, but in Gramsci's view it obscures and mystifies more than it reveals.

> It is apparent that Perri is not directly familiar with the simple life of the Calabrians through his own emotional and psychological experience, but that he makes use of the old regionalist clichés.... The absence of any historical sense is intentional, since this enables him to treat all folklore themes as a homogenous mass, whereas in reality they differ greatly in space and time. (Gramsci 1975b: 2201f., Q23)

Gramsci is referring here to a procedure within culturalism that ascribes and typifies particular characteristics, something that can frequently be observed in present-day studies on migration (Apitzsch 1995). Gramsci returns to the real historical background to migration processes by discussing FIAT's policies for the recruitment of migrant labourers. He refers to Agnelli's policy in 1925–26, when 25,000 Sicilians were recruited as labour migrants for the factories in Turin. The attempt failed miserably. The Sicilians, who were supposed to live in barrack-like accommodation where strict internal discipline was maintained, fled in droves from the factory to nearby farms in search of work. The criminal records of those years reinforced even more the Sicilians' reputation as brigands.

What is interesting here is that Gramsci's treatment of the event does not include any reference to general cultural peculiarities of the Sicilians. Instead, he sees it as a continuation of the old struggle between the Piedmontese and the Sicilians, between the industrial North and the peasant South. The migrants, who originally came on a 'voluntary' basis, recognised immediately on entering the barracks that there was a connection between migration and the history of their colonisation. For Gramsci, the Sardinian chronicler who can draw parallels very quickly with the state of virtual war between the Piedmontese and the Sardinians, these Sicilians and their ways of behaving are in no sense 'alien'.

Gramsci, using a methodological approach familiar to us from eth-nomethodology and psychoanalysis, reverses the angle of vision to that of 'the alien' himself. It is not the immigrants that are alien, since the causes for their collective behaviour are easily identified; instead, those groups and social formations that come into being in the large factories as a consequence of capitalist factory owners' behaviour are the subjects that are alien not only for politicians and political scientists but also for ordinary people. This is an aspect that Gramsci discussed even before the Ordine Nuovo period, shortly after the end of the First World War, and to which he often returned in the *Prison Notebooks*. Unlike other Marxist theorists, Gramsci finds the idea of all proletarians uniting both abstract and insufficient – what interests him instead is the specifically new that comes into being in the melting pot of the large factory. For Gramsci it is important that the new can only be created when what happens to the subjects in this process is autonomously grasped as something essentially new. In one of his first articles about 'Socialism and Culture', written in 1916 (Gramsci 1975a: 22ff., SG), Gramsci quotes Novalis to show that the prerequisite for understanding the alien is the understand-ing of oneself. In 1916, Gramsci termed this a 'transcendental' aspect. By linking the 'transcendental' component of early Romanticism with Vico's work on the 'First Corollary concerning the speech in poetic characters of the first nations', he then goes a step further in his analysis of the 'alien'. The members of the dominant minority do not have to 'understand' the majority, but instead it is the subordinated groups who should discover themselves and thereby develop their universal claim to equal civil rights.

What makes Gramsci's writings such a rich source of material today for solving the problems of multinational and multicultural coexistence is the fact that he does not reduce the social problems associated with differing degrees of modernity to the relationship between native people and foreigners, but defines these differences as a problem of modern consciousness generally. Modern consciousness is characterised for him by the fact that only through 'folkloristic' distortions is it able to retain certain moments of its rural prehistory and the counter-knowledge rooted in and dominated by the process of modernisation. The relationship of such sedimented collective experience to industrial society is by no means identical to the relationship between traditional and modern societies; *this difference in degree of modernity is much rather a crucial defining aspect of modern society itself.* Gramsci developed this aspect with extraordinary clarity in his 27th prison notebook. According to his analysis, so-called 'folklore' research cannot be conducted in isolation from 'official' world views in the dominant society.

Gramsci's reflections on folklore are provoked by a question that might be posed today in the context of migration from rural to post-industrial areas, without losing any of its relevance. Gramsci states his position on the question as to whether or not folklore should be taught at teacher-training establishments. 'To deepen the impartial culture of the teachers? To show them the object that they should not destroy?' (Gramsci 1975b: Q23§13). Gramsci poses this question in precisely the same sense in which one could ask today whether it is necessary to include an introduction to alien cultures in teacher-training courses. The answer, for Gramsci, will depend significantly on whether the introduction of such new syllabus content is nothing more than 'firing broadsides at folklore' – in other words, to convince the younger generations of migrants that they are caught up in a culture that must be overcome, or which is seen 'as an eccentricity, an oddity or a picturesque element' – or whether such cultural activity should be seen as a serious matter which should also be taken seriously. In Gramsci's view, the issue is not to choose between the illusory alternatives of pluralism and universalism – in other words, the point is not whether one accepts the Ptolemaic system as an element of folklore or whether it is combatted as archaic and a barrier to progress. Both reactions would be an expression of thought that is confined by categories of cultural difference, one in which the culture of the subaltern masses is disqualified out of hand as something backward and as something that has therefore to be removed from the dominant culture.

Gramsci therefore sees the debate between universalists and relativists as a 'mock battle'. The real issue for him is to identify within historically real 'common sense', in all its specific variations, that reformative element which Solon and Vico had already mentioned, namely the consciousness of fundamental human rights and the dignity and worth of each individual human being. If, by contrast, popular consciousness as 'pre-history in the present' obstructs such reformative strivings, it can easily prove to be an element hostile to the simple individual and something he must rid himself of, since 'folklore has always been linked to the culture of the dominant classes, and has extracted elements that have become joined with existing traditions' (Gramsci 1975b: 1105).

The principal concern (and Gramsci refers here to the Catholic population in Italy, as befits his specific historical situation) should be to assess the extent to which a new 'reformed' *civiltà* could arise from the complex of popular culture.

> Only in this way will the teaching of folklore be more efficient and really bring about the birth of a new culture among the broad popular masses, so that the separation between modern culture and popular culture of folklore will disappear. An activity of this kind, thoroughly carried out, would correspond on the intellectual plane to what the Reformation was in Protestant countries. (Gramsci 1988: 362)

Today, however, in Western societies individual developments and crises of migrants, not only of the first, but also of the second generation, are often purposively explained in terms of the closed cultural context of the society of origin in order to arrive at a 'better understanding'. Especially in studies conducted in the fields of education, sociology and cultural anthropology, the society of origin is being interpreted unquestioningly in the name of cultural identity as something 'immutable'. A contrast is thus constructed, creating two clinically separated worlds with an opposition between their respective central components. Once this polarity has been established, it will control subsequent perceptions, thus reinforcing the prejudice and vice versa. The migrant is locked within the ideological structure of his/her society of origin, while at the same time Western values are assumed to be the superior ones.

The debate on the multicultural society is barely able to include the question of societal sub- and superordination. As long as the population of rich industrial countries continues to be underclassed by immigrants, the stress on cultural identity can have a certain functional utility, in the sense of subordination under the dominant culture. The question of cultural relations cannot be discussed without referring it back to the question of hegemonic structures and the reflection on subalternity. As the historical example of the Reformation shows, Gramsci is thinking of a fundamental change in consciousness throughout society, of a new *civiltà*.[1] Without such a reform of consciousness, political changes are unthinkable.

For Gramsci, the revolutions between the seventeenth and nineteenth centuries in Europe ran parallel to a mental reformation that involved overcoming corporatism as well as dogmatic universalist tendencies. The same has still to take place in Italy 'because national consciousness was formed and indeed had to be formed through the conquest over two forms of culture: town hall particularism on the one hand, and Catholic cosmopolitanism on the other' (Gramsci 1975b: 1801, Q15).

Also Italian liberal cosmopolitanism should be substituted by an 'interested cosmopolitanism' that understands the phenomenon of migration as the specific relation of the Italian peasant masses to the world.

Traditional Italian cosmopolitanism would have to become cosmopolitanism of the modern type, i.e. it would have to ensure the best conditions for the development of the Italian 'uomo-lavoro', wherever in the world he might happen to be – not as a citizen of the world, to the extent that he is a 'civis romanus' or a Catholic, but to the extent that he is a producer of 'civiltà'. (Gramsci 1975b: 1988, Q19)

This quote is expressive of Gramsci's very own personal aim – to apply a universalist spirit to the critique of particularist and folklorist elements in the 'plurality of cultures', i.e. to recognise the gesture of submission that these elements entail, but also to identify the universal or the global in the particular, in the subaltern, in the 'foreign'. This is the struggle against any sociological analysis of everyday culture which is 'permanently afraid that modernity is going to destroy the object of (its) study' (Gramsci 1975b: 1506).

Gramsci's thoughts regarding the so-called 'subaltern social strata' (*Prison Notebooks*, vol.27, as well as many other writings on cultural hegemony) appear to supply a wealth of ideas relating to precisely this problem. Gramsci's concept permits us to base our analysis not only on *one* but on *many* cultures within a given society. At the same time, however, it is clear that the 'many cultures' cannot be separated from the context that binds them to the structures of domination in both the country of origin and the country to which they emigrate. The concept of 'national culture' takes effect for Gramsci at this point: as a hegemonic framework in which dominated and subordinate cultures encounter each other. This means that 'popular' or 'folk' culture cannot be reduced to national culture, or vice versa (cf. Gramsci 1975b: 1660f.). Because dominant and subordinate cultures are described in terms of their opposition and their mutual interdependency, it is necessary to reflect further on the process by which the entire complex develops and the direction that that development takes.

THE SOUTHERN QUESTION AND
THE PROBLEM OF SUBALTERNITY

Gramsci's famous essay 'Some Aspects of the Southern Question', written prior to his imprisonment in November 1926 and never corrected or completed before being published in the exile journal *Lo Stato Operaio* in Paris in 1930, is very different from a popular political pamphlet. Theoretically, the analysis of the Southern question is coherent with the analysis of culturalist interpretations of peasant migrants from the South in the *Prison Notebooks*.

> It is well known what kind of ideology has been disseminated in myriad ways among the masses in the North, by the propagandists of the bourgeoisie: the South is the ball and chain which prevents the social development of Italy from progressing more rapidly; the Southerners are biologically inferior beings, semi-barbarians or total barbarians, by natural destiny; if the South is backward, the fault does not lie with the capitalist system or with any other historical cause, but with Nature, which has made the Southerners lazy, incapable, criminal and barbaric – only tempering this harsh fate with the purely individual explosion of a few great geniuses. (Gramsci 1988: 173)

Politically, the text represents a very complicated positioning of Gramsci in relation to three sides: (1) to the members of the now illegal Italian Communist Party concerning the Southern question, defending the former Ordine Nuovo group; (2) to the Soviet Communist Party as a statement for the cooperation of workers and peasant masses instead of the repression of the latter by a proletarian dictatorship (cf. Vacca 2012); (3) to the decisive and theoretically new social element, the 'Southern Intellectuals', some of whom fought at the side of the workers within the 'Biennio Rosso' in 1919/20 in Turin. Gramsci's introduction of the role of intellectuals either for the integration of the peasant masses into the agrarian bloc, or in breaking up this alliance and leading the peasants into the new model of hegemony means a new interpretation of the 'Philosophy of Praxis' and a new understanding of subalternity of the South. According to him, the intellectuals are not *interpreting* social movements, but they are themselves organic *elements* of the formation of hegemony.

We have already said that Southern Italy represents a great social dis-integration. The formula can be applied not only to the peasants, but also to the intellectuals. It is a remarkable fact that in the South, side by side with huge property, there have existed and continue to exist great accumulations of culture and intelligence in single individuals, or small groups of great intellectuals, while there does not exist any organization of middle culture.... Well, the supreme political and intellectual rulers of all these initiatives have been Giustino Fortunato and Benedetto Croce. In a broader sphere than the stifling agrarian bloc, they have seen to it that the problems of the South would be posed in a way which did not go beyond certain limits; did not become revolutionary.... In this sense, Benedetto Croce has fulfilled an extremely important 'national' function. He has detached the radical intellectuals of the South from the peasant masses, forcing them to take part in national and European culture. (Gramsci 1988: 182f.)

This is a frequently quoted, but at the same time 'under-analysed' central argument of Gramsci's thoughts on the Southern question, as Edward Said reminds us (Said 1994: 49). In fact, we have to ask: how could the 'great intellectual' Croce 'force' radical Southern intellec-tuals to detach themselves from the peasant masses and take part in cosmopolitan 'European culture'? Gramsci puts together not just one, but two arguments that interpret the positioning of these intellectuals in an overly simple way. Also Said himself simplifies the solution to some extent when he explains Croce's historical position: 'Croce himself, a most impressive and notable figure in Italy, is seen by Gramsci with characteristic shrewdness as a southern philosopher who finds it easier to relate to Europe and to Plato than to his own crumbling meridional environment' (ibid.: 49). This evaluation underestimates the enormous liberating role that Benedetto Croce played for the radical Italian youth before and during the First World War, a social group within which also Gramsci is positioning himself. On 17 August 1931, during his imprisonment in Turi when Gramsci is most intensively studying Croce and analysing his theory in the *Prison Notebooks*, he writes in a letter to his sister-in-law Tatiana Schucht about the Turin group of students around Professor Umberto Cosmo that he himself belonged to:

But it seemed to me that both myself and Cosmo, like many other intellectuals of that time (that is to say, during the first fifteen years of the century) found ourselves on a common ground that was as follows: we (felt) we were participating wholly or in part in the movement of moral and intellectual reform initiated in Italy by Benedetto Croce, whose first point was this, that modern man can and must live without religion, and that means without religion, revealed, positive, mythological, or whatever else you want to call it. This point seems to me even today the major contribution to world culture made by modern intellectuals, I regard it as a civil achievement that must not be lost. (Gramsci 1994: 56, LR Bd. 2§86)

What Benedetto Croce had brought to this radical youth was thus the impression of liberation from the Catholic Church and its 'stifling agrarian bloc', introducing instead liberalism as 'religione della libertà' (as Croce himself called it). This concerned also the peasant masses of the South. 'In Italy the peasant question, through the specific Italian tradition, and the specific development of Italian history, has taken two typical and particular forms – the Southern question and that of the Vatican. Winning the majority of the peasant masses thus means, for the Italian proletariat, making these two questions its own' (Gramsci 1988: 173).

The problem for Gramsci and the Ordine Nuovo Group in Turin in 1919 and 1920 was that Croce had made the first step of liberation from the Vatican and thus taking radical intellectuals with him, but failed to make the next step of presenting an ideology and political option that would bring these masses out of their social disintegration and subalternity. Instead, Gramsci sees Croce as a prime example of the great intellectual from southern Italy on account of his functional support for the regional and social divisions of the country.

At the same time, a wrong and dangerous alliance of peasants and Southern intellectuals was arising in the form of a new syndicalism. According to Gramsci, 'syndicalism is a weak attempt on the part of the Southern peasants, represented by their most advanced intellectuals, to lead the proletariat' (Gramsci 1978: 450). In prison notebook 13 Gramsci comes back to the question of syndicalism and refers to it as a problem of subalternity:

Here we are dealing with a subaltern group, which is prevented by this theory from ever becoming dominant, or from developing beyond the economic-corporate stage and rising to the phase of ethico-political hegemony in civil society, and of domination of the state.... It is undeniable that in it, the independence and autonomy of the subaltern group which it claims to represent are in fact sacrificed to the intellectual hegemony, since precisely theoretical syndicalism is merely an aspect of laissez-faire liberalism. (Gramsci 1988: 210f., GR)

Already in his sketch on the Southern question in 1926, Gramsci sees the dangerous development of this new liberalism into nationalism. Paradoxically, those 'Southernists' brought up again the question of emigration, but not emigration of Southern peasants to the industrial North and thus forming a part of the industrial working class, but instead emigration by way of colonisation of the African continent. 'The phenomenon of emigration gave birth to the idea of Enrico Corradini's "proletarian nation"; the Libyan war appeared to a whole layer of intellectuals as the beginning of the "great proletariat's" offensive against the capitalist and plutocratic world' (Gramsci 1978: 450). Corradini wrote studies of the Italian emigration in North and South America as well as North Africa. He 'advocated colonial expansion into Africa so that Italians should go abroad as conquerors rather than as cheap labour' (Hoare, in Gramsci 1978: 506, n.255). In 'Some Aspects of the Southern Question' Gramsci underlined that 'left organs of social democracy ... and Mussolinism too soon fell under the control of the "Southernists".... Everyone remembers that, in fact, when Mussolini left *Avanti!* and the Socialist Party, he was surrounded by this cohort of syndicalists and Southernists' (Gramsci 1978: 451).

Thus, Gramsci demonstrated with the example of the topic of migration that it was intellectuals who were decisive for the formation of the subalternity of the masses as well as for the political turn of society as a whole.[2]

DISPARITIES AND POSSIBLE ALLIANCES IN MIGRATION PROCESSES TODAY: THE HETEROGENEITY OF NEW POLITICAL ACTORS

Are there any aspects of Gramsci's essay on 'Some Aspects of the Southern Question' still valid today in more than a merely historical dimension? Here we might consider the two young intellectuals Gramsci got to know in the context of the Ordine Nuovo group, Piero Gobetti and Guido Dorso, whom he mentions at the very end of his unfinished essay. Gobetti had lost his life in his struggle against fascism in 1926 at the age of 25 years, and Gramsci's considerations about his important role can be read like a eulogy to him.

Gramsci regards Gobetti with evident warmth, appreciation, and cordiality as an individual, but his political and social significance for Gramsci's analysis of the southern question – and it is appropriate that the unfinished essay ends abruptly with this consideration of Gobetti – is that he accentuates the need for a social formation to develop, elaborate, build upon the break instituted by his work, and by his insistence that intellectual effort itself furnishes the link between disparate, apparently autonomous regions of human history. (Said 1994: 50)

Said underlines that Gramsci has this very important, unheard of idea that intellectuals – and Gramsci even says *only* intellectuals – can create the links between disparate regions of the world, rich and poor, regions of emigration and regions of immigration. What has to be added is that Gramsci – in contrast to other Western Marxists like Lukács in 'History and Class Consciousness', for example – does not believe that the intellectual can have this important role only as a member of a revolutionary party but – on the contrary – typically might perform it as someone who consciously does not join the party but insists only in the importance and seriousness of his intellectual effort. Gobetti's and Dorso's main idea was the *'Rivoluzione liberale'* and the *'Rivoluzione meridionale'* (the latter is the title of Dorso's most important book from 1925), a revolutionary liberalism that sharply criticised the late outcomes of the Italian Risorgimento as a perverted liberalism that had left out the rural and proletarian masses and in its actual amoral form after the First World War made the phenomenon of 'transformism' to the Fascist movement possible. Nevertheless, Gobetti remained a radical liberal and did not become communist; his journal and his main literary work had both the title *Rivoluzione liberale*. Gramsci defended this not as a minor deficit but instead as a necessity of Gobetti's and Dorso's being intellectuals.

Gobetti, in practice, served us ... with a series of Southern intellectuals who through more complex relationships, posed the Southern question on a terrain different from the traditional one, by introducing into it the proletariat of the North (of these intellectuals, Guido Dorso is the most substantial and interesting figure). Why should we have fought against the *Rivoluzione liberale* movement? Perhaps because it was not made up of pure communists who had accepted our programme and our ideas from A to Z? This could not be asked of them, because it would have been both politically and historically a paradox. Intellectuals develop slowly, far more slowly than any other social group, by their very nature and historical function. They represent the entire cultural tradition of a people, seeking to resume and synthesize all of its history. (Gramsci 1978: 461f.)

With regard to his interpretation of the important political role of intellectuals Gramsci is here – in the autumn of 1926, while expressing his philosophy of new alliances for the moral and cultural reform of the masses – in coherence with the Congress of Lyon from the beginning of the same year. This philosophy leads Gramsci at the end of his prison years to formulate the idea of the '*Costituente*' (Constituent Assembly) as the aim to achieve in order to fight fascism – together with a multifaceted coalition of anti-fascists (cf. Vacca 2012: 145ff.).

It must be stated, however, that this idea is not as mature in the manuscript of 'Some Aspects of the Southern Question' as in the *Prison Notebooks* and in the *Letters from Prison*. Many contradictions are to be found in Gramsci's manuscript when he tries to defend the revolutionary position of the young Ordine Nuovo group that had envisaged the conquest of the state as the next step. It is not by accident that Gramsci's article was published in 1930 in the journal *Quarto Stato* with the editorial note that the text could not be completed by Gramsci before his imprisonment and that the author would probably have made corrections if he had been able to do so (Spriano 1975: 248, n.1). Gramsci in his manuscript quotes an article from *L'Ordine Nuovo* No.3, January 1920 which – as he remarks –

> sums up the viewpoint of the Turin Communists: ... The economic and political regeneration of the peasants should not be sought in a division of uncultivated or poorly cultivated lands, but in the solidarity of the industrial proletariat. This in turn needs the solidarity of the peasantry and has an 'interest' in ensuring that capitalism is not reborn economically from landed property ... By introducing workers' control over industry, the proletariat will orient industry to the production of agricultural machinery for the peasants ... By smashing the factory autocracy, by smashing the oppressive apparatus of the capitalist State and *setting up a workers' state* that will subject the capitalists to the law of useful labour, the workers will smash all the chains that binds the peasant to poverty and desperation. (Gramsci 1978: 442; emphasis added)

Still sticking to this revolutionary spirit, the Turin workers' councils after the occupation of the factories refused the FIAT board's proposal that the workers should take over the firm and run it as a cooperative (Gramsci 1978: 449). Gramsci reminds us of the fact that the same happened in Reggio Emilia:

At Reggio Emilia, a problem arose similar to the one at FIAT: a big factory was to pass into the hands of the workers as a cooperative enterprise. The Reggio reformists were full of enthusiasm for the project and trumpeted its praises in their press and at meetings. A Turin communist went to Reggio, took the floor at a factory meeting, outlined the problem between North and South in its entirety, and the 'miracle' was achieved: the workers, by an overwhelming majority, rejected the reformist, corporate position. (Gramsci 1978: 453)

Gramsci's comment on the result of these refusals is quite astonishing:

In April 1921, 5000 revolutionary workers were laid off by FIAT, the Workers' Councils were abolished, real wages were cut. At Reggio Emilia, something similar probably happened. In other words, the workers were defeated. But the sacrifice that they had made, had it been useless? We do not believe so: indeed, we are certain, that it was not useless ... In any case, so far as the peasants are concerned, such proof is always difficult, indeed almost impossible. (Ibid.: 454)

Obviously, for him as for the Turin communists, it was so important to avoid the impression of agreeing with the formation of a workers' elite that it was worth every sacrifice. The only concession Gramsci makes on this defeat is: 'Seven years have gone by and we are seven years older politically too. Today, certain concepts might be expressed better' (Gramsci 1978: 442). As we all know, seven years later, in the autumn of 1926, Italy had experienced the dictatorship of Mussolini's Fascist state. In his manuscript on the Southern question, shortly before his own imprisonment, Gramsci does not speak any more about the coming 'dictatorship' of the proletariat, but still expresses the political vision of the winning of 'state power' by the proletariat before it could reach intellectual hegemony: 'The proletariat, as a class, is poor in organizing elements. It does not have its own stratum of intellectuals, and can only create one very slowly, very painfully, *after the winning of state power*' (Gramsci 1978: 462; emphasis added). In this text, it is very unclear which concrete political and time perspective Gramsci sees for the taking over of 'state power' and thus for resolving the Southern question. The strategy becomes more and more a question of a general moral orientation against workers' corporativism, not of a concrete political perspective of alliances. Anyway, in a letter to Tatiana Schucht five years later, in November 1931, Gramsci states about his speech at the congress of Lyon in January 1926 – as a directive that had to be approved by the congress (as it was) – 'that the work to be done was that of "political organization" and not insurrectional attempts'.[3] The question remains how the workers and their 'political organization' would be able to win 'state power' before they had escaped from their intellectual and organisational subalternity. Gramsci no longer speaks about 'smashing' the capitalist state (as Ordine Nuovo did in 1920), but he envisages winning the consensus of the 'majority' of the Italian population. In the autumn of 1926 Gramsci expects that

> a class which aims to lead the peasants and intellectuals ... can win and build socialism only if it is aided and followed by the great majority of these social strata. If this is not achieved, the proletariat does not become the leading class: and these strata (which in Italy represent the majority of the population), remaining under bourgeois leadership, enable the state to resist the proletarian assault and wear it down. (Gramsci 1978: 448f.)

It is remarkable that Gramsci foresees for this a very long time period; he repeats that the self-educational work that has to be done by the intellectuals as well as by the workers and peasant will 'develop slowly'. This is in total contradiction with the quick, spontaneous move of the Turin workers in the moment of capitalist crisis, quoted in the introduction of his article. Later on, in the *Prison Notebooks*, Gramsci will harshly criticise spontaneity of this type when he speaks about Rosa Luxemburg's famous book from 1906 on the general strike: *Massenstreik: Partei und Gewerkschaften*:

> This little book, in my view, constitutes the most significant theory of the war of maneuver applied to the study of history and the art of politics.... It was a rigid form of economic determinism, made worse by the notion that effects of the immediate economic factor would unfold at lightning speed in time and space. (Gramsci 1992: 161f.)

Which insights can we draw from these historical analyses for the present situation in Europe concerning its split into wealthy and poorer states, the latter mostly in the South and East of the Union? What does 'political organisation' mean for the solution of the Southern question? Is the migration from South and East to North and West comparable with the situation of Italy at Gramsci's times? And what about the migration from outside of Europe into it from all parts of the Mediterranean?

We might be tempted to compare the fight for hegemony in the new Italian nation state during the Risorgimento with the European situation today. The comparison will not always lead to positive solutions, but might help to prevent the wrong alliances and cultural ascriptions Gramsci described. He showed how dangerous it is to enforce Politics of Identity with regard to the supposedly subaltern populations 'at the margins'[4] of the European continent, whether these were the excluding and ethnicising view of migrants from the side of nationalist parties in immigrant societies, or ideologies of superiority from the side of religious or self-defined ethnic immigrant communities. As already quoted, Gramsci saw that the Libyan war was understood by the fascists and the reactionary 'Southernists' as 'the beginning of the "great proletariat's" offensive against the capitalist and plutocratic world.' (Gramsci 1978: 450). This meant that Italian proletarians should go to Africa – this time not as marginalised migrants as in other parts of the world, but as ethnically hegemonic colonisers. Today politicians of the 'Lega Nord', on behalf of the Northern Italian 'Padano' population, try (often successfully) to position workers from Northern Italy against immigrants, e.g. those from North Africa who cross the Mediterranean Sea in order to escape the consequences of colonialism and postcolonialism.

But what can intellectuals do in this situation? How can they create links 'between disparate regions of human history', as Said put it?

I want to refer to the example of a group of intellectuals, dispersed in different parts of Europe, who made it possible to obtain a positive sentence from the European Court of Human Rights (*Europäischer Gerichtshof für Menschenrechte*, EGMR) in favour of a disparate group of boat people who had tried to flee to Italy but instead were 'pushed back' to Libya to which they didn't belong and had never wanted to go. What happened?[5]

During the night of 6–7 May 2009 following a shipwreck a boat of the Italian *Guardia di Finanza* (a police unit controlling taxes and customs) took 231 migrants on board 35 miles from the Italian island of Lampedusa. Instead of bringing the migrants to Lampedusa, however, they brought them to Tripoli and turned them over to the Libyan authorities without asking for their names, the reason why they had to flee and where they had intended to go.[6] It was the first 'push back' operation of Berlusconi's minister Roberto Maroni from Lega Nord. Two journalists from *Paris Match* were on the boat and documented the case in their journal (14 May 2009). As a result of this documentation, the lawyers Giulio Lana and Andrea Saccucci in the name of 24 'pushed back' persons accused the Italian state of violating human rights. The EGMR on 23 February 2012 decided on all points against the state of Italy, acknowledging that the victims were entitled to seek asylum even in extraterritorial parts of the Mediterranean. Many actors from the civil societies of different European countries had helped to win this case.

Analysing this case using Gramsci's categories one can say that a subaltern group of migrants had succeeded in helping to establish a liberal–progressive concept of human rights within the juridical sphere of Europe against the conservative hegemonic project in the national political sphere of Italy. The migrants were subaltern not because of their common class structure and/or education and nationality. On the contrary: the migrants on the ships that bring them to Europe via the Mediterranean Sea are very diverse with respect to all the mentioned categories. Often they are well educated and have been affluent in their countries of departure. What makes them all 'subaltern' is the ex-colonial and postcolonial history they have gone through and whose consequences they suffer. Intellectuals can create links between them by reconstructing the communalities of their history. Moreover, they are able to enforce a common moral–juridical European space constituted by law and to give migrants access to this space.

These considerations take us back to the very last sentences of Gramsci's uncompleted essay, dedicated to Piero Gobetti's work of intellectual leadership: 'This is gigantic and difficult, but precisely worthy of every sacrifice (even that of life, as in Gobetti's case) on the part of those intellectuals (and there are many of them, more than is believed) – from North and South – who have understood that only two social forces are essentially *national* and bearers of the future: the proletariat and the peasants' (Gramsci 1978: 462; emphasis added). Interestingly, Gramsci's last thought is dedicated to the idea of the Italian nation that is to be reborn out of the idea of the solidarity of intellectuals and the masses, instead of being founded on the colonisation of the Mediterranean South. This idea might today be rethought with respect to Europe as a possible multi-national nation. The European Union has citizens, but it is still a 'non-state' (Wiener 1998). Therefore it is able to solve neither the problem of the necessary solidarity among its citizens (as we can see in the Greek example) nor that of its Southern frontier. A moral progress of Europe, however, is to be seen today in the juridical sphere, as we have seen with the example of the ruling of the EGMR of February 2012 and the solidarity of intellectuals who made this sentence possible through their actions. This could be the nucleus of an alternative European moral hegemony, based on practices which go far beyond national egoisms and the concept of a 'fortress Europe'.

NOTES

1. In the debate he conducted with Henri De Man, Gramsci demands a '*catarsi di civiltà moderna*' (Gramsci 1975b: 1506) to replace De Man's psychology of depraved worker consciousness, which found considerable acceptance during Italian fascism. Gramsci

accuses De Man of being a 'scholarly student of folklore who is permanently afraid that modernity is going to destroy the object of his study' (Gramsci 1975b: 1506).

2. See also §57 and §58 of Gramsci's first notebook and Joseph Buttigieg's notes in Gramsci 1992: 165f.; 457–66.

3. The intervention to which Gramsci refers here has been published in English translation in Gramsci 1978: 313–39.

4. Antonio Gramsci gave his notebook 25, which is totally dedicated to the theory of subalternity, the title: 'Ai margini della storia' (At the Margins of History).

5. A chronology and analysis of the case is to be found in Pichl and Vester 2014.

6. Documented in the Italian film *Closed Sea* by Stefano Liberti and Andrea Segre, http://marechiuso.blogspot.de

REFERENCES

Apitzsch, U. 1995. 'Lavoro, cultura ed educazione tra fordismo e fascism'. In G. Baratta and A. Catone (eds). *Antonio Gramsci e il Progresso Intellettuale di Massa*. Milan: Edizioni Unicopli.

Gramsci, A. 1975a. *Scritti Giovanili 1914–1918*. Turin: Einaudi.

—— 1975b. *Quaderni del Carcere: Edizione Critica dell'Instituto Gramsci*, ed. V. Gerratana (4 vols). Turin: Einaudi.

—— 1978. *Selections from Political Writings, 1921–1926*, ed. and trans. Quintin Hoare. London: Lawrence and Wishart.

—— 1988. *A Gramsci Reader*, ed. David Forgacsz. London: Lawrence and Wishart.

—— 1992. *Prison Notebooks*, ed. Joseph A. Buttigieg, vol.i. New York: Columbia University Press.

—— 1994. *Letters from Prison*, ed. Frank Rosengarten (2 vols). New York: Columbia University Press.

Pichl, M. and Vester, K. 2014. 'Die Verrechtlichung der Südgrenze: Menschenrechtspolitiken im Grenzraum am Beispiel des Hirsi-Falls'. In Forschungsgruppe 'Staatsprojekt Europa' (Hg.), *Kämpfe um Migrationspolitik*. Bielefeld: Transcript.

Said, E.W. 1994. *Culture and Imperialism*. New York: Vintage Books.

Spriano, P. 1975 *Storia del Partito comunista italiano* (8th edn), vol.ii: *Gli anni della clandestinità*. Turin: Einaudi.

Vacca, G. 2012. *Vita e pensieri di Antonio Gramsci 1926–1937*. Turin: Einaudi.

Wiener, A. 1998. *'European' Citizenship Practice: Building Institutions of a Non-State*. Boulder, CO: Westview Press.

3

Countering Hegemony through a Park: Gezi Protests in Turkey's Migrant Neighbourhoods

Nazlı Şenses and Kıvanç Özcan

On October 2012, the AKP (Justice and Development Party) government initiated the Taksim Pedestrianisation Project in Istanbul, which aimed to transform Taksim Square by building a residential centre, a shopping mall, a mosque and a copy of a nineteenth-century Ottoman artillery barracks, among many other constructions. However, all these required the demolishing of Gezi Park, which is the green area situated in the middle of the Square. Five trees in the Park were uprooted on 27 May 2013. After this, a few activists began to stay in tents in the park so as to prevent its total destruction. Their environmentalist reaction ignited the wick of the biggest social protest in the country's history. The use of disproportionate police force against the activists in the park and the uncompromising rhetoric of the prime minister at the time, Tayyip Erdoğan, escalated the tension, which reached to its peak when security officers burned down the tents of activists at dawn on 30 May. From then onwards the number of protesters in Taksim Square sharply increased and protests spread across the country. The human cost of the disproportionate use of police force in the following weeks was heavy: the International Federation for Human Rights (FIDH 2014: 9) stated that between 31 May and 15 July 2013, 8,163 people were wounded as a result of the police brutality during the protests. Official reports indicated that 5,341 people were detained between 28 May and the first week of September (Bianet Independent Communication Network 2013). The death toll was eleven; of these, three lost their lives through excessive exposure to tear gas. Due to the continuing police violence and the government's reckless discourse, the number of protesters skyrocketed. Protests took place in almost all cities of Turkey, with the participation of more than 3 million citizens (FIDH 2014: 14). In short, a Pandora's box had opened up in Turkey.

Environmental concerns were an auxiliary motive behind the protests. Already existing discontent against the government's authoritarian neoliberalism and accompanying illiberal policies targeting social life erupted in the form of nationwide protests. More specifically, demolishing Gezi Park presents a flawless example of AKP-style hegemony, which is based on an authoritarian neoliberal policy framework coupled with a religious–sectarian discourse. Provocation of the construction sector, commodification of common spaces and urban regeneration projects have long become lynchpins of the government's neoliberal policies, which have led to accumulation by dispossession of the masses in many cities and depredation of the environment.

The protests, which lasted nearly three months, brought together various social groups from different classes, spatialities, political parties and voluntary organisations and having diverse identities and ideologies. Recalling Antonio Gramsci's suggestion in 'Some Aspects of the Southern Question', this chapter seeks to explain the participation of these heterogeneous groups of actors in the Gezi protests as a significant development in countering a dissolving hegemony. According to Gramsci, forming an alliance in Italy between the Northern proletariat and the Southern peasants was a prerequisite for changing the hegemonic structure in the country. The Gezi protests have indicated that an alliance between different classes, spatialities, ethnic and religious identities in Turkey might be formed to challenge the current hegemonic order in Turkey. During the Gezi protests common concerns arising out of this heterogeneity formed a united front against the state. The tension in civil society dealt a blow to the government and its associates. Cumulative anger, which arose from environmental concerns, precarious working conditions and the erosion of democracy, led to a solidarity that represents a deep transformation, an organic kind of crisis, rather than merely a conjunctural development that had erupted on the spur of the moment on 31 May 2013. Deriving its inspiration from a Gramscian perspective, this chapter sheds light on the multidimensional and multi-spatial nature of these contestations and analyses the heterogeneity of subaltern groups in the protests, with a specific focus on internal migrants as the 'urban minorities': the residents of migrant neighbourhoods in Istanbul and Ankara where fierce clashes occurred during the protests. We argue that the protests in these neighbourhoods coloured the whole process with a distinct hue. In migrant neighbourhoods, the Gezi protests took a specific character compared to other local confrontations during the protests. Thus, the nature of the protests in these migrant neighbourhoods should be elaborated further, especially in terms of their contribution to forming alliances with other neighbourhoods against the hegemonic order. Our study thus contributes a distinct and overlooked perspective to the existing literature on the Gezi protests, first by adopting a Gramscian framework, and second by scrutinising the role of migrants and migrant neighbourhoods in the Gezi protests. In our analysis, we lean on Gramscian concepts such as hegemony, historical bloc, organic versus conjunctural, and civil society versus state in order to delve into Gezi.

The next section analyses the path leading to the Gezi protests by taking the government's neoliberal and authoritarian policies into account. Then we further elaborate our theoretical framework in relation to Gramscian concepts and theoretical arguments. Following that, we analyse the actors involved in the Gezi protests with a specific focus on urban minorities living in territorially stigmatised neighbourhoods in Istanbul and Ankara. We conclude by reflecting on a possible alliance between the urban minority and other actors involved in the Gezi protests.

CONTEXTUALISING THE GEZI PROTESTS

Since coming to power in 2002, the AKP government has enacted many laws with the aim of regulating working life. Such laws and regulations have led to disorganisation of the working classes 'through deunionization, low wages, precarization, intensification of workloads, erosion of social benefits and increasing workers' debts' (Ercan and Oğuz 2014: 114). According to the OECD.Stat (2015) indicators, 9.5 per cent of the workforce were members of a union in 2002, but this ratio decreased to 4.5 per cent in 2012. Working conditions have deteriorated too since 2002. For instance, while 72,344 people had work-related accidents in 2002, this number had risen to 191,247 by 2013 (*Hürriyet* 2014). Turkish Assembly for Workers' Health and Work Security statistics reveal that the number of workplace deaths soared from 872 in 2002 to 1,235 in 2013 (Müller 2014). The number of work health and safety inspections declined from 27,000 in 2005 to 8,000 in 2013 despite the fact that the number of workers increased in the meantime (Yazar 2014). These figures indicate the precarisation of working conditions and the exploitation of the workforce resulting from the government's neoliberal policies. Turkey's growing population has been turned into a flexible labour force (Kuymulu 2013: 277). Flexibility, exploitation and precarisation targeted not only industrial manual workers but also professionals such as physicians, nurses, teachers and lawyers (Ercan and Oğuz 2014: 122–9). In other words, precarity has gained a definitive character and become a uniting force for all sections of the working class in Turkey. The statistics quoted above and widespread precarity as their unavoidable outcome indicate that a situation akin to an organic crisis was prevalent before the Gezi protests. These precarised sections of the working class were actively present during the Gezi protests (ibid.: 129). Social groups' dissatisfaction with the system manifested itself during the Gezi protests which involved a heterogeneous group of actors with varying economic interests but with similar economic costs and suffering.

Additionally, commodification of common spaces, urban regeneration and transformation of neighbourhoods and large-scale construction projects has been the trademark of state policies that again represented the government's hegemony. For the promotion of the economic growth of the country, the construction sector has been made the dominant sector on which the government's hegemonic model was built (Çavuşoğlu and Strutz 2014: 135). These construction-related projects are multifunctional for the government first in the sense of developing the relations between the government and the construction companies. As long as the government satisfies its cronies by creating rent, fidelity relations are being established between the government and construction sector. Kerem Öktem (2013) describes the government's understanding of growth as neoliberal developmentalism which prioritises rent generation and the interests of government-linked companies over urban heritage and natural resources. Large-scale construction projects, such as the third Bosphorus Bridge, the third airport in Istanbul, the Artvin Yusufeli Dam and hydroelectric power plants, are neither environment friendly nor based on the consent of local people. As a result, these projects face harsh criticisms and the protests of environmentalists. The government has suppressed such environmental protests by force when it could not produce consent. For instance, local people's environmental demonstration against the construction of a hydroelectric power plant on the rivers in the Solaklı Valley in July 2012 culminated in the intervention of the gendarmerie and the arrest of 110 villagers (DTF 2012).

Another function of government-backed construction projects is their potential for controlling political opposition or 'dissident' populations: urban regeneration and transformation projects sweep away the potential political opposition from the marginalised neighbourhoods close to Istanbul city centre, such as Sulukule, Okmeydanı, Tarlabaşı and Gazi. Dissident populations of these neighbourhoods are relocated, and their daily life practices are transformed forever. As previously mentioned, via these projects common spaces are presented for the use of government cronies in the construction sector. Judith Whitehead (2013: 296) argues that accumulation by dispossession impoverishes the masses or leads to the formation of new working classes for the informal sector.

Whitehead also reminds us that the state's attempts to divide the masses by dispossession could link diverse groups (ibid.: 297). This could explain how diverse groups within marginalised neighbourhoods of Istanbul and Ankara developed the solidarity ties with other protesters that we witnessed during the Gezi protests. With regard to the demolition of Gezi Park, the interests of capital were put above the interests of the ordinary inhabitants of Istanbul (Kuymulu 2013: 275). This explains the victimisation of the inhabitants of dispossessed neighbourhoods, which makes meaningful the participation in the protests of various social groups, including subaltern communities from different socio-economic backgrounds and spatialities. The participation of people from the previously mentioned neighbourhoods is the specific concern of this chapter, since we think that these populations significantly added to the heterogeneity of the actors in the Gezi protests.

As a final note on the path leading to the Gezi protests, one should also refer to the government's intensifying authoritarian tendencies, especially after the 2007 elections. At the expense of losing its liberal supporters, the government cadre has taken a majoritarian stand and started to govern as if the victory in the elections gave them the right to rule arbitrarily. Winning 49 per cent of the votes in subsequent elections and regaining the majority of seats in the parliament in the 2011 elections further exacerbated this stance. After the 2011 elections, the government has widely employed a discourse in which its electoral support has been presented as the 'national will'. Authoritarian policies of the government have gone far beyond the distorted interpretation of the election results. The day-to-day life practices of various segments of society have been targeted and defamed by the government's policies and discourse. Secular people, women, Kurds, Alevis, socialists, environmentalists ... all are under fire.

The government's authoritarian stance over the elections and majoritarian understanding in the parliament has blocked channels of expression and representation for the masses who did not vote for the AKP. As the government has consolidated its power more and more through elections, which are based on the ten per cent threshold system, its tolerance against the opposition has declined, judicial institutions have become biased, and critics of the government have been jailed for various reasons (Acemoğlu 2013). Such authoritarian tendencies of the government, when coupled with an economic–corporate interest in the economic sphere, have further alienated various groups of people and turned them into 'minorities'. Thus, the hegemony that the government attempted to establish across various subaltern groups at the beginning of the 2000s has started to dissolve. That manifested itself most clearly during the Gezi protests, which brought together a wide variety of social and economic groups: environmentalists, anarchists, students, workers, professionals, women, LGBT individuals, ethnic minorities, football fans and many others. Barring the avenues for criticism has fuelled the growing anger of the masses and opened the doors for street protests.

The heterogeneity of actors within the Gezi protests resulted from the suffering of diverse groups and the diversification of antagonisms. Stuart Hall (1986: 16) says that 'the actual social or political force which becomes decisive in a moment of organic crisis will not be composed of a single homogenous class but will have a complex social composition'. Diverse antagonisms defined the social character of the Gezi protests. Recalling Hall's idea that society was polarised along the broadest front of antagonism (ibid.: 16), the Gezi protests showed the degree of polarisation within society. The united front against the government reflected the constellation of diverse interests and concerns.

MIGRANT NEIGHBOURHOODS AND SPATIALITY PRACTICES

In this chapter we argue that the category of migration, albeit ignored in most studies on the Gezi protests, has played an important role during the protests and requires further elaboration. More specifically we argue that the solidarity networks and attempts to form an alliance against the government's hegemony should be taken into account also in relation to migrant neighbourhoods in the metropolitan cities. The Gezi protests have presented an opportunity to crack the hegemonic order of the government, which is also based on the construction of borders and the marginalisation of migrants for the sake of neoliberal policies. Deepening precarity is more visible in migrant neighbourhoods and this trait made these neighbourhoods an important element of alliance during the protests. Acknowledging the argument that migrants constituted an important part of the new heterogeneity involved in the protests enables us to better understand the complex nature of the protests. We argue that a certain kind of migratory background in fact defined some of the protesters' socio-economic and political positions that were reflected in the protests.

This particular theoretical concern on migratory background contributes an original perspective to an already large literature on Gezi. More specifically, some studies in the literature focus on the relationships between urban space, its transformation as a result of neoliberal policies and the Gezi protests (see, for example, Çavuşoğlu and Strutz 2014;

Kuymulu 2013; Moudouros 2014; Örs 2014) and many others focus on the class structure of Gezi protests (Boratav 2013; Ercan and Oğuz 2014; Keyder 2014; Wacquant 2014). The two lines of research do not address each other. However, we think that bringing these findings together, the two different lines of research point to an important but unaddressed issue: how the distribution of urban space as the result of a long process of migration (re)creates the subaltern classes and affects their involvement in the Gezi protests. Such a perspective enables us to focus on how the trajectory of internal migration has created impoverished neighbourhoods in big cities, and how these neighbourhoods' residents actively took part in the Gezi protests since their living spaces and lifestyles had been targeted by the government's decade-long neoliberal and authoritarian policies, including urban renewal projects. Gramsci argues that space is a constructed phenomenon which comes into existence as the result of specific social relations (Jessop 2007: 105). The migrant neighbourhoods mentioned above have gained a distinct political identity thanks to the internal migration waves of the last decades. The government's authoritarian neoliberalism and religious discourse have posed a vital threat to the identity of these neighbourhoods.

In the Turkish context, internal migration is a result of a combined effect of both economic and political dispossession (Ercan and Oğuz 2014: 123). The economic dispossession happened between the late 1940s and the early 1980s mainly as a result of mechanisation in agriculture and market-oriented production, which left many peasants unemployed. As a result, millions had migrated to urban centres in Turkey, contributing to the increase in the urban population (Çelik 2005: 139). Migration resulting from political dispossession happened especially during the end of the 1980s and 1990s, when Kurds were forced to leave their lands as a result of the armed struggle between the military and the PKK (*Partiya Karkerên Kurdistan*: Kurdistan Workers' Party). Kurds from eastern and south-eastern Anatolia were caught between evacuation of their villages by the military, the emergency rule of 1987 (*OHAL*), and the pressure they were under to support the PKK (Çelik 2005: 139).

Societal tensions, deteriorating economic conditions in rural areas and political discourse which aggrandised the Turkish Sunni and Islamic character of the state have hastened internal migration and explain how Alevi and Kurdish people began to congregate in the large cities in the 1970s and 1980s. During the forced migration of Kurdish people to large cities, the migrants have experienced discrimination and hardship in integration into the city in general and into the already existing migratory networks in particular (Erman 2001: 988). 'As a result, they have created their own communities, usually in the most disadvantaged locations, and have ended up with impoverished lives and social stigma, creating a suitable atmosphere for radical action and social fragmentation' (Erman 2001: 988). In other words, Alevi and Kurdish migrants in large cities have gathered together in their own communities within neighbourhoods that are continuously being territorially stigmatised and marginalised through public, political and media discourses. Gazi, Okmeydanı and Tarlabaşı in Istanbul and Tuzluçayır in Ankara are examples of such neighbourhoods; these are the places where the Gezi protests also found significant support and where fierce clashes took place between protesters and the police.

Coming to power in 2002, the government has furthered the spirit of the 1980 military coup by excluding the Alevi and Kurdish populations.[1] For instance, the government has refrained from officially recognising Cemevi[2] as a place of worship and does not hesitate to associate legal Kurdish political parties with terrorism. Furthermore, city neighbourhoods with dense Alevi and Kurdish populations (especially in Istanbul and Ankara) have become targets of urban renewal and regeneration projects and the government's religious rhetoric. The prime minister's 2012 inauguration in Okmeydanı of the convent of archers, which had disappeared a century ago, exemplifies the government's attempts to stamp Ottoman–Turkish–Sunni imprints on the migrant neighbourhoods (Perouse 2015).

Thus, internal migration has developed a group of a very specific subaltern class in some of the urban areas. These people, whom we call the urban minority, are living precarious lives in poor neighbourhoods. We think that their participation in a seemingly middle-class revolt carries important implications for the possibility of forming new alliances among subaltern classes in Turkey. In 'Some Aspects of the Southern Question', Gramsci emphasised 'that the fundamental concept of the Turin communists was ... the political alliance between Northern workers and Southern peasants, to oust the bourgeoisie from State power' (Forgacs 2000: 172). Gramsci's narrative on the spatial distinction between the South and the North inspires us to rethink the relation between the urban minority and the middle classes of Gezi. Although the Gezi protests have included different kinds of actors, the most vocal groups were those who may be considered as the middle classes. Following Gramsci, we focus on the relationship between the middle classes and the urban minority. Our focus derives mainly from the fact that it is especially the Kurdish and Alevi minorities who reside in migrant neighbourhoods who contradict the idea of homogeneous middle-class participation in the Gezi protests.

THE ACTORS IN THE GEZI PROTESTS

With regard to the actors who took part in the Gezi protests, there are various social groups, in the sense in which Gramsci employed the term. '"Social group" is clearly used in the *Notebooks* not simply as a substitute for class, but rather to identify the differing groupings of people that come together politically' (Ekers and Loftus 2013: 30). The concept is very useful in understanding the actors involved in the Gezi protests. What we saw there was a juncture of diverse antagonisms in which, as we saw above, many different classes, ethnic groups and religious groups coalesced against the government. On the one hand these people as a whole could be regarded as one large social group who came together challenging an already dissolving hegemonic order. On the other hand, each of them separately can be considered as a social group, since each was putting forward group-specific political demands as well (the demands of women versus those of secularists, for example). With more than 35 professional bodies, civil-society organisations, environmentalist groups and trade unions, Taksim Solidarity Platform, the leading organisation of the Gezi protests, reflects this heterogeneous structure (Pope 2013).

Inspired by this heterogeneity in the protests, there has already developed a rich literature analysing the socio-economic composition of Gezi protesters and supporters (see, for example, Boratav 2013; Bürkev 2013; Ercan and Oğuz 2014; Keyder 2014; Tonak 2013; Tuğal 2013; Wacquant 2014; Yörük and Yüksel 2014). A popular question in this literature is whether or not the Gezi protests were the protest movement of the newly emerging middle classes. As an illustration, the study by Erdem Yörük and Murat Yüksel (2014) uses survey data in order to make sense of the socio-economic backgrounds of Gezi protesters and supporters, and to discover whether or not there is a middle-class dominance in the protests. Adopting the class categories developed by Alejandro Portes and Kelly Hoffman (2003), Yörük and Yüksel find that '[t]he largest single group of protesters was from the manual formal proletariat (20 per cent), the informal proletariat (18 per cent), the petty bourgeoisie (11 per cent), professionals (6 per cent), executives (5 per cent), and capitalists (4 per cent)' (Yörük and Yüksel 2014: 111). The survey from which they attain these numbers was conducted in Istanbul and Izmir in December 2013 and it 'was based on a stratified random sample of 3,944 respondents' (ibid.: 110). However, the proletarian

COUNTERING HEGEMONY THROUGH A PARK · 49

proportion of the Gezi protesters was lower than that of the population as a whole. In other words, although the proletariat had the absolute numerical majority during the protests, their participation rate was low when compared to their overall presence in the general population. By contrast, the rate of participation was higher than in the population as a whole among professionals, executives and capitalists, and according to Yörük and Yüksel '[t]he high rate of participation within the middle and upper classes created the impression of a predominantly middle-class crowd' (ibid.: 113).

From a different perspective, Korkut Boratav (2013) argues that although the working class did not participate in the protests with their own organisations or programmes, this does not mean that members of the working class were absent from the protests altogether. Therefore, heterogeneity in terms of class composition should be acknowledged for the Gezi protests. The working classes (in the sense of 'industrial labour' or 'manual formal proletariat' and the 'informal proletariat') were as much present as the middle classes (mainly in the sense of profession-als). Having observed this heterogeneity in twenty-first-century social movements, Tanıl Bora (2014) argues that the global opposition waves between 2011 and 2013 were characterised not only by the participation of middle classes but also by the 'contact' between the middle classes and every variety of the 'lower strata' and the 'damned'. This was the case for the Gezi protests too. Workers (whether organised or not), the unemployed, the impoverished, the marginal in the technical economic sense, Kurdish dissidents, and Alevis, all of whom are neutralised through ghettoisation, had all taken part in the protests (ibid.: 24). Therefore, for Bora, what is significant in the Gezi protests is this *contact* between those from the so-called middle classes and those from the lowest ranks of the social strata. These groups came together and stayed side by side. In a domain that is constantly being defined as an area of middle-class revolt, the organised and unorganised working classes were present too – the oppressed, the marginal, outcasts in some cases – in short, those considered not to be 'respectable' citizens (ibid.: 26).

From a similar perspective Yörük states that '[t]he protest originated from a middle-class habitus but swiftly expanded into working-class squatter house areas, especially to ones in which Kurdish and Alevi minorities are highly numerous and the socialist Left is powerful.' (2014: 425) The involvement of those minorities is significant for our purposes in this chapter, where we aim to present a theoretical reflection bringing together migration, Gramsci and the Gezi protests. Bora (2014) argues that those who claim that the middle classes were dominant during the Gezi protests, ignore those that took place in the neighbourhood of Berkin Elvan.[3] The neighbourhood of Berkin Elvan is called Okmeydanı, and is the home of a large Alevi population. We argue that it is in fact the participation of the residents of these neighbourhoods that has deepened the heterogeneity of the actors in the Gezi protests, since their participation has brought a spatial dimension to the protests that can be understood by utilising a Gramscian perspective on spatial practices. Such neighbourhoods represent political geographies within the urban landscapes, reminiscent of the dichotomy between the Italian South and the North as depicted by Gramsci's writings on the Southern question. These neighbourhoods host a migrant and politically active population, as a broader category. The daily practices and life courses of their inhabitants are relatively more precarised in comparison with those in other parts of the city.

MIGRANT ACTORS OF MIGRANT NEIGHBOURHOODS ...

The rest of this section elaborates more on a couple of such neighbour-hoods and their involvement in the Gezi protests. We focus on the Okmeydanı and Gazi neighbourhoods in Istanbul and the Tuzluçayır neighbourhood in Ankara. The importance of these neighbourhoods, when compared to other parts of the two cities, is that they were formed as a result of internal migration of Alevis and Kurds from all over Turkey, mostly for political reasons. We argue that the populations of these neighbourhoods add up to a significant social group within an already heterogeneous body of actors in Gezi.

Okmeydanı is one of the neighbourhoods where the Gezi protests were highly concentrated and where people had faced brutal police inter-ventions. Throughout June 2013 protest movements took place within the neighbourhood leading to fierce clashes with the police. Forums and solidarity platforms had been established within the neighbourhood to discuss the ongoing protests and desired system of governance. These forums and platforms followed the decisions of the Taksim Solidarity Platform. This was an example of how a distinct social group joined an alliance formation with various other social groups, and contributed to the formation of a united front in countering the governments' hegemony. What is more important is that the relative isolation of the Okmeydanı population from the rest of the city and its marginalisation has started to dissolve as a result of these alliances (Sendika.org 2013a). This relative isolation of the population relates to the fact that the neigh-bourhood had been formed mainly by internal migrations. Most of the people had migrated from cities such as Sivas, Tokat, Erzincan, Giresun and Ordu in the 1960s, 1970s and 1980s.[4] The majority of the inhabitants are Alevis. Following that, dissident or revolutionary movements have been another characteristic of the public spaces in the neighbourhood (Kurt 2008: 8–9). Since 2012, the neighbourhood has been the target of urban transformation policies (Evrensel 2015) that face significant resistance on the part of its population. According to Ercan Kesal,[5] the local population of Okmeydanı still retain ties with the places from which they had migrated. Nevertheless, they are resisting the urban transformation policies, which are forcing them to leave the neighbourhood. Kesal states that when these people migrated from various parts of Turkey and settled in Okmeydanı, the area was covered in mud, lacked roads, and was of no value to anyone. However, now the locals are faced with the possibility of a second wave of migration as a result of urban transformation policies (*Diken* 2014). This situation has contributed to their politicisation, which came into play also during the Gezi protests.

The Gazi neighbourhood of Sultangazi in Istanbul also carries a similar migratory background. It is the home to Kurdish and Alevi migrants from the eastern regions of Turkey (Marcus 1996: 25). The neighbourhood is among these urban spaces where Gezi protests took place. People gathered around the Gazi Cemevi and walked towards the highway where they were subjected to police intervention with tear gas and water cannons (Sendika.org 2013b). However, the history of the Gazi neighbourhood includes various other social movements involving Alevis, Kurdish minorities and Leftist organisations. In 1995, the neighbourhood had witnessed one of the most violent clashes between the police and Gazi's Alevi inhabitants, who were demonstrating against earlier attacks on teahouses in the neighbourhood by unknown gunmen. There were rumours that the police had been involved in the shooting. The demonstrations lasted for several days and 17 people were killed in the clashes (Çelik 2003: 152).

Finally, Tuzluçayır is a neighbourhood in Ankara that is close to the city centres at Ulus and Kızılay. Tuzluçayır's inhabitants participated in large numbers in Gezi protests during the summer of 2013. They protested in the centre of Tuzluçayır and also marched towards Kızılay, the city centre. Such protests had been stopped in most cases by brutal police interventions (Sendika.org 2013c). Most of the people of Tuzluçayır are Kurdish or Alevi migrants who have moved to Ankara for political or economic reasons. The neighbourhood has been considered one of the most politicised areas in Ankara, especially since the 1960s. Most of the inhabitants are on the left of the ideological spectrum. Many leftist organisations were established, and in the 1960s and 1970s the neighbourhood was known as the 'little Moscow'. In recent years, Tuzluçayır has also been the target of urban transformation projects in which squatter houses are destroyed and apartment buildings are constructed (Metin 2009: 91–92).

These neighbourhoods were politicised even before the Gezi protests – their populations were already contesting their social positions in urban life and under the Turkish political system. However, what is novel is that for the first time they participated in a protest movement together with the rest of the urban population, raising the possibility of a future alliance between these groups and others. People from these neighbourhoods do not belong to the group of the 'middle classes' described in the literature on the Gezi protests and for that reason their participation contradicts the argument that Gezi was a middle-class uprising. The population of these neighbourhoods forms a distinct social group in the Gramscian sense. They suffer directly from the government's neoliberal policies in the construction sector that came under the name of urban regeneration and transformation; they are targeted and marginalised by the government's religious discourse. Moreover, poverty and precarity are common within the neighbourhoods. However, for the purposes of this chapter the most important commonality for these neighbourhoods' population is their migrant and minority background. Their neighbourhoods were established as a result of (usually forced) migrations throughout Turkey, and today urban renewal projects, religious – mostly sectarian – policies and the authoritarian stand of the government have formed an insecure atmosphere for the residents of these neighbourhoods. Since the population of these neighbourhoods actively took part in the protests, all these characteristics have been represented in the Gezi protests and deepen the heterogeneity of the actors which is challenging the hegemony.

CONCLUDING REMARKS

The Gezi protests of the summer of 2013 share some important similarities with the global social movements of the past year or two. Similar to the revolutions in Arab cities discussed by Verdeil, the Gezi protests are urban in nature (Verdeil 2011). For Immanuel Wallerstein, Gezi is even a 'continuing process of what started as the world-revolution of 1968' together with similar uprisings in Brazil or in Bulgaria (Wallerstein 2015). As one common characteristic of these protests, Wallerstein states that they not only 'assault' the current government in power but also question the 'very legitimacy of the state' itself. This common feature may be a reason why the protests involve such a heterogeneous collection of social groups. Each one is targeting in its own way the hegemony of the state. In line with Wallerstein's argument, Michael

Hardt argues in an interview on the Gezi protests that demanding a new form of democracy is one of the commonalities of these protests (Semercioğlu and Ayyıldız 2014). As we have seen, the heterogeneous groups of actors of the Gezi protests brought together people from a wide variety of organised and unorganised dissident social groups. For that very reason, in Hardt's words, 'Gezi raised the prospect of overcoming divisions across all axes ... : gender and sexuality, the religious/secular divide, the Kurdish question, and composition of labour – and there are undoubtedly others' (Hardt 2014). Put shortly, the Gezi protests put forward a new agenda. This chapter aims to understand one specific social group within this heterogeneity: the urban minorities, living in migrant neighbourhoods of Istanbul and Ankara. Our study focuses on those groups who can be considered the quintessential members of subaltern classes: the marginalised urban poor. Their marginality has been constructed on their migrant background, sectarian identity, political position and spatial practices. These parts of the city remained isolated from the rest, stigmatised as underdeveloped and marginal. However, during the Gezi protests their populations joined up with the rest of the city, the middle classes, students, women and many others, in countering the government's hegemony. This participation was also important in itself as it has the potential of reminding the rest of the urban population that they have common expectations and demands from the state. Thus a possible alliance has been formed.

Looking through a Gramscian lens at the Arab Spring of 2011, especially the revolts in Tunisia and Egypt, Stefan Kipfer argues that '[t]hese were urban revolutions not because they grew out of central city spaces in the capitals but because they were produced by spatial dynamics of mobilization that articulated various points in the countries' differentially urbanized landscapes' (Kipfer 2013: 98).

Most of the residents of the neighbourhoods that we have examined have Alevi and Kurdish identities, and their participation in the protests is politically very significant too since this participation has the prospect of overcoming the prejudices associated with these neighbourhoods and their inhabitants. As was argued by Bora (2014) the Gezi protests have put people of the middle classes in contact with the urban poor (among others) and it is this contact that generates the prospect of finding a common ground by transforming the participant groups in order to counter the hegemony of the current political structure.

Kipfer's interpretation of the relations that Gramsci established between the peasants and the proletariat for building a hegemonic bloc is especially important for understanding the relation between the urban minorities and the middle classes of Gezi. According to Kipfer (2013)

'Gramsci recognized that hegemonic politics required much more than a recombination of "autonomous" social forces – some rural, some urban – in an additive and instrumental project of coalition building. Linking urban with rural forces required a transformation of both, and thus also a break with "the aversion of the country for the city" and the "hatred and scorn for the 'peasant'" he observed in his own time' (ibid.: 95). Thus, in order for this contact that took place during the Gezi protests between the urban minority and the middle classes to lead to a meaningful coalition, both sides would have to abandon an earlier mode of thinking about their and others' interests. Especially, the middle classes should get rid of their prejudices that see these neighbourhoods and their inhabitants as 'threats' to their way of city life, and this has to do with challenging the hegemonic discourses marginalising the urban minorities. Neoliberal authoritarianism and the stigmatising policies of the government have created diverse antagonisms by posing threats for both the middle classes and the urban poor, and this in turn has led to the establishment of solidarity networks and the unification of various groups. Gramsci says:

> [t]he first problem to resolve, for the Turin communists, was how to modify the political stance and general ideology of the proletariat itself, as a national element which exists within the ensemble of State life and is unconsciously subjected to the influence of bourgeois press and bourgeois traditions. It is well known what kind of ideology has been disseminated in myriad ways among the masses in the North, by the propagandists of the bourgeoisie: the South is the ball and chain which prevents the social development of Italy from progressing more rapidly. (Gramsci 1978: 444; Forgacs 2000:173)

Like the peasants of the South, the urban minority is portrayed within hegemonic discourses as the sources of all the criminal activity, poverty and informality within the city. Thus, in order for this contact to turn into a possible counter-hegemonic bloc in the future, first the middle classes should save themselves from 'the influence of bourgeois press and bourgeois traditions'. The Gezi protests provided a significant venue in which to start this transformation.

NOTES

1. Since 2009, the AKP government has been initiating some policy moves in regard to the solution of the Kurdish question, commonly known as the 'peace process'. However, both the government's sincerity and the methodology employed have constantly been called into question. After the 7 June elections, the so-called 'peace process' collapsed,

followed at the end of July by armed clashes between the Turkish security forces and the PKK.
2. Place of worship for Alevi community.
3. Berkin Elvan was 14 when he was hit in the head by a gas canister fired by police, while on his way to a bakery in his neighbourhood. He remained in a coma for 269 days and died on 11 March 2014. Hundreds of thousands of people participated in his funeral. The prime minister at the time, Erdoğan, implied he was a 'terrorist'.
4. These cities are located near each other in the north-eastern part of Turkey: Giresun, Ordu and Tokat are in the Black Sea region, Sivas is in Central Anatolia and Erzincan is in Eastern Anatolia.
5. Ercan Kesal is an actor and a medical practitioner. He established a private hospital in Okmeydanı in 1997 and since then had been able to observe and experience the daily practices of the neighbourhood.

REFERENCES

Acemoğlu, D. 2013. *Development won't ensure democracy.* www.nytimes.com/2013/06/06/opinion/development-wont-ensure-democracy-in-turkey.html?_r=0
Bianet Independent Communication Network. 2013. *Police releases Gezi Resistance report.* www.bianet.org/english/crisis/151583-police-%20releases-gezi-resistance-report
Bora, T. 2014. 'Gezi ve orta sınıf'. *Birikim* (June).
Boratav, K. 2013. 'Olgunlaşmış bir sınıfsal başkaldırı: Gezi direnişi'. In Ö. Göztepe (ed.). *Gezi Direnişi Üzerine Düşünceler.* Ankara: NotaBene Yayınları.
Bürkev, Y. 2013. 'Sınıf, toplumsal muhalefet ve siyasal rejim açısından haziran isyanı'. In Ö. Göztepe (ed.). *Gezi Direnişi Üzerine Düşünceler.* Ankara: NotaBene Yayınları.
Çavuşoğlu, E. and Strutz, J. 2014. 'Producing Force and Consent: Urban Transformation and Corporatism in Turkey'. *City* 18(2).
Çelik, A.B. 2003. 'Alevis, Kurds and Hemsehris: Alevi Kurdish Revival in the Nineties'. In P.J. White and J. Jongerden (eds). *Turkey's Alevi Enigma: A Comprehensive Overview.* Leiden: Brill.
——2005. '"I miss my village!" Forced Kurdish Migrants in Istanbul and Their Representation in Associations'. *New Perspectives on Turkey,* 32.
Diken [Internet newspaper]. 2014. *Ercan Kesal: Okmeydanı'nda yaşayanlara 'buraları çok kıymetli, artık boşaltın' deniyor.* www.diken.com.tr/ercan-kesal-okmeydaninda-yasayanlara-buralari-cok-kiymetli-artik-bosaltin-deniyor/
DTF [Demokratik Türkiye Forumu]. 2012. *Günlük İnsan Hakları Raporu.* www.tuerkeiforum.net/trw/index.php/17–18_Temmuz_2012-Günlük_İnsan_Hakları_Raporu
Ekers, M. and Loftus, A. 2013. 'Gramsci: Space, Nature, Politics'. In M. Ekers et al. (eds). *Gramsci: Space, Nature, Politics.* West Sussex: Wiley-Blackwell.
Ercan, F. and Oğuz, Ş. 2014. 'From Gezi Resistance to Soma Massacre: Capital Accumulation and Class Struggle in Turkey'. *Socialist Register* 51.
Erman, T. 2001. 'The Politics of Squatter (Gecekondu) Studies in Turkey: The Changing Representations of Rural Migrants in the Academic Discourse'. *Urban Studies* 38(7).
Evrensel Newspaper. 2015. *Beyoğlu Belediyesi'nden 'iptal edilen eski plan' açıklaması.* www.evrensel.net/haber/103970/beyoglu-belediyesinden-iptal-edilen-eski-plan-aciklamasi
FIDH. 2014. *Bir yılın ardından Gezi.* http://1807.tihv.org.tr/wp-content/uploads/2014/05/BirYilinArdindanGezi.pdf
Forgacs, D. 2000. *The Antonio Gramsci Reader.* New York: New York University Press.
Gramsci, A. 1978. *Selections from Political Writings, 1921–1926,* ed. and trans. Quintin Hoare. New York: International.

Hall, S. 1986. 'Gramsci's Relevance for the Study of Race and Ethnicity'. *Journal of Communication Inquiry* 10(2).

Hardt, M. 2014. *Innovation and Obstacles in Istanbul One Year after Gezi*. www.euronomade. info/?p=2557

Hürriyet [newspaper]. 2014. İşte yıllara göre işçi ölümleri. www.hurriyet.com.tr/ ekonomi/27588984.asp

Jessop, B. 2007. *State Power: A Strategic-Relational Approach*. Cambridge: Polity Press.

Keyder, Ç. 2014. *Yeni orta sınıf*. http://bilimakademisi.org/wp-content/uploads/2013/09/ Yeni-Orta-Sinif.pdf

Kipfer, S. 2013. 'City, Country, Hegemony: Antonio Gramsci's Spatial Historicism'. In M. Ekers et al. (eds). *Gramsci: Space, Nature, Politics*. West Sussex: Wiley-Blackwell.

Kurt, F. 2008. *Making of Community in the Margin: The Case of Okmeydanı*, unpublished MA thesis. Istanbul: Bogazici University.

Kuymulu, M.B. 2013. 'Reclaiming the Right to the City: Reflections on the Urban Uprisings in Turkey'. *City: an analysis of urban trends, culture, theory, policy, action* 17(3).

Marcus, A. 1996. '"Should I Shoot You?": An Eyewitness Account of an Alevi Uprising in Gazi'. *Middle East Report* 199.

Metin, Ş. 2009. *Rethinking the Implications of Flexibilisation of Labour Markets: The Case of Home-Based Production in Tuzluçayır*, unpublished MA thesis. Ankara: Middle East Technical University.

Moudouros, N. 2014. 'Rethinking Islamic Hegemony in Turkey through Gezi Park'. *Journal of Balkan and Near Eastern Studies* 16(2).

Müller, H. 2014. *The Dire State of Labor Rights in Turkey*. www.turkeyanalyst.org/ publications/turkey-analyst-articles/item/346-the-dire-state-of-labor-rights-in-turkey. html

OECD.Stat 2015. *Trade Union Density*. http://stats.oecd.org/Index.aspx?DataSetCode=UN_ DEN

Öktem, K. 2013. *Contours of a New Republic and Signals from the Past: How to Understand Taksim Square*. www.jadaliyya.com/pages/index/12088/contours-of-a-new-republic-and-signals-from-the-pa

Örs, İ.R. 2014. 'Genie in the Bottle: Gezi Park, Taksim Square, and the Realignment of Democracy and Space in Turkey'. *Philosophy and Social Criticism* 40(4–5).

Perouse, J.F. 2015. *Okmeydani: A Targeted Territory*. www.jadaliyya.com/pages/index/21373/ okmeydani_a-targeted-territory

Pope, H. 2013. *Erdogan Can Win by Engaging Turkey's Park Protesters*. www.bloombergview. com/articles/2013-06-06/erdogan-can-win-by-engaging-turkey-s-park-protesters

Portes, A. and Hoffman, K. 2003. 'Latin American Class Structures: Their Composition and Change during the Neoliberal Era'. *Latin American Research Review* 38(1).

Sendika.org [Internet newspaper]. 2013a. *Okmeydanı'nın da artık bir 'Dayanışması' var*. www.sendika.org/2013/06/okmeydaninin-da-artik-bir-dayanismasi-var/

—— 2013b. *Gazi halkı 18 gündür direniyor: Polis saldırdı, halk direndi*. www.sendika. org/2013/06/gazi-halki-18-gundur-direniyor/

——2013c. *Ankara AKP faşizmine karşı duruyor (dakika dakika)*. www.sendika.org/2013/06/ ankara-akp-fasizmine-direniyor-dakika-dakika/

Semercioğlu, C. and Ayyıldız, D. 2014. *Michael Hardt: Çokluk örgütlenmek zorunda*. http:// meseledergisi.com/2014/06/michael-hardt-cokluk-orgutlenmek-zorunda/

Tonak, A.E. 2013. 'İsyanın sınıfları'. In: Ö. Göztepe (ed.). *Gezi Direnişi Üzerine Düşünceler*. Ankara: NotaBene Yayınları.

Tuğal, C. 2013. 'Resistance Everywhere: The Gezi Revolt in Global Perspective'. *New Perspectives on Turkey* 49 (Fall).

Verdeil, E. 2011. *Arab Cities in Revolution: Some Observations.* www.metropolitiques.eu/
Arab-Cities-in-Revolution-Some.html

Wacquant, L. 2014. *Urban Inequality, Marginality and Social Justice.* http://istifhanem.com

Wallerstein, I. 2015. *Uprisings Here, There, and Everywhere.* http://iwallerstein.com/
uprisings/

Whitehead, J. 2013. 'Accumulation through Dispossession and Accumulation through
Growth: Intimations of Massacres Foretold?'. In M. Ekers et al. (eds). *Gramsci: Space,
Nature, Politics.* West Sussex: Wiley-Blackwell.

Yazar İ. 2014. İş kazalarında toplu ölümler arttı. www.zaman.com.tr/ekonomi_
is-kazalarinda-toplu-olumler-artti_2254177.html

Yörük, E. 2014. 'The Long Summer of Turkey: The Gezi Uprising and its Historical Roots'.
South Atlantic Quarterly 113(2).

—— and Yüksel, M. 2014. 'Class and Politics in Turkey's Gezi Protests'. *New Left Review* 89.

4

Gramsci in Slices: Race, Colonialism, Migration and the Postcolonial Gramsci

Miguel Mellino

(UN)BROKEN LINES

Decoding the semblance of the postcolonial Antonio Gramsci is not an easy task. To follow the postcolonial *traces* of Gramsci (uses of Gramscian concepts within cultural, Indian Subaltern or postcolonial studies) is to immerse oneself in something of a Borgesian universe and give up all possibility of finding a (logical) Ariadne's thread to guide one through the maze. It is to find yourself in a garden full of paths that fork for ever. This assumption should be an axiomatic principle for whoever undertakes to explore this territory: bouncing from path to path into the postcolonial Gramsci means abandoning oneself to a voyage of no return; confronting unknown (*other*) semblances of his thought, but at the same time, losing his *singularity* as a figure. In short, it means disassembling or deconstructing Gramsci, rather than pinning him down.

This is in itself a logical consequence of the globalisation of the *Notebooks*, or, taking up Dipesh Chakrabarty's metaphor, of what might be called the 'provincialisation' of the Italian 'communist' reading of Gramsci (cf. Capuzzo and Mezzadra 2012). However, the primary assumption about this 'provincialisation' of Gramsci's work, the postcolonial readings of his writings, is that we now have to confront Gramsci in slices. In other words, postcolonial readings of Gramsci's oeuvre propose more of a *translation* of some of his key concepts in *other* and specific historical contexts than an analytical or (even) critical continuation of his particular Marxist perspective.

It is the very material nature of the *Notebooks* – their structure as a continuing work in progress – that permitted this translation or appropriation. This imprint of Gramscian thought derives not simply from the inherently *conjunctural* articulation of many of his theses and concepts, from the development of a system of thought in continuous revision, but from the eminently tactical and political quality of his 'philosophy of praxis'. However, to emphasise the radically contingent nature of many Gramscian concepts is not to suggest any fragmentariness of his thought, and even less that his Marxism lacks coherence or is lacking any internal *master* narrative (of any explicit continuity throughout its intricated development).

Intertwining this contingent nature of Gramscian thought and the postcolonial 'deconstruction' of his work, I want to suggest two things – two assumptions that seem to me important when attempting a comprehension from *within*, as it were, of postcolonial *translations* of Gramscian thought. The first is quite obvious: it is not accurate to define what can be called the 'Gramscian moment' in cultural, subaltern or postcolonial studies merely as a variation of current 'Gramscianism' (see Thomas 2009). The cultural and postcolonial turn to Gramsci is more complex. The second assumption is highly connected to the first: 'Gramscianism' within these fields cannot be considered without taking into account the politics of 'post' thinking. It could be argued that the postcolonial turn to Gramsci is one of the main 'theoretical symptoms' of the emergence of 'heterogeneity' – and hence of new political subjects – as a structural feature of contemporary global capital.

POST-GRAMSCI/POST-MARXISM

First of all, the idea of dealing with Gramsci in slices is intended to evoke something perhaps a little obvious: in postcolonial and subaltern studies, the work of Gramsci has come to be configured as one of many reference points and not, by any means, their determining or dominant component.

At first glance, the Subaltern Studies project on India would seem to contradict this statement. Yet, even if we are dealing here with a collective of historians defining itself from the outset by one of the more famous terms of Gramscian thought, their project, when taken as a whole seems difficult to classify as solely Gramscian. Some of the most influential theoretical assumptions of the Indian Subaltern Studies group seem to be in open contradiction to Gramsci's Marxian perspective. Consider, for example, the work of Ranajit Guha (1988; 1997; 1983), particularly his idea of a historical–political space of *autonomy* of the subaltern or *masses* (peasants) within Indian history – whereas autonomy means here to locate peasants' political subjectivity, i.e. the meaning of their anticolonial insurgences, outside the discursive grammar of any Western grand narrative, whether centred on the modern (liberal–bourgeois) nation state or on the emergence of the proletariat as a 'class' or as a historical subject; otherwise, take Partha Chatterjee's (1993) and Chakrabarty's (2000) critiques of the masses' 'politics of education' pursued by the Indian National Congress after the achieved independence. We are confronting here two assumptions that have little to do with the construction of a socialist political hegemony as theorised by Gramsci (following Lenin) in the *Notebooks*. As has been noted, the importance Gramsci conceded to the cultural (or superstructural) dimension – to the sphere of cultural consent – in the construction of a hegemonic project, of the socialist state, did not in itself mean to suggest a *valorisation* of subaltern cultures, and even less to question the main premises of historical materialism or of dialectics – as necessary key approaches to capitalism and to the deployment of its political antagonisms (Frosini 2003).

Having said this, I do not intend to suggest a philological approach to postcolonial uses of Gramsci. There would be no point, since the outcome can be taken for granted. Little can be gained from asking, as does, for example, Jean-Loup Amselle, if 'post-colonial authors invoke the *true* thought of the celebrated Italian theorist or a reconstructed image of him' (Amselle 2008: 162). These kinds of rough philological interrogations end up as dull syllogisms. The answer is contained in the question from the start. Conversely, it is more helpful and politically significant to try to understand what the postcolonial reading of Gramsci is about. What I am suggesting is to read Gramsci's work in the light of postcolonial critique (of subaltern and cultural studies) and not the other way around. This seems to me the only way of gaining any intellectual or political profit.

Our discourse could be summarised thus: considering cultural, postcolonial and subaltern studies as simply Gramscian approaches seems utterly beside the point. It would be more appropriate to affirm that within these perspectives, many critical theorists have had to pass through some key or nodal points of Gramsci's work in a particular and contingent historical moment – just as they passed through the work of other authors such as Barthes (Guha), Althusser (Hall), Derrida (Spivak), Lacan (Laclau), Foucault (Said and Chatterjee), Heidegger (Chakrabarty) – to outline something like what Stuart Hall has called a 'complex Marxism' (Hall and Jefferson 1976). Their aim was to sketch a theoretical–political approach to cultural history and especially to the world of different subaltern classes – or colonial others – that could *still* be Marxist (at least during the 1970s and 1980s), but explicitly breaking with that economistic and Eurocentric Marxism historically promoted by Communist Parties and their own organic intellectuals. No wonder if we are describing the shift that would lead to the emergence of so-called post-Marxism, namely a mix of Marxism and post-structuralism of which Ernesto Laclau's work represents perhaps its 'ideal type'.

Secondly, the idea that postcolonial approaches to Gramsci are working only with slices of his work is simply to stress the 'politics of theory' pursued by 'post' (postmodern, postcolonial) thinking: the use of theory as a toolbox (Foucault and Deleuze 1972), as a 'concrete and applied practice' aimed at the comprehension of conjunctural or specific political questions rather than as a mere abstract epistemo-logical expertise, theoretical system or master narrative. From the 'post' standpoint, the adoption of ready to use grand-theory systems, rather than simply 'going on theorising', to quote again a well-known expression of Stuart Hall (Hall 2006; 2007), would be to fall back into the philosophy of history, colonial historicism or orientalism at the base of Western knowledge. Chakrabarty's project of 'provincialising Europe' summarises, rather incisively, this kind of postcolonial *Weltanschauung*: what is to be done is to get away from theory as 'exhaustive taxonomy' (Derrida) or as 'master narrative', otherwise we are going to be trapped forever in the (colonial) question of Subject and History (with capital S and H, revoking Althusser's Marxism).

I am not assuming here – as many Marxist critiques do – that postmodern/postcolonial criticism of master narratives stands for futile and solipsistic pleasures in micro-narration, for compulsive cultural relativism or simply self-satisfied celebrations of the disappearance of material overdetermination (of classes), and even less for the impossibility of putting into practice real politics of social and cultural emancipation. It could be argued that the 'politics of theory' in 'post' theoretical approaches deploys itself in what might be called an 'anti-dialectic' direction: getting out of the 'grand narration' or 'historicist' discourse surely means emphasising the *coloniality* of any universal idea of History (or Subject), but also the impossibility of any (eventual) dialectical re-integration of the whole (to say it with Lukács), that is, of ever being able to re-enter that particular Garden of Eden in which consciousness can be reconciled with itself.

It is in this sense then that postcolonial Gramsci means Gramsci in slices. Highlighting the various ways in which Gramsci's uniqueness was dissolved (deconstructed), the unravelling of the crux that holds together the 'nodal point' (Lacan) of any consciousness, can bring to light something extremely significant not only about the present of 'this big and terrible world' – to use Gramsci's suggestive expression – but also about Gramsci himself. This is what is meant by reading his work in the light of postcolonial critique.

TRAVELLING THEORY: TRAVELLING GRAMSCI

To describe the strategy of our discourse more effectively it might be useful to recall one of the most well-known of Edward Said's writings, *Traveling Theory* (1983). In this essay, Said reminds us that ideas and theories, just like people, travel: from one situation to another, one time to another, one perspective to another. It is by this movement that they end up, inevitably, experiencing the pressure of the different circumstances they encounter. Said's suggestion is to focus on those specific contingencies that have in some way inspired an *anomalous* reconfiguration of a particular theoretical perspective. For this anomaly can show us a great deal about the *limits* of these theories: it could be argued that delocalisation or *translation* of European theories into non-Western contexts, into places and situations far removed from their places of origin, like 'mimicry' (Bhabha 1994) of imperial cultures by colonial subjects, has always been a fundamental phase in that process of 'provincialising Europe' invoked by Chakrabarty.

According to Said, it is only by concentrating on swerves and contingencies inherent in the journey that we can judge if a single theory and its main assumptions are reinforced or if instead they lose consistency or, to put it in another way, if ideas and concepts connected to a certain place, time, culture or national context mutate completely when translated into different contexts or epochs. In this way, recording the theory 'then' and 'now', assuming the encountering/antagonism of theory (in this case Gramscian) with something *untranslatable* to it, would mean confronting not with Gramsci himself, but with a wider political world, with its epochal transmutations, its openings and closures, in other words, with its constitutive *conjunctural* feature – it is worth noting that this is precisely the Gramscian imprint on Said's argument. To put it in the terms of our own discourse: focusing on the anomalies of postcolonial translations of Gramsci's toolbox can surely help us understand something about the economic and political configuration of contemporary world or global (postcolonial) capitalism.

Let's start by fixing a point we have already anticipated: Gramsci's appeal to cultural and postcolonial studies lies more in 'populist' and 'anti-historicist' tensions (*postcolonial* tensions) running through his work than on his assumptions about colonialism, as they are articulated in *L'Ordine Nuovo* or scattered throughout the *Notebooks*. It could be argued that not even his famous reading of '*la quistione meridionale*' (the Southern question) in Italy as another peculiar case of 'internal colonialism' holds a particularly central position in the space allotted to Gramsci in these fields of study. Certainly, Gramscian characterisation of the Risorgimento's nationalism as a 'passive revolution' is well known and often quoted: indeed, Indian Subalternist historians have never ceased tracing analogies between this description by Gramsci and the political situation in postcolonial India, characterised by the regressive political limits of the Indian National Congress Party's nationalism. In any case, as we shall see, it is not Gramsci's theorising on the '(post-)colonial situation' that attracts the attention of Indian critiques such as Guha, Chakrabarty or Spivak, but rather the 'anti-historicist' tensions running through the Gramscian archive. This is not surprising, since Gramsci's ideas on colonialism and imperialism appear far less elaborated than those of, say, Trotsky about global capitalism as 'combined/uneven development' and even not really distant from Lenin's positions. Furthermore, it was precisely this kind of traditional Marxist perspective, when dealing with colonial/imperial/national questions that Subalternist historians were attempting to leave behind, even through a particular interpretation of Gramsci's oeuvre.

RACE, MIGRATION AND THE DECOLONISATION OF WESTERN MARXISM: STUART HALL'S GRAMSCI AND THE CRISIS OF ENGLISHNESS

Gramsci's writings entered into British Marxist debate in the late 1950s (Forgacs 1989), but their impact on British cultural studies could not be measured until the late 1970s, through the work of Raymond Williams (1978) and, mainly, Hall (1980; 1986). Paradoxically, compared to what was happening in Italy at the time, in Britain Gramsci was at the centre of milieus still marked by the propelling force of New Left cultural politics, and hence was situated in domains of the British Left in open dissent with the dogmatic Marxism promoted by 'official' Communist Parties and organisations. As Hall himself explained, in cultural studies the interest in Gramsci grew from attempts to create a renovated 'complex Marxism' (1976), neither Eurocentric nor economistic, capable of a sensitive handling of 'the relative autonomy of the different spheres' of social totalities or, to say it in an Althusserian way, of the constituent role of culture, representations and ideology in the production of social worlds (Hall 1976; 1980; 1992b). However, this attention to Gramsci was symptomatic of a rather different political moment in Britain than that from which the New Left had emerged. We are now at the beginning of the 1970s. On the one hand, students are still in revolt, new social movements (especially feminism) continue to rise; but on the other hand at that time was emerging a general impression about the exhaustion of the post-war economic boom and hence the feeling that the country might be on the brink of a deep social and economic crisis. But these are years of intense and persistent *racial* conflicts, a period characterised by ever more frequent riots of black and Asian communities against what might be called the British state's neo-colonial management of post-war migration (Hall et al. 1978; CCCS 1982).

It is at this point that a radical shift becomes apparent in the history of the Centre for Contemporary Cultural Studies (CCCS) in Birmingham. During this period a radical anti-humanism began to emerge within the centre as a key understanding of Western colonial (and British) culture. By radical anti-humanism I mean the radical questioning of all the fundamental premises of European humanism, but above all the *deconstruction* of the (Western) notion of history. Clearly, this criticism did not take the form of mere theoretical production; it was itself the result of extended political struggles, namely those of antiracist, migrant and feminist movements, but also of those tacitly present global decolonisation movements that can be commonly conceptualised as insurrections of different (other) histories against the hegemony of (Subject) History with a capital H. In Hall's words, 'it is the moment of the emerging of the margins (migrants, blacks, women, colonial subjects, youth, the working classes etc.) into the centre' (Hall 2000), or of the *supplements'* revolt against modern sovereign subject master narratives and hence of their radical demand for the right to self-representation (both of political and cultural autonomy). It is from this gradual disintegration of consensus and authority at the base of the immediate post-war period social pact, that Thatcherism emerges as an 'authoritarian and populist' way to 'govern the crisis' (Hall et al. 1978; Hall 1988).

The significance of this shift in the history of British cultural studies – behind the emergence of this radical anti-humanism – could be effectively conceptualised as the emergence of what Jean-Francois Lyotard has called '*the differend*' (Lyotard 1983). This *differend* is generated by the manifestation and fulfilment of *difference*, that is by the collapse of that humanistic philosophy of history erected by Western knowledge as the fundamental pillar of traditional humanities and social sciences. Hall is rather eloquent on this point: one of his more quoted articles is entitled 'The Emergence of Cultural Studies and the Crisis of Humanities' (1990). Its main assumption is that cultural studies arose from the progressive critique of humanism and those specific disciplines on which it was fundamentally based: especially history and literature, not by chance the two principal institutional vehicles and custodians of national identity. Drawing on Hall's assumption it is possible to define (the archive of) cultural studies as a *symptom* of the disintegration of Englishness at the very core of the United Kingdom, namely of the corroding of traditional

British identity, of white and Euro-Western Subject, as a mere variation of the modernity grand narration.

This is the historical context in which Hall's *anomalous* interpretation of Gramsci emerged. It is helpful to stress, assuming Said's ideas on travelling theories, the *anomaly* of Hall's uses of Gramsci: since it has produced a *non-historicistic* reading of Gramsci's thought. Indeed, what Hall is proposing is a use of Gramscian theories and concepts aimed not at the outline of a general theoretical system, but at the comprehension of very specific phenomena (such as Thatcherism, post-Fordism, new politics in the domain of popular culture, the articulation of race, racism, and postcolonial ethnicities in post-war Britain) and *beyond* any form of 'historicist imaginary', that is *outside* the grammar of that political imagination that shaped Gramsci's thought (despite the atypical nature of his 'philosophy of praxis').

Hall's essays such as 'Race, Articulation and Societies Structured in Dominance' (1980), 'Gramsci's Relevance for the Study of Race and Ethnicity' (1986) or the famous 'The Hard Road to Renewal: Thatcherism and the Crisis of the Left' (1988) are inspiring examples of his postcolonial 'anti-historicist' use of Gramsci's toolbox. In these works, Hall turns to the Gramscian archive to bring into focus more effectively the way in which capitalism and the modern nation state had always been active agents in the production of 'racially structured societies' (Hall 1980) – in other words, how they operate through mechanisms of what might be called 'differential inclusion of subjects and populations'. Thus these writings convey, rather suggestively, a radical critique of Western capitalist modernity and its presumed *inherent* universalism. Contrary to what traditional Marxist theories inspired by Kautsky, Hilferding and Trotsky, as well as Second International orthodox Marxism, had assumed on uneven and combined development, Hall's writings aimed to show how the global expansion of capitalist modernity (intertwined with questions of race) did not produce a homogenisation or a levelling of world economy and labour, but rather a ceaseless proliferation of differences, heterogeneities and hierarchies. It is essentially from this starting assumption that every 'historicist' or 'teleological' perspective (liberal–bourgeois or Marxist) concerning the development of capitalism becomes not only ill-founded, but above all *colonial* and Eurocentric: since they assume as a *universal* model the *modalities* of European capitalist development and, particularly, its *form* of class struggle.

We need to emphasise that the 'non-historicist' interpretation of Gramsci conveyed in these works by Hall has been legitimised to some extent by the reading of the *Notebooks* by Althusser and a few years later by Laclau (1977). As Peter Thomas recalls, 'the anti-historicist and anti-humanist perspectives Althusser had brought into sharper focus through his critique of Gramsci became formative for an entire generation' (Thomas 2009: 8), but mainly they are still 'representative of more general "images of Gramsci" in both the Marxist and wider intellectual culture' (ibid.: xix). Hall is clearly one of the best examples of this 'Althusserian Gramscianism'. Let us remember, for example, the recurrence through these writings of expressions such as 'overdetermination', 'relative autonomy of the spheres', 'complex and articulated totalities', but also of the critique of every kind of simplistic or *univocal* determinism. It seems to me *symptomatic* that Hall expresses himself through these concepts in proposing a Gramscian perspective, or that he considers the main contribution of Gramsci to have been to induce us to think of different social formations as the product of particular 'articulations' and thus as phenomena that are 'historically specific' (Hall 1986). It is through these concepts that Hall requires us to define current multicultural societies as 'racially structured societies', to consider these social formations as the product of a global capitalism that has historically worked *even through* differences, regional variations, cultural, gender and racial particularities, never deploying any rule of homogeneous development.

Gramsci never makes the mistake of believing that, because the general law of value has the tendency to homogenise labour power across the capitalist epoch, that therefore, in any concrete society, this homogenisation can be assumed to exist. Indeed, I believe Gramsci's whole approach leads us to question the validity of this general law in its traditional form, since, precisely, it has encouraged us to neglect the ways in which the law of value, operating on a global as opposed to a merely domestic scale, operates through and *because* of the culturally specific character of labour power, rather than – as the classical theory would have us believe – by systematically eroding those distinctions as an inevitable part of a worldwide, epochal historical tendency. Certainly, whenever we depart from the 'Eurocentric' model of capitalist development (and even within that model) what we actually find is the many ways in which capital can preserve, adapt to its fundamental trajectory, harness and exploit these particularistic qualities of labour power, building them into regimes (Hall 1986: 26).

The main suggestions and anomalous nature of the (postcolonial) reading of Gramsci bequeathed by Hall arises clearly from this passage. It is by way of Gramsci that Hall tries to highlight the *conjunctural* features of capitalist development and the spread of Western modernity across the globe. He is thus opposing any reading of the history of other societies and their joining/colliding with capitalism from within a Eurocentric framework theoretically built on its unique reference to the historical development of European modernity (and of European working classes) or, rather, on a certain hegemonic (historicist) way of imagining its historical evolution. In summary: underlining the conjunctural *nature* of social formations, Hall is invoking *non-historical* and *non-teleological* readings of the relationship between 'formal subsumption' and 'real subsumption' of labour to capital outlined by Marx. In Hall's vision, a historicist reading of this relationship would inhibit an adequate (non-Eurocentric) understanding of real capitalist development: for a 'unitary logic' of capital has never existed. Hall then passes through Gramsci in order to go even further: in his scheme, differing from Gramsci, history (capitalism) no longer operates within a *dialectic* unity. We are therefore far beyond 'humanist–historicist' imaginaries: we must open to historical difference rather than trying to force history into a dialectical scheme. It is through this 'Gramscian' assumption that Hall requires us to decolonise Western Marxism.

THE SUBALTERN OF SUBALTERN STUDIES: THE CRISIS OF THE POSTCOLONIAL INDIAN STATE

The emergence of the Indian Subaltern Studies approach is linked to the crisis of Western grand narrative (in its bourgeois–nationalist version) as a project of universal collective emancipation. Subaltern Studies has arisen in the context of the crisis of the postcolonial state from the failure of the Indian bourgeoisie in its attempt to speak for the entire nation (Guha 1988: 38) and hence to produce a truly universal citizenship. The crisis of the postcolonial Indian state was also effectively highlighted by the emergence of Maoist Naxalite guerillas in an important region of the country, or rather by the eruption at the beginning of the 1970s of peasant rebellions in Western Bengal, which raised radical questions about the nation-building process (and the politics of citizenship) promoted by the Congress Party (see Young 2001). Although the Indian historical and political context greatly differs from that of the United Kingdom, it is not difficult to draw analogies with the contingencies of postcolonial British history (emergence of the margins, of race, in the metropolitan territory of the former empire) which were the backdrop for Hall's Gramscian reading. In both cases, we are witnessing what, drawing on Jacques Rancière, we might call the insurgence 'of the part of those without any part' (Rancière 1995).

It is within this particular political context that the central axis of the Subaltern Studies project began to take shape: Guha gathers together a group of historians with the intent of launching a new historiography, centred on the comprehension of the role of subaltern classes (and mainly the recurring peasants' rebellions) in Indian history. The aim of the project, therefore, was the production of a new historiography that would go beyond the mere reproduction of colonial or elitarian–nationalist encoding of subaltern subjectivities' forms and expressions, namely of those who had made most of Indian history, through their rebellions against colonial power, but were not able to write about it.

It could be said that Subaltern Studies shaped their project from the outset with a particular set of questions: How can we write and stay close to the masses? How can we understand the anticolonial insurrections of Indian peasants from the nineteenth century onwards without expropriating the subjectivity of the insurgents (as had happened in colonial and elitarian–nationalist versions of history)? In Guha's more specific terms, how can we be *within* history, intended as historicity – as the history not of the state but of common people (Guha 2002)? It is from these questions that the Gramscian category 'subaltern' begins to become significant. Yet, from the very point of view of the collective, the name 'subaltern' ends up becoming something like a *signifier* (see Spivak 1988b), that is it has become something entirely different from what it represented for Gramsci.

In effect, differing from Gramsci's perspective, Indian historians seemed to be saying that in order to recover subaltern subjectivities, peasants must remain on (or need to be put back to) the margins of History (of historicism): peasant rebellions cannot be understood in their political, cultural and subjective specificity from within any modern grand narrative (colonial, nationalist, Marxist), for the very reason that these represent tools of knowledge *external* to their socio-cultural world. It is in this way that the term 'subaltern' is transformed into a *signifier*, since it does not have to carry the weight of any grand narrative on its shoulders. Subalterns are those on the margins of history: subjects immersed in the autonomous space (which does not mean archaic or traditional) of their own historicity. As from various perspectives Guha (1988), Spivak (1988a, 1988b) and Chakrabarty (2006) insist, subalterns do not constitute something similar to a traditional historical subject. In Chakrabarty's assesment:

> I think there was something salutary in the structuralist side of Guha's work, in his insistence that the subject of an insurgency was collective and in his refusal to see this collective either additively – as a collection of individuals – or as a unity having a psychology of its own. In other words, as I have already said, this was not a subject whose history could be written on a biographical model of birth and subsequent growth towards maturity (the model long prevalent, for

instance, in labour histories of the sixties and seventies). A subject without a biography, a subject without a psychology, a subject without a continuous existence in historical time, a subject coming into being only in specific conjunctures – all this sounds like a plethora of contradictions. What kind of a subject was this? This familiar criticism, however, simply misses the point. One can see in the twists and turns of Guha's complicated thoughts that even the idea of the subject – an autonomous, sovereign being – had to be 'stretched' (in Fanon's sense of the word) in order for the word ('subject') to be pliable at all in the context of subaltern history. (Chakrabarty 2006: 21)

The question opened by Subaltern Studies, but already laid out systematically and groundbreakingly a few years earlier by Said in *Orientalism* (1978), is extremely significant. It is a question not of an anthropological kind, it does not ask simply how to understand the other beyond Eurocentric frames, or how to decolonise our modes of knowledge, but it is mainly a question of politics: in the sense that it poses problems of theoretical representation on the one hand, and of political representation on the other. And they are extremely significant to our political time: how can we understand contemporary movements of subjectivation without legitimising what Spivak has called a new form of 'epistemic violence' (Spivak 1999), namely a discursive strategy that ends up depriving the subjects we are examining of their subjectivity? In short: how can we identify and conceive a revolutionary subject, given the constitutive heterogeneity of what we might call postcolonial global capitalism? I will come back to this point in my conclusion.

For now it is more important to emphasise that the problematic opened up by Subaltern Studies poses more general questions about politics and decolonisation of knowledge and archives. Two of the more suggestive analyses of these subaltern questions are certainly, 'Can the Subaltern Speak?' (1988a) and 'Deconstructing Historiography' (1988b) by Gayatri Spivak. Through these texts, Spivak openly raises an epistemological problem that remained only latent in the first of Guha's works and that might be summarised thus: how can we think the 'Real' (in a Lacanian sense) in its immanence without closing it through theoretical categories that remain alien to it, that is through categories that tend to lose their historicity (their precise historical–geographical root), becoming, by virtue of the relationship between knowledge and power, Europe and the Third World, universal, transcendent, hypothesised, reifying expropriating concepts? This is perhaps one of the biggest critical interrogations raised by the use of the Gramscian subaltern concept within Subaltern Studies.

As a mode of conclusion, I want to suggest that from a Subaltern Studies perspective, the concept of subaltern becomes intelligible in what can be called an 'anti-conceptual' guise, namely as a (Maoist) concept close to the masses (to the historical–local dimension of peasants' consciousness); as a kind of 'dissolving concept', an opening (not closure) concept, as a radically democratic and above all anti-historicist concept. My suggestion is also that the application of other Gramscian concepts such as the 'passive revolution', 'historical bloc', 'hegemony' or 'dominance without hegemony' (see Chatterjee 1986; Guha 1997) to the history of India are inscribed within this radically anti-historicist (postcolonial) perspective, as a central part of that project which Chakrabarty a few years later is to call 'provincialising Europe'. It could be argued therefore that what most famous Subaltern Studies works have tried to underline, drawing on their analysis of the particular *translation* processes of Western modernity into Indian cultures, is that there is no *unitary* logic to capital. As Chatterjee explains:

People can imagine themselves in empty homogeneous time; they do not live in it. Empty homogeneous time is the utopian time of capital. It linearly connects past, present, and future, creating the possibility for all of those historicist imaginings of identity, nationhood, progress, and so on that Anderson, along with many others, have made familiar to us. But empty homogeneous time is not located anywhere in real space – it is utopian. The real space of modern life consists of heterotopia. (Chatterjee 2004: 6–7)

As in the case of Hall, hence, even the Indian Subalternist historians passed through Gramsci seeking to go further. It is by using Gramsci as a starting point, but also by reading Gramsci against the grain, that the Subaltern Studies group began to decolonise the historiography of India; to restore the political nature, the category of politics, to the traditional forms of Indian peasant rebellions, whether against the colonial state before or the postcolonial state after. Yet, it is an operation that could only have been conceived by sacrificing the uniqueness (the coloniality) of Gramscian thought itself.

CONCLUSION: POSTCOLONIAL GRAMSCI, POSTCOLONIAL GLOBAL CAPITALISM AND MIGRATION STUDIES TODAY

Current debates on the meanings of the postcolonial as a key signifier of our present condition are seldom connected to debates on the historical transformations of capitalism. Although it is now assumed that the development of postcolonial studies has certainly broadened historical knowledge on the constitutive role of colonial/racial governmentalities in the formation of both modern capitalist world market and nation-building processes, the postcolonial signifier has hardly ever been mobilised to define present capitalist formations. While it has become commonplace to define contemporary subjects, politics, cultures, societies and cities as postcolonial (postcolonial migrants, postcolonial Britain, postcolonial Paris, not to say postcolonial India or postcolonial theory) it is still quite unusual to name contemporary global capitalism as postcolonial. We are dealing here with one of the most striking paradoxes of postcolonial theory: it is hard to assume that anything like a postcolonial condition can exist independently of anything like postcolonial capitalism.

Why then such a failure? It could be argued that it arises directly out of the very discursive turn that nurtured the emergence of postcolonial theory. Postcoloniality has been mostly concerned with the decolonisation of knowledges and cultures, namely with the disruption of dominant Western representations of the rest of the world and its 'ethnographic authority' (Clifford 1988) in the articulation of imperial global dominance. Drawing on Spivak (1999) and Sanjay Seth (2007) it could be said that postcolonial theory's main political task has been right from the beginning – since the disruptive appearance of Said's *Orientalism* (1978) – to unmask Western historical epistemic privilege as epistemic (colonial) violence. However, as Hall pointed out in his well-known controversy with Arif Dirlik, what has resulted from the discursive/cultural turn and its abandonment of classical political-economy perspectives, 'has been, not alternative ways of thinking questions about economic relations and their effects, as the conditions of existence of other practices, inserting them in a "decentred" or dislocated way into our explanatory paradigms, but instead a massive, gigantic and eloquent disavowal' (Hall 1992a: 244).

My argument here is that it is possible to begin to fill this gap precisely by drawing on postcolonial readings of Gramsci. As we have seen, Hall's and Subaltern Studies' readings of Gramsci have revealed important hitherto unknown or under-theorised features about the uneven historical global working of capital. Thus it is from this specific re-reading of Western Marxism in the light of postcolonial Britain and India, combining it with some of the best postcolonial studies on contemporary global capital (see for example Mbembe 2001; Venn 2006; Ong 2005; Sanyal 2005), that I suggest contemporary global neoliberal capitalism should be addressed through a specific materialistic reading of the postcolonial signifier.

There is an obvious strategic political value to be gained, and hence to be spent, in social struggles by defining contemporary global capitalism as postcolonial capitalism. What do we mean then by postcolonial capitalism? First of all, the signifier 'postcolonial' is useful to name a capitalist order still highly dependent on 'new and permanent processes of primitive accumulation' (Sanyal 2005) and 'accumulation by dispossession' (Harvey 2004). Many Marxist and post-Marxist scholars – albeit from different perspectives – have emphasised this aspect of the working of contemporary global capital in their recent writings (Escobar 1995; Harvey 2004; Sanyal 2005; Samaddar 2009; Hardt and Negri 2009; Van der Linden 2009; Bonefeld 2011). However, by appealing to the postcolonial signifier in naming contemporary capitalist formations, my aim is to stress both the coloniality underlying such processes and the colonial roots of its modes of domination and subjectification (Quijano 2000). Significantly, in current literature on the causes of contemporary financial crises there is no reference to the long historical and structural dependence of capitalism on colonialism. Hegemonic political economy – either in liberal/conservative or in left/Marxist discourses – still considers colonialism merely an (ended) historical stage in capitalist accumulation. Conversely, to understand better the roots of the present economic meltdown, we need to reconsider colonialism, or colonial capitalism, and imperialism as key historical processes in the shaping of modern capitalist regimes of exploitation. I argue that contemporary over-accumulation crises rely on the coloniality of contemporary capitalist rule: in the global production and proliferation of what Ahiwa Ong calls 'different sovereign subjects and spaces' (Ong 2005).

Indeed, in spite of hegemonic neoliberal discourse and its claims to the universality of market relationships and to the formal homogeneity of modern Western citizenship, contemporary global capital is still driven by colonial and imperial logics of accumulation, that is, it can constitute itself only by producing political, economic and juridical heterogeneous spaces and therefore articulating what we can call specific and differential forms of incorporation of territories, cultures, knowledges, and subjects into its domain. I would argue that this form of differential incorporation has its roots in colonial capitalism: 'neoliberalism as exception', to recall Ong's quoted work (2005), cannot be understood without taking into account the role of colonial rule in shaping capitalist modernity. However, this assumption remains vague in Ong's text.

These differential forms of incorporation involve new and very different types of (material and immaterial) enclosures, as well as the increasing privatisation and hierarchisation of citizenship and knowledge, the ethnic spatialisation of local and global urban spaces, and the constitution of heterogeneous or multiform regimes of labour that crisscross national boundaries. In *The Wretched of the Earth* Fanon has defined the colonial space as a 'protean and uneven space' (2007: 64): in the colony – unlike homogeneous metropolitan territories – 'slavery, bondage, barter, cottage industries and stock transaction exist side by side' (ibid.). It could be argued that nowadays 'this protean and uneven space', this combination of different and hierarchised forms of labour, extends even through the so-called advanced capitalist countries. It is precisely in these terms that I that suggest contemporary global capitalism can be conceived of as postcolonial capitalism.

Struggles around migration and citizenship in Europe are a privileged arena from which to regard contemporary neoliberal capitalism as postcolonial capitalism. Moreover, contemporary European postcolonial citizenships should be considered as symbol and allegory of postcolonial capitalism. In examining the question of citizenship in Europe, and in particular contemporary struggles around the status of migrant labour, it becomes possible to grasp what is at stake in postcolonial capitalism. It is thus in the light of the becoming of what can be called the 'heterogeneity of labour' as a constitutive feature of global capital that postcolonial readings of Gramsci might become a helpful toolbox for approaching contemporary conflicts and struggles. At this point, it must be clear why – from my point of view – Hall's and the Subalternist historians' Gramscian turn to decolonise Western Marxism really matters.

REFERENCES

Amselle, J. 2008. L'occident décroché: Enquêtes sur les poscolonialismes. Paris: Stock.
Bhabha, H. 1994. The Location of Culture. London: Routledge.
Bonefeld, W. 2011. 'Primitive Accumulation and Capitalist Accumulation: Notes on Social Constitution and Expropriation'. Science and Society 75(3): 379–99.
Capuzzo, P. and Mezzadra, S. 2012. 'Provincializing the Italian Reading of Gramsci'. In N. Srivastava and B. Battacharya (eds). The Postcolonial Gramsci. London: Routledge.
CCCS (ed.). 1982. The Empire Strikes Back: Race and Racism in 70s Britain. London: Hutchinson.
Chakrabarty, D. 2000. Provincializing Europe: Postcolonial Thought and Historical Difference. Oxford: Princeton University Press.
—— 2006. 'Subaltern History as Political Thought'. In V. Metha and T. Pantham (eds). Political Ideas in Modern India: Thematic Explorations. New Delhi: SAGE.
Chatterjee, P. 1986. Nationalist Thought and the Colonial World: A Derivative Discourse. Tokyo: Zed Books.
—— 1993. The Nation and Its Fragments: Colonial and Postcolonial Histories. New Jersey: Princeton University Press.
—— 2004. The Politics of the Governed. New York: Columbia University Press.
Clifford, J. 1988. The Predicament of Culture: Twentieth Century Ethnography, Literature and Art. Cambridge (MA): Harvard University Press.
Escobar, A. 1995. Encountering Development. Princeton: Princeton University Press.
Fanon, F. 2007 [1961]. The Wretched of the Earth. New York: Grove Press.

Forgacs, D. 1989. 'Gramsci and Marxism in Britain'. *New Left Review* 1/176, July–August: 69–88.

Foucault, M. and Deleuze, G. 1972. 'Les intellectuals e le pouvoir'. *L'Arc* 49: 3–20.

Frosini, F. 2003. *Gramsci e la filosofia: saggio sui Quaderni del carcere*, vol. 211. Rome: Carocci.

Guha, R. 1983. Elementary Aspects of Peasant Insurgency in Colonial India. New Delhi: Oxford University Press.

—— 1988. *An Indian Historiograohy of India: A Nineteenth-century Agenda and Its Implications*. Calcutta: K.P. Bagchi.

—— 1997. *Dominance without Hegemony: History, Power and Colonial India*. Cambridge, MA and London: Harvard University Press.

—— 2002. *History at the Limit of World-History*. New York: Columbia University Press.

Hall, S. 1980. 'Race, Articulation and Societies Structured in Dominance'. In M. Baker and M. Diawar (eds). *Black British Cultural Studies*. Chicago: Chicago University Press.

—— 1986. 'Gramsci's Relevance for the Study of Race and Ethnicity'. *Journal of Communications Inquiry* 10(2): 5–27.

—— 1988. *The Hard Road to Renewal*. London: Verso.

—— 1990. 'The Emergence of Cultural Studies and the Crisis of Humanities'. *The Humanities as Social Technology* 53: 11–23.

—— 1992a. 'Cultural Studies and Its Theoretical Legacies'. In L. Grossberg, C. Nelson and L. Treichler (eds). *Cultural Studies*. London: Routledge.

—— 1992b. 'When was the Post-Colonial? Thinking at the Limits', in Chambers, I. and Curti, L. (eds), The Postcolonial Questions. Common Skies, Divided Horizons. London: Routledge: 242–257.

—— 2000. 'The Multi-Cultural Question'. In B. Hesse (ed.). Un/settled Multiculturalisms: Diasporas, Entanglements, Transruptions. London: Zed Books.

—— 2006. *Il soggetto e la differenza: Per un'archeologia degli studi culturali e postcoloniali*, ed. Miguel Mellino: Rome: Meltemi.

—— 2007. 'Epilogue: Through the Prism of an Intellectual Life'. In *Culture, Politics, Race and Diaspora: The Thought of Stuart Hall*, ed. B. Meeks. Kingston and Miami: Ian Randle Publishers; United Kingdom: Lawrence and Wishart.

—— et al. (eds). 1978. *Policing the Crisis: 'Mugging', the State and Law and Order Society*. London: Hutchinson.

Hardt, M. and Negri, A. 2009. *Commonwealth*. New York: Belknap Press.

Harvey, D. 2004. *The New Imperialism*. Oxford: Oxford University Press.

Laclau, E. 1977. *Politics and Ideology in Marxist Theory: Capitalism, Fascism, Populism*. London: Verso.

Lyotard, J. 1983. *Le differend*. Paris: Les Editions de Minuit.

Mbembe, A. 2001. *On the Postcolony*. Berkeley and London: University of California Press.

Ong, A. 2005. *Neoliberalism as Exception: Mutations in Citizenship and Sovereignty*. Durham, NC: Duke University Press.

Quijano, A. 2000. 'Coloniality of Power, Eurocentrism and Latin America'. *International Sociology* 15(2): 215–32.

Rancière, J. 1995. *La mesentente: politique et philosophie*. Paris: Galilee.

Said, E. 1978. *Orientalism*. London: Routledge & Kegan Paul.

—— 1983. 'Traveling Theory'. In *The World, The Text and the Critic*. Cambridge: Harvard University Press.

Samaddar, R. 2009. *Emergence of the Political Subject*. New Delhi: SAGE Publications India.

Sanyal, K. 2005. *Rethinking Capitalist Development: Primitive Accumulation, Governmentality and Post-Colonial Capitalism*. London and Delhi: Routledge.

Seth, S. 2007. *Subject Lessons: The Western Education of Colonial India*. Durham, NC: Duke University Press.

Spivak, G. 1988a. 'Can the Subaltern Speak?' In C. Nelson and L. Grossberg (eds). *Marxism and the Interpretation of Culture*. Chicago: University of Illinois Press: 271–313.

—— 1988b. 'Deconstructing Historiography'. In R. Guha and G. Spivak (eds). *Selected Subaltern Studies*. Oxford: Oxford University Press.

—— 1999. *A Critique of Postcolonial Reason: Toward a History of the Vanishing Present*. Cambridge, MA and London: Harvard University Press.

Thomas, P. 2009. *The Gramscian Moment: Philosophy, Hegemony and Marxism*. Leiden and Boston: Brill.

Van der Linden, M. 2009. 'Unfree Labor as Primitive Accumulation'. *Capital and Class* (February): 23–38.

Venn, C. 2006. *The Postcolonial Challenge: Toward Alternative Worlds*. London: SAGE.

Williams, R. 1978. *Marxism and Literature*. Oxford: Oxford University Press.

Young, R. 2001. *Postcolonialism: An Historical Introduction*. Oxford: Blackwell.

Part II

Solidarity and Alliances

5

Political and Social Alliances: Gramsci and Today

Derek Boothman

One of the first aspects of Antonio Gramsci's thought to be looked at seriously inside and outside Italy was that of social and political alliances: it is also a constant theme of relevance as much outside as within Europe, its 'home continent'. And it is to Gramsci's writings, probably more than to those of any other single theorist of strategy of the left, that one would turn for the question of alliances. What is of interest is the extent to which his approach is valid in a current context and what, instead, needs to be updated for changed circumstances, while still taking into account his own specific situations and overall methodological framework. The present chapter attempts to indicate some possible lines of reconstruction of his approach to alliances, as expressed in both the prison and the pre-prison period, and in the second part to outline some ways in which his approach may or should be rethought now, referring specifically to aspects of Britain and immigration there.

THE *PRISON NOTEBOOKS* AND BEFORE: GRAMSCI'S REASONING ON HIS EXPERIENCE

Most readers of Gramsci both outside and inside Italy look first of all at the *Notebooks* for a guide to his theorisation of the politics and policies of alliances. This is only part of the picture. The *Notebooks* contain many historical generalisations, but an appreciation of his own experience, in Italy at the beginning of the 1920s, in Moscow as a leader of the International, and then on his return to Italy and nomination as general secretary of the Italian Communist Party (PCI), also helps shed light on his approach to alliances.

A useful starting point is provided by the letters he wrote before his arrest (1926) and subsequent imprisonment under fascism. Here, his experience in Moscow as the PCI's main representative on the executive and presidium of the Communist International provides a very useful insight. In a key letter written while still in exile (in Vienna), due to a pending arrest warrant in Italy, he observes that 'in central and western Europe, the development of capitalism has created not only broad proletarian strata but also, and for that very reason, an upper stratum, the working-class aristocracy, with its appendages of trade-union bureaucracy and social democrat groupings' (Gramsci 2014: 227).[1] A first problem posed here is therefore that of the unification of the various components of the working class, although, as he was to write in one of the last letters before his arrest, in the countries outside the soviet state 'the great working masses', although 'stratified politically in a contradictory way, [were] tending in their entirety towards unity' (ibid.: 378).[2] (Here 'soviet' is written with a small letter to emphasise its true meaning as an elective council, rather than 'Soviet' with a capital letter, almost as an adjective of nationality.) Not without reason, Gramsci writes 'tending' in order to emphasise, as did other Marxists in the dialectical tradition, that no outcome can be predicted in advance. As he later wrote from behind the prison walls, 'in history as it really is', such as happens in a clash between social forces, 'the antithesis *tends* to destroy the thesis, the synthesis that emerges being a supersession without one being able to tell in advance what of the thesis will be "preserved" in the synthesis' (Gramsci 1995: 342, Q10I§6, emphasis added).[3]

The stratification hindering unity in the urban working-class forces was fairly complex, but that of the social forces in the countryside, with whom an alliance might be formed, was even more complicated. Scattered through the *Notebooks* are references to various types of land-holding and land-working in the countryside, so that in a count of the various types that together constitute the peasantry, one easily arrives at double figures. Some of these had roots going back at least to the later Roman Empire, and features of the various systems were often combined, as well as – to further complicate issues – sometimes undergoing change. In the pre-fascist period, where land-workers' trade union organisations were strong, successful moves were being made towards less servile forms of agricultural labour relations, while on the other side of the socio-economic divide, political representatives of the big landowners were attempting to prevent the consolidation of land-workers into a single class.[4] Additionally, Italy was divided geographically into macro-areas each of which, within their respective countrysides, had their own agrarian characteristics. Such a complexity means that what Gramsci proposed as a worker–peasant alliance, along the lines of what was being attempted in the young soviet state, would have to come to terms with different problems from those of a peasantry that had emerged from serfdom only just over half a century previously. What the situation required, then, was not just a worker–peasant alliance within a republican state (a 'Workers and Peasants' Government') but what, towards the end of his stay in Moscow, Gramsci began to define as a 'Federal Republic of the Workers and Peasants': the alliance aimed at had not therefore to be considered as merely 'a problem of class relations, but also and especially as a territorial problem'. This innovative way of posing the question of alliances was then further developed in the essay 'Some Aspects of the Southern Question', on which he was working at the time of his arrest (Gramsci 1978: 441–62). Gramsci states explicitly that the above watchword would be an 'optimal ideological preparation' in Italy as the equivalent to the 'political centralisation given ... by the Communist Party' together with 'administrative decentralisation, and ... recognition of the status of the local popular forces' that, in his reading of life in Russia, characterised the state there (Gramsci 2014: 171; 241).[5]

What seems to be missing here is a recognition of other social groups that were present – not the stratum of the 'working-class aristocracy' in the western European countries – but, for example, the technical strata, the small-scale retailers, the artisans, etc. The most likely explanation for this seeming omission probably lies in part in his direct experience of and participation in the events of the 'Biennio Rosso' – the 'red two years' in Turin in 1919–20. In a report to the International, which he wrote and shortly afterwards published in his review *L'Ordine Nuovo*, he devotes little space to the question of the popular, but non-proletarian, urban strata, simply giving a numerical breakdown of their strength and noting that they were allies of the advanced workers: three quarters of Turin's half a million inhabitants were working class, many of them internal immigrants from other parts of Italy. Within these workers, engineering workers and metalworkers numbered about 50,000, while there were about 10,000 white collar and technical staff, most of them directly or indirectly dependent on FIAT. Gramsci writes of these latter employees that 'they work in the big factories, are organised in big Trade Unions belonging to the Chamber of Labour,[6] have gone on strike side by side with the workers, and the majority of them – if not all – have therefore acquired the psychology of the proletariat, the psychology of those who are fighting against capital for the Revolution and for Communism'. With these groups, the workers' Factory Councils succeeded in establishing the close relations essential for attaining 'the workers' self-government of production'.[7]

This was Gramsci's position in mid-1920 immediately after the victorious citywide general strike that united these social groups; his report is, naturally, highly coloured by the events leading up to and including the strike. On a re-reading now, he seems to downplay the importance of other aspects of the situation, such as the difficulties created by the reformist leadership of the official trade union and the Socialist Party.[8] He returns to the question of the 'Trade Union bureaucracy' several times, on one occasion – not without reason – accusing its 'whole machinery' of having stopped the strike spreading to the province and of having prevented 'the working masses of the rest of Italy following Turin's example'. The reformist leadership had attempted to sabotage the growing movement, just as it did a couple of years later (summer 1922) in a countrywide strike, supported in theory by every shade of left opinion from the reformists themselves, through various other socialist currents, to the young, only eighteen-months-old, Communist Party, the libertarians and the strategically important anarcho-syndicalist railway workers' union. Gramsci's first assessment from his new vantage point in Moscow was that the strike had demonstrated the 'revolutionary capacity of the masses', their 'enthusiasm and fighting spirit, despite the treachery of the leaders, despite the lack of technical and spiritual preparation they had been left with by these leaders' (Gramsci 2014: 118–21).[9] He later revised this judgment, deciding that the strike had driven the industrialists and the Crown into the arms of fascism (Gramsci 1971b: 164)[10] which came to power only three months later, albeit for the first four years in a theoretically still democratic state. What Gramsci is posing here is the basic question of working-class unity, and indeed, even in the letter of 26 October 1926 quoted above, he seemed confident that the various communist parties influenced 'all the political strata of the great mass of people, [and] represented[ed] its tendency toward unity': they were 'moving on a fundamentally favourable historical terrain despite the contradictory superstructures' (Gramsci 2014: 378).

In principle, the question of alliances, with the masses in the countryside and with non-proletarian strata in the towns and cities, did not initially, in the wake of the Biennio Rosso, seem to raise too many problems in Gramsci's mind, although his addition of 'if not all', cited above, does seem to indicate a partial revision of an initially over-enthusiastic assessment. He continued to maintain much of his original optimistic view: in a key early paragraph of his *Prison Notebooks* he states that 'the instrumental masses – at least through their own organic intellectuals – exercise an influence over the technicians', where 'instrumental' has its usual Gramscian meaning of 'subaltern' or 'subordinate' (Gramsci 1996: 202, Q4§49, headed by him 'The Intellectuals').[11] In this same paragraph, he also begins to analyse the different types of intellectual, including the technical ones, and a more complex situation emerges than the one he was outlining in 1920. Here, in the paragraph of the *Prison Notebooks* mentioned, and in its reformulated version in Notebook 12 (on education and 'the history of the intellectuals'), he states that, broadly speaking, Italy was divided between South and North, and, within this division, between rural and urban areas. The Southern rural bourgeoisie produced, in general, officials, especially in the state apparatus, and representatives of the free professions, while the urban (predominantly Northern) bourgeoisie tended to produce technicians (Gramsci 1971a: 12, Q12§1). This question of the different types of intellectual occurs frequently in the *Notebooks*, and represents Gramsci's return to the problem of the psychological attitude of the intellectuals towards the 'fundamental classes':

> Do they have a 'paternalistic' attitude towards the instrumental classes? Or do they think they are an organic expression of them? Do they have a 'servile' attitude towards the ruling classes, or do they think that they themselves are leaders, an integral part of the ruling classes? (Gramsci 1971a: 97, Q19§26)

In other words, he does not here suggest that they are necessarily, or at all automatically, allies of the advanced workers, namely intellectuals who, as had happened in the factory council movement, had 'acquired the psychology of the proletariat'.

This view of the intellectuals, novel for its time, may be contrasted with Karl Mannheim's conception of them as a 'relatively classless stratum which is not too firmly situated in the social order' (Mannheim 1962: 154–5). From a different stance, the Trotsky of the 1904–6 period seems to define the specifically Russian *intelligenčija* as almost a class in itself in arguing for a future 'democratic dictatorship', not just of the proletariat and peasantry, but of the 'proletariat, peasantry and intelligentsia' (Trotsky 1969: Chapter V of *Results and Prospects*: 'The Proletariat in Power and the Peasantry').

When we take into consideration concepts used in the *Notebooks* like 'intellectual bloc' – either a conservative one or an 'intellectual–moral bloc which can make politically possible the intellectual progress of the mass' (Gramsci 1971a: 332–3, Q11§12) – we begin to see an even further innovation and differentiation in function and type of the intellectuals. Why, then, as Anne Showstack Sassoon asks, did Gramsci continue to use the word 'intellectual' rather than 'petit-bourgeois' or even 'déclassé'? Her answer is that an analysis of these strata of society in terms of 'social or economic class' is inappropriate, while it is 'too limited' to call the people in them 'specialists' (Showstack Sassoon 2000: 42–50, see especially p.46).

The differentiation among intellectuals can be almost as complex as that among what Gramsci variously refers to as the 'peasant class', with the great variation in ownership, tenure and relations of production mentioned above.[12] He seemed confident that at some levels there was a 'tendency towards unity in the peasant class'.[13] The extremely variegated nature of the agricultural workers, with the added complication of territorial differences among them, meant that by mid-1925, in the South, 'up to now there has been no real and proper peasant organization' (Grieco 1925: 61–4). Despite fascist repression, however, relatively successful moves had been made only a few months before to launch a peasant defence organisation there, and the land-workers' union, like other mass organisations, continued to function, though at a greatly reduced level (Spriano 1967: 413–14). Then, later on that year, the all-important non-communist figure of Guido Miglioli, leader of the 'white' (i.e. catholic) peasant trade union in the Po Valley, began to work with the Communist Party, at both the national level and the international one, through the Comintern's sister organisation for peasants, the Krestintern.

At this point we can define a picture of the PCI's alliance strategy in the mid-1920s, just before fascism established its full dictatorship, banning other political organisations and jailing many of its opponents – including, of course, Gramsci. It was not then envisaged by the PCI that there should or could be other proletarian parties in a state under proletarian leadership. As an authoritatively written but unsigned letter from a top leader of the PCI to a Socialist Party parliamentary deputy puts it:

one can only conceive of the dictatorship of the proletariat being achieved through the party of the proletariat, while if there are TWO (or three or more) parties of the proletariat no state of the proletariat exists but a democracy, albeit more radical than bourgeois democracy in the proper sense, destined to succumb under the hammer blows of capitalist reaction. (Full text in the Comintern Archives: see file 513-2-45: 99–101)

This position finds a parallel in the *Prison Notebooks*, where Gramsci writes of the 'passage of the troops of many parties under the banner of a single party which better represents and sums up the needs of the entire class'. He contrasts this with the 'demagogic promises' of the 'traditional ruling class', for whom 'violent solutions' may be reached through 'charismatic' leaders or 'men of destiny'; the reference here is to Mussolini and the rightist dictators of other, especially European, countries of that era (Gramsci 1971a: 210 and 211, Q13§23; the translation given here is slightly adjusted).

The question regards not just a proletarian party, but the social allies of the urban working class: what was their political expression to be? Gramsci was against the formation of, for example, peasant parties, possibly having in mind Bulgaria, where Stambolijski, the Peasant Party prime minister assassinated by rightist forces in 1923, had committed the fundamental error of having 'counterposed countryside to city, not at all the peasants to the bourgeoisie, but the peasants to the city in its entirety, and thus also to the proletariat' (letter from Vienna to the Central Committee of the PCI of 19 April 1924; Gramsci 2014: 289). In this context, the Bulgarian Vasil Kolarov (a Comintern leader with a brief to follow Italian affairs) expressed his fears to the Italian Party regarding 'the creation of a national peasant organisation [which] might in the long run constitute a real peasant party'. However, according to Ruggero Grieco, head of the PCI agrarian section, 'the Italian communists have held firm on this essential point', the Party's policy being that the poor peasants 'may and should fulfil their revolutionary role through a unitary and independent organisation of their own, which is neither a Party nor a Trade Union' (Spriano 1967: 472).[14]

A similar policy applied to the intellectual sectors. And in both cases Gramsci deals with the question of social blocs: those of the class adversaries and of real or potential allies. The most representative figure of an ally among the intellectual strata was that of the left liberal Piero Gobetti – where 'intellectual' is to be understood as an organiser of culture, here a new culture, and therefore partially overlapping with Gramsci's concept of some types of intellectual. Rather like his judgment on Miglioli, Gramsci's assessment of Gobetti was that he 'was not a communist, and would probably never have become one', but the radical liberalism espoused by Gobetti and his circle converged with Gramsci's Ordine Nuovo group in being based on collective rights, no longer just the individual ones that characterise classical liberalism.

Early on in the *Notebooks* Gramsci writes of parties 'in dictatorial states' (including those of a 'democratic dictatorship') that, while representing one class and only one class, nevertheless maintain an equilibrium with the other unhostile classes ('*classi non avversarie*') and ensure that the development of the represented class takes place with the consent and assistance of the allied classes.

And in the rewritten version of this paragraph, with the more general 'group/s' substituting 'class/es', he adds after the last phrase, 'if not out and out with that of groups which are definitely hostile' (first draft Q4§10, now in Gramsci 1996: 152; for the rewritten version [Q13§ 21, on Machiavelli] see Gramsci 1971a: 148).

On the one hand, what emerges clearly is that part of his strategy was to single out what was of value both in past thought and in that of the current adversaries. 'Definitely hostile' groups is presumably an indirect reference by Gramsci to the New Economic Policy that followed the period of 'war communism' in Russia. Of this event, he rhetorically asked of the Russian working class: 'Are you, the badly dressed and underfed worker, the dominator, or is it rather the Nepman in his furs with all the goods of the earth at his disposal?' (Gramsci 2014: 375). And in Italy this approach meant assessing what could profitably be learned from, for example, the 'intellectual bloc' headed by conservative figures, such as Benedetto Croce and Giustino Fortunato, who together were the leaders 'of liberal democratic culture' (Gramsci 1995: 463, Q10II§591). They, in a different way from prestigious left figures such as Gaetano Salvemini, posed the Southern question as a 'national problem capable of renovating political and parliamentary life' (Gramsci, 1971a: 72, Q1§149). Thus, here, Gramsci took seriously those who, while being of the right, in practice might be more advanced on certain issues than others who were nominally more progressive and further to the left in the orthodox political spectrum.

On the other hand, what also emerges is a hoped-for single party representing the urban working class, united under its most advanced sector, as it was in the Turin of 1919–20. This would weld together – see above – the various stratifications of 'the great working masses', including those of the countryside in their associations and organisations. There is, additionally, ample documentation of a wide variety of intellectual and cultural organisations and associations mentioned in passing, or discussed in greater depth, in the *Prison Notebooks*, such as to ensure a pluralism, albeit at that time not of parties as such.

GRAMSCI, ALLIANCES, BRITAIN

All this seems a far cry from the current situation in the 'advanced' industrial societies: to call them 'post-industrial' may be a misnomer since to a large extent production has been relocated elsewhere. Here a geopolitical comment of Gramsci's comes to mind, namely 'if India and China were to become modern nations with great volumes of industrial production', then this would rupture the 'current equilibrium' with a consequent 'shift in the axis of American life from the Atlantic to the Pacific seaboard' (Gramsci 1995: 196, Q2§78; Gramsci 1992: 328). But while touching on migration, either in search of work (the case of southern Italy) or following capital (as in the case of Germany; both forms are mentioned in Q1§149; Gramsci 1992: 228–9), he does not go in any depth into migration on a vast scale. This is left by him for subsequent development via the countryside–city relationship and the South–North one, both fruitful metaphors for present-day analysis and understanding.

Migration into Britain from abroad, here including Ireland, is no new phenomenon. On the one hand, the slave trade deposited people from Africa in the ports and big cities, while on the other people fleeing religious persecution, whether Huguenot weavers in the seventeenth century or Ashkenazi Jews two centuries later, meant posing the question of relations between the newcomers and the established population.

The newer immigrants can, in approximate terms, be dated back to the years immediately succeeding the Second World War, starting from when, in 1948, the *Empire Windrush* docked in London with immigrant men and women from the West Indies who were needed to ease the labour shortage for the post-war reconstruction of Britain. Some years later, it was the turn of Indians, Pakistanis and Bangladeshis, who came to work, in part, in the latter stages of the textile industry of the North, and settled not only there but in cities elsewhere. And it was to these immigrants – formerly called the 'coloured' communities – that, by the early to middle 1960s, what remained of British fascism switched much of its attention. Anti-immigrant stances spilled over into sections of the Conservative Party, as exemplified in racist electoral campaigns by individual candidates and, towards the end of that decade, into the rise of anti-immigrant policies on the Conservative right, associated with the name of Enoch Powell. But the second generation black community in London, influenced by the United States Black Power movement, was now beginning to assert itself and recognise, more than in the past, its own group identity.

At that time the situation in Britain was more complex than many on the left thought. Unemployment had begun to rise, but to levels that in the second decade of the twenty-first century would be judged more than acceptable. The trade union left – and other movements outside the institutional structures of the Labour movement – offered great hope as an alternative to an official Labour Party leadership that, for example on Vietnam and labour relations, had become discredited. At the start of the 1970s, Scottish shipbuilders staged a 'work-in' in their closure-threatened shipyards, and twice in a couple of years the coalminers went on strike, with widespread public support. The Conservative administration, elected in 1970, was brought down as a consequence of the second of these strikes. Again, the Labour Party was returned to power and it seemed there would be plain sailing. However, the cracks were widening.

Schematising greatly, one could say that in this situation some sections on the left continued with a 'workerist' policy of keeping up and intensifying wages pressure, which in their view would lead to increased efficiency in industry, and hence to a general increase in well-being and even a redistribution of income. The 'advanced' parts of the trade unions would thereby bring sufficient numbers of other people over to form a strategic majority for further advance, but had the weakness of, for example, ignoring possible wage contributions to inflation. Others interpreted differently the changes going on at that time in society due to the rise of the 'new movements' in the 1960s and early 1970s, arguing that an alliance between the traditional Labour movement and these new social phenomena was necessary; however it required different approaches to that propounded by the 'workerists'. These 'non-workerists' were, with all the weaknesses this entailed, opposed to what they considered a 'corporativist' stance and argued that the sacrifice of short-term economic gains would be outweighed by democratic control in industry and also in society at large, taking to heart Gramsci's dictum that 'there can, and indeed must, be hegemonic activity even before the rise to power' (Gramsci 1971a: 228–9, Q19§24). This latter strategy, if allied to the defence of living standards especially of the lowly paid workers – consisting, among others, of women, immigrants and, more and more, younger workers – could be a basis for an alliance, encapsulated in the formula of an Alternative Economic Strategy (AES). The various interpretations of the AES were, however, hard to put into practice after an economic crisis struck in 1976, with the consequent IMF-imposed cutbacks in public expenditure which, as ever, hit the most vulnerable sectors of the population, including the immigrant communities. Apart from the economic consequences, these were also subject to harassment at the social and institutional levels, and the lack of popular democratic control – over the police in particular – meant that protests and self-defence were ineffectual against racist attacks. The anti-fascist demonstration at Lewisham (1977), the death during the 1979 election campaign of the anti-racist campaigner Blair Peach, almost certainly at the hands of a police officer, and then the riots at Brixton (1981) over the lack of immigrant community rights, all involving mass arrests of the democratic forces, stand out in the mind like the communist-led defence of London's East End Jewish community in the 1930s. The situation was dire, both for those from the Indian subcontinent and for the West Indian communities and their British-born offspring.

The left in all its variants was, however, too weak to be able to weld together a social alliance. And additionally, what they were neglecting was the question of who actually formed – and represented – the working class around whom an alliance was to be built. A striking example at the institutional level is the fact that from the outbreak of the Second

World War until the 1980s there was no elected Member of Parliament from what are classed as ethnic minorities, and even during the 1983–87 parliament the MPs from these minorities could be counted on the fingers of one hand (four Labour and one Conservative).[15]

Two converging figures stand out in the debate on the questions of those years, a debate which for once had political results. One is Eric Hobsbawm who, in an initial article (1978), tried to analyse the reasons for the impasse in which he considered the entire Labour movement had found itself, drawing attention to changes in the structures of British society such as tertiarisation and domestic deindustrialisation. The other was the British Jamaican Stuart Hall, whose complex ancestry and the plurality of cultures contained in it gave him the right to be considered a member of a number of ethnic minorities.

Hall was the first major figure to question received assumptions about the nature of the British working class and the questions of class- and other types of identity (Hall 1986). Strongly influenced by Gramsci (as was Hobsbawm), one sees analogies between Hall's approach to non-class identity and problems of alliances as set out by Gramsci, in Hall's view to be found most of all in the above-cited essay on 'Some Aspects of the Southern Question'. Among other things, Hall was in effect questioning what being 'English' or 'British' actually means: for example, through immigration from Ireland, 'Irishness' is one component of 'Englishness'; and these (predominantly catholic) immigrants together with newer ones have modified the religious composition of Britain, a far-from-negligible aspect of society. Immigration has also changed in part the occupational structure of places such as North Manchester, Leeds and the East End of London, with Pakistani or Bangladeshi substitution of the Jewish population in the clothing industry, in the process giving an important boost to youth fashion in particular. The Indian community on the other hand has the reputation of containing a relatively high proportion of middle-class business people, although this does not seem to transfer at all automatically into greater support for the Conservatives.

The ethnic composition of Britain has changed a lot even since the 1991 census (see endnote 15), which makes Hall's attack on the myth of the homogeneity of the working class in the late 1970s even more prescient than it appeared at the time. And non-homogeneity goes further than just the ethnic make-up of society. Recent figures show that 'non-white' immigrants have an initial unemployment rate double that of recent 'white' immigrants (Papademetriou, Somerville and Sumption 2008) and, while this rate for the main six ethnic minority immigrant groups has improved over the last generation, it has still not converged with that of the 'native white' ('non-ethnic minority') population. For women, the position is worse, since the gap between women in the 'non-white' immigrant groups and their 'native white' counterparts has remained constant over the same period (1993–2009) as in the Papademetriou et al. paper, at an unemployment rate for immigrant women that is rather more than 20 per cent greater than that for 'non-ethnic minority' women.[16] Within the ethnic minority immigrant communities, there are also divergences on the educational front: in maths and English, Chinese and Indian children come out well, but the situation of children of Caribbean descent is worrying; they begin school on the whole in no worse a position than the other major 'non-white' ethnic minorities but, by the end of compulsory schooling, have fallen to the last position among these minorities (See Dustmann, Frattini and Theodoropoulos 2015: fig.5, p.15). If one looks at what education should lead to – employment – one finds that current (2015) long- and short-term unemployment rates in the key 16 to 24-year-old age group are higher than at any time over the last two decades, having reached 14.4 per cent, i.e. more than 150 per cent greater than the national average for everyone (just under 6 per cent); as regards long-term unemployment, for 'native white' young people the rate has fallen very slightly (ca. 2 per cent) since 2010, while the equivalent rate among black, Asian and minority ethnic communities has risen by 49 per cent.[17]

Regarding other aspects, little progress has been made since two famous publications of nearly half a century ago looked at class difference and discrimination in Britain. In his early socio-linguistic educational surveys, Basil Bernstein noted the prevalence of restricted linguistic codes among the underprivileged (overexploited) classes, observing that 'a great deal of potential ability is being lost' (Bernstein 1971: 31). Unknown to him, a similar position emerges in the last of Gramsci's *Prison Notebooks* (Gramsci 1985: 179–88, Q29) where he examines among various things the barriers to mastering language in children from subaltern backgrounds, one conclusion being that whenever the language question is posed, the question of reorganising 'cultural hegemony' goes hand-in-hand with it. The second publication, the classic 1967 *May Day Manifesto* of the 'old' New Left, deals among many things with educational gaps between the children from manual workers' and from middle-class families. Differences between the 'haves' and the 'have nots' may be narrower than in the 1960s but, as demonstrated in a recent (2010) report on educational achievement, again by the Rowntree Foundation, they are nowhere near disappearing (Hall, Williams and Thompson 1967; Rowntree Foundation 2010). The analogy with unemployment and wage rates of recent 'non-white' immigrants – see above – is quite apparent. The intellectual content of work is on the increase, but the disparities apparent between classes – and also between immigrant communities – indicates an under-fulfilled potential, with negative consequences for social development.

All this raises a number of questions, some of which find their analogy in Gramsci's various writings. In working towards some sort of juncture, first one has to resolve the question of the relation between class and national, ethnic and/or cultural identity. This means at one level ensuring that there is an adequate basis for a multi-ethnic, multi-national state in which the popular forces may become hegemonic: in other words, it means taking seriously and transferring and updating to present conditions Gramsci's notion of the 'national–popular'. As noted above, Gramsci spoke of 'stratifications' in the industrially developed nations, and also of strong regional disparities. A task before today's left, paralleling that of the regional issue, is that of overcoming the type of 'vertical' differentiation represented by ethnicity. And on top of this, attention has partially been drawn to differences within the immigrant communities themselves: while the offspring of some ethnic minority groups are well equipped for contributing to a knowledge-based society, gender- and ethnic-based disparities mean this is not the case across the board. The net result is that individuals, groups, and society at large are losing out. And within this context, even to speak of a 'knowledge-based' society – the workers there being analogous to Gramsci's 'technicians' – without any further breakdown, means ignoring social and economic stratifications that reach their apex in what may be summed up in the phrase 'the City of London'. The task is to single out which strata, as in the case of Gramsci's analysis of city and countryside relations (with the ramifications present in both his peasantry and present-day technical workers), are to be targeted as potential members of a progressive alliance.

The regional question, as well as being deeply rooted in British society, is also present in an extremely acute form in the European Union. All this makes the construction, not of some notional 'people' at the international level, but of a union of popular forces at that level, difficult – possibly even more difficult than in Gramsci's time. For all these factors, Hall's question is pertinent: 'Where is the class as a political subject, where is the class as an organizational force ... which other elements can join in an alliance?' Pessimistically and perhaps almost despairingly, he added 'This is the element that is disappearing',[18] a viewpoint similar to Hobsbawm's in the above-mentioned 'Forward March' article. This approach is open to question since, it may be argued against 'postmodernist' interpretations, it tends to overlook the redeployment of production outside the countries of the first industrial revolution and the industrial working class outside the metropolitan countries. As Hall realised, however, the international aspect comes quickly to the fore. The question is posed of a new internationalism that takes much more seriously the strategic role of the industrial proletariat outside its historical geographical base. And this last problem, again posed by Hall in the video interview quoted, is one of no easy solution. It is not sufficient to ask how to form an alliance at the popular–national level: what is the solution the left can offer to the problem of alliances represented at the popular–*inter*national level?

NOTES

1.   Letter of 9 February 1924 to Palmiro Togliatti and other communist leaders in Italy. After Gramsci's imprisonment, Togliatti succeeded him as the most important leader of the PCI, usually in the post of general secretary.
2.   Gramsci to Togliatti, 26 October 1926, after the latter's advice not to transmit officially a letter of Gramsci's, written on behalf of the Political Bureau of the PCI, to the Central Committee of the Bolshevik Party.
3.   Cf. also Q10II§41xvi: 'one cannot – without being arbitrary – assert what will be conserved ... without falling into ideologism' (Gramsci 1995: 376).
4.   See Q1§44 (Gramsci 1992: 136–51). For Gramsci's rewritten form (Q19§24), see Gramsci 1971a, p.76; in the latter volume, see also, e.g., p.283 for other categories of land workers.
5.   Letters of 23 September 1923 (from Moscow) and 1 March 1924 (from Vienna), to the PCI Executive and then to Togliatti and Mauro Scoccimarro (another PCI leader) respectively.
6.   The Chambers of Labour correspond, for example, to the Trades Councils in Britain, as the organisations uniting all the Trade Union branches in a given territorial area.
7.   These words are taken from Gramsci's original manuscript of a report to Moscow, recently rediscovered in the Comintern Archives. For the version he revised for publication, see *L'Ordine Nuovo* (Einaudi, Turin, 1975 [1954]), pp.176–86, especially pp.177–8 and 184 for the passages included here. The report, with its variations, is scheduled for publication in Italian and in an English translation in a forthcoming issue of the online *International Gramsci Journal*.
8.   It should here be remembered that the entire left outside the anarchist movements was still within a very variegated Socialist Party, and that the Communist Party as such was still a few months away from being formed.
9.   Gramsci and Ersilio Ambrogi (then the other PCI Comintern Executive member), letter to Grigorij Zinov'ev, president of the Comintern Executive, 28 August 1922.
10.   Reprint of Gramsci's article 'The Elections', first published in the first issue of the new series of *L'Ordine Nuovo*, March 1924.
11.   We use the accepted Gramscian convention – a calque of the original Italian – and call 'paragraph' what in English would normally be called a section.
12.   Cf. Gramsci's letters to the Executive Committee of the PCI of 23 September 1923 (from Moscow) and to the Party Central Committee (from Vienna) of 10 February 1924 (in Gramsci 2014: 171; 233). For the idea that peasants are a separate class, cf. his notes in the Communist Party Archive held at the Gramsci Institute in Rome (APC 513-1-112: 4) and his report to the Central Committee in preparation for the Party's Third Congress (Lyon, January 1926) , *L'Unità*, 20 December 1925.
13.   Fragmentary notes in Gramsci's handwriting in the PCI archives (APC 513-1-112: 4).

14. Spriano 1967, p.472, with Grieco's comment on Kolarov is quoted in a footnote on the same page.
15. After the General Election of May 2015, there are now around 40 MPs having some sort of ethnic minority background in their recent ancestry – around 6 per cent of the total, compared with recent estimates of about 14 per cent of the population who identified themselves as belonging partly or wholly to one or more than one ethnic minority. The analysis by the Joseph Rowntree Foundation of the most recent censuses indicates a doubling since 1991 of the 'non-white' population in England and Wales (therefore excluding Scotland and Northern Ireland) to a figure now of around 14 per cent of the whole: www.ethnicity.ac.uk/medialibrary/briefings/dynamicsofdiversity/how-has-ethnic-diversity-grown-1991-2001-2011.pdf
16. The comments here on ethnic minority immigrant groups, both men and women, are necessarily schematic: for an analytical breakdown, see Dustmann, Frattini and Theodoropoulos 2015.
17. Daniel Boffey in *The Observer*, 22 February 2015; official figures for ethnic minority unemployment from the House of Commons Library, quoted by Matthew Taylor in *The Guardian*, 10 March 2015.
18. Stuart Hall, video interview with Giorgio Baratta and the present author (director Massimiliano Bomba), London, 2008.

REFERENCES

Bernstein, B. 1971. *Class, Codes and Control*, vol.i. London: Routledge and Kegan Paul.

Dustmann, C. Frattini, T. and Theodoropoulos, N. 2015. 'Ethnicity and Second Generation Immigrants'. www.ucl.ac.uk/~uctpb21/Cpapers/Ethn_2gen_revision_C1.pdf

Gramsci, A. 1971a. *Selections from the Prison Notebooks*, ed. and trans. Q. Hoare and G. Nowell-Smith. London: Lawrence and Wishart.

—— 1971b. *La costruzione del partito comunista 1923–1926*. Turin: Einaudi.

—— 1978. *Selections from Political Writings, 1921–1926*, ed. and trans. Q. Hoare. London: Lawrence and Wishart.

—— 1985. *Selections from Cultural Writings*, ed. D. Forgacs and G. Nowell-Smith, trans. W.Q. Boelhower. London: Lawrence and Wishart.

—— 1992. *Prison Notebooks*, vol.i, trans. J. Buttigieg. New York: Columbia University Press.

—— 1995. *Further Selections from the Prison Notebooks*, ed. and trans. D. Boothman. London: Lawrence and Wishart.

—— 1996. *Prison Notebooks*, vol.ii, trans. J. Buttigieg. New York: Columbia University Press.

—— 2014. *A Great and Terrible World: The Pre-Prison Letters*, ed. and trans. D. Boothman. London: Lawrence and Wishart.

Grieco, R. 1925. 'Report to the PCI Central Committee, 11–12 May 1925', Comintern Archives, file 513-1-296.

Hall, S. 1986. 'The Relevance of Gramsci for the Study of Race and Ethnicity'. *Journal of Communication Studies* 10(5).

—— Williams, R. and Thompson E. (eds). 1967. *May Day Manifesto*. London.

Hobsbawm, E. 1978. 'The Forward March of Labour Halted'. *Marxism Today* (September).

Mannheim, K. 1962 [1936]. *Ideology and Utopia*, trans. L. Wirth and E. Shils. New York: Harvest Books.

Papademetriou, D, Somerville, W. and Sumption M. 2008. 'Observations on the Social Mobility of the Children of Immigrants in the United States and United Kingdom'. In *Social Mobility and Education*. London and New York: Carnegie Corporation/Sutton Trust.

Rowntree Foundation. 2010. *The Importance of Attitudes and Behaviour for Poorer Children's Educational Attainment*. Rowntree Foundation.

Showstack Sassoon, A. 2000. 'Gramsci's Subversion of the Language of Politics'. In *Gramsci and Contemporary Politics*. London and New York: Routledge.

Spriano, P. 1967. *Storia del Partito Comunista*, vol.i: *Da Bordiga a Gramsci*. Turin: Einaudi.

Trotsky, L. 1969. *The Permanent Revolution* and *Results and Prospects*, trans. B. Pearce. New York: Pathfinder Press.

6

Gramsci, Migrants and Trade Unions: An Irish Case Study

Mary Hyland and Ronaldo Munck

For all his iconic status as guru of Western Marxism, it is often forgotten that Antonio Gramsci is a political figure from the global South. We develop here a Gramsci as migrant and trade union organiser who forged a radically anti-economistic perspective on trade unionism and who promoted the need for an alliance between industrial workers and their 'others', whether internal or transnational migrants. This perspective serves well to illuminate the story of inward migration in Ireland in the 1990s and the way in which the trade unions forged a hegemonic alliance against any xenophobic reactions and helped create, along with migrant-oriented NGOs, a new 'common sense' through which migrants became the 'new Irish' and not 'non-Irish' as they were first dubbed, in a quite possibly unintentional form of xenophobia. Likewise, the Irish case may serve to enrich the international debate on social-movement unionism.

A SOUTHERN PERSPECTIVE

Gramsci was born in 1891 into an impoverished Sardinian family, suffered all sorts of humiliations and lived in a world which did not speak 'Italian' and believed in spell-casting and the supernatural. The cultural nationalism of his Sardism would give way to the more universal creed of socialism when he moved to the industrialised North in his mid-twenties to attend university. Gramsci was a migrant and he took with him the Southern question throughout his life and its ending in Mussolini's jails, where he wrote his great *Prison Notebooks*. When he was discovered in the Anglophone world in the 1970s he was used to provide cover for the turn to Euro-communism. A stress was placed on the 'universal' value of the *Prison Notebooks* and Gramsci as the theorist of the superstructure. It is only recently that a grounded Gramsci, fully reintegrated into Italian history, society, politics, culture and geography, has re-emerged (see Capuzzo and Mezzadra 2012). It is this Gramsci that we deploy here to illuminate a recent engagement in Ireland with migration, as it turned (along with Italy) from labour exporter to labour importer in the 1990s.

In Turin, Gramsci began to work with the trade unions and played the key 'organic intellectual' role in the great strike wave of 1919–20 (see Williams 1975). He was only too aware of the divisions that had been created between the Northern industrial workers and the Southern peasants who saw the first as a privileged caste. The making of the working class in Italy in the period from 1911, when Gramsci arrives in Turin, to the breakout of the mass strikes in 1919 occurred, as elsewhere, through a significant process of uprooting of peasants from the land. Internal migration (and international migration to peripheral countries like Argentina) was an integral formative element in the social life of workers during that period. Gramsci was well placed to bridge the gap between the Northern industrial workers (see his often positive account of Fordism for example) and the social world of the rural dweller where popular understanding (*senso comune*) was still largely forged through the medium of folklore. This political strategy for socialism in Italy was thus necessarily based on a worker–peasant alliance which was anything but an empty political formula.

In 'Some Aspects of the Southern Question' (1926), his last major publication before he was imprisoned, he outlined very concretely what he meant by the worker–peasant alliance. For Gramsci the one undoubted merit of the Turin communists was that they had brought the Southern question forcibly to the attention of the Northern workers. The subjugation by Northern capitalist interests of the South of Italy to a semi-colonial status and the racialisation of its inhabitants had to be contested by the social class that aspired to bring in a new social order. The necessary alliance between town and countryside would, in our era, arguably translate into an alliance between workers in the global North and those in the global South. The proletariat can only, according to Gramsci, 'become the leading [*dirigente*] and dominant class to the extent that it succeeds in creating a system of class alliances which allows it to mobilise the majority of the population' (Gramsci 1978: 443). To become a national leading class, workers and their organisations need to be internationalist in their own outlook and reject any divisions created in their ranks by the powerful and the ignorant.

In practice Italian trade unions did not live up to these expectations and Gramsci was quite critical of them. When workers develop trade unions to obtain a better price for their labour power, they are not in themselves agents of social transformation. By taking on this role, trade unions accept an economistic reading of workers (who 'sell' their labour power) and the ideological hegemony of the capitalist order. Against the reformist socialists of his day he rejected the notion that collective bargaining could lead to socialist transformation. Rather, according to Gramsci, 'the trade union is nothing more than a commercial society, of a type purely capitalistic' (cited in Annunziato 2011: 123) in its role of seeking the maximum price for labour power. He also railed against the trade union leaders of his day who 'are just like the mandarins, men of a higher social caste ...who disdained their subjects' (ibid.: 125). Gramsci contrasted this situation to the 'voluntarism' of those workers and leaders engaged in the factory councils, which broke with economism and industrial legality.

Overall Gramsci always argued that there was nothing fixed about the nature of trade unionism. As he put it:

> There is no specific definition of a trade union ... the union becomes a determined definition and, therefore, assumes a determined historical form when the strength and will of the workers who compose it, impress upon it a direction, and impose upon its actions those ends which are affirmed by their definition. (Cited in Annunziato 2011: 120)

As is the case with all social institutions, the trade unions are shaped by, but also shape, the broader context in which they exist. In specific conjunctures – for example the Turin general strike in which Gramsci was involved – trade unions can take on progressive orientations and cease to be just a passive reflection on workers roles in the capitalist production process. Above all, Gramsci recognised the contradictory role of social institutions, not least that of the trade unions. Going beyond the dominant reformist/revolutionary dichotomy, he recognised the fluid nature of trade unionism as a site for political intervention and one where 'the will of workers could achieve the transformation of the trade union struggle from its narrow corporatist and reformist outlook, to the terrain of revolutionary struggle' (Gramsci 1977: 104).

From a broader perspective, it is clear that it is the concept of hegemony which is the cornerstone of Gramsci's analysis of modern capitalism and within which a transformative vision of trade unions needs to be situated. For Gramsci, hegemony is the process through which a social class produces itself as historical subject. It moves beyond narrow class interest to achieve consensus across society. It requires a process of leading rather than merely dominating the rest of society. The hegemonic class dominates society through the institutions of political society (state government) and civil society (state society). The main usage of the concept of hegemony refers to how the dominant classes create a historical bloc, but it can also be deployed in relation to the strategy of the subaltern or dominated classes. In particular, in the complex societies of the West, the subaltern classes, and their political organisations, may begin to contest the dominant power bloc and begin to form a more progressive hegemony. Particularly in civil society – that space between the state, the economy and the household – alternative forms of organisation and visions for social transformation may emerge.

In the struggle for hegemony both the dominant and the dominated groups vie to construct a 'common sense' which will have wide consensus across society. We can think of the role of the market, of migrants and even of trade unions themselves, where the struggle for meaning and the elaboration of a 'common sense' pits different political meanings against one another. For Gramsci, each social group has its own *'senso comune'* (good sense) which articulates a conception of social life. What is crucial for Gramsci is that 'common sense is not something rigid and stationary, but is in continuous transformation' (Gramsci 1985: 419–21, Q24§4). Thus we might see how the social role of migrant workers, for example, can be understood quite differently by various social groups and those conceptions may change over time. In a delightful phrase, Gramsci refers to how 'common sense creates the folklore of the future' (ibid.). So, in contemporary struggles over political and cultural hegemony, what becomes part of *'senso comune'* and what does not will play key roles.

A Gramscian perspective on migrants and trade unions today would need to take account of the concepts developed here. There are many similarities sociologically and politically between translational migrants today and internal migrants of the past. Although no two historical periods are the same, it would be a mistake to believe that stronger borders in the past would have prohibited immigrants from maintaining ties with their home countries or circulating between states. That would be overemphasising the differences within the distinction between past and present states. However, the means of communication and of travelling obviously have changed. Likewise we have seen new regulatory systems of mobility developing over time. The new discipline of transnational migration studies has tended to operate as though intra-national migration is somehow a completely different phenomenon, but we might usefully take migration as a complex and fluid process within and across national boundaries. The sociological and political similarities are such that a Gramscian perspective can usefully be applied to both forms of migration. With globalisation, the making of the working class has of course become a transnational as much as a national process. Trade unions can react in different ways to the arrival of new workers from overseas. A xenophobic turn is possible (even probable in some cases) but sometimes they react with the customary belief that 'a worker is a worker' (regardless of creed, national origin, etc.). What is clear, though, following Ernesto Laclau (who developed Gramsci's theory of hegemony in a 'post-Marxist' direction) is that when trade unions meet migrant workers we are dealing with a 'contingent process of political articulation in an open ensemble whose elements had purely relational identities' (Laclau 1996: 117) and thus are mutually constitutive. In brief, following Gramsci's personal, as well as intellectual, example we should always seek to foreground worker agency and not assume passive acceptance of the status quo.

The story of Ireland, migrants and trade unions that follows is grounded in these broad theoretical concepts and also, hopefully, enriches them. There are many different ways to 'apply' Gramsci to labour relations, from Euro-communism (see Ackers 2014 for an example) to the more libertarian approaches of some chapters in this book. For our part, we take certain key themes such as hegemony and common sense as framing concepts, and work on the assumption that both trade unions and migrants have been changed through the struggle and did not simply play pre-allotted roles. Also from Gramsci we take the importance of the union organiser and the fluid nature of trade union politics.

AN IRISH SOLUTION?

Modernisation theories argue that the transition from an industrial to a service economy erodes the basis for union organisation. The major structural changes that, in previous decades, worked in favour of trade unions – the decline of agriculture and traditional household services, expanding public employment and increased bureaucratisation in industry and services – are now reversed, given current trends of privatisation, downsizing and outsourcing (Ebbinghaus and Visser 1999). While it is the case that such a transition erodes the basis for traditional union organisation, it also challenges unions to consider new approaches and provides space for envisaging, and engaging with, social transformation. Unions are increasingly adopting new roles, new social functions and new interventions vis-à-vis the workforce, in this case migrants and ethnic minorities. While the initial response of the Irish trade unions was slow, we now note a concerted attempt at reaching out beyond the bastions of formal employment.

METHODOLOGY

The case study to follow is based on empirical research carried out with the Irish Congress of Trade Unions (ICTU) and a number of its constituent unions in the period April 2011 to February 2013. It involved a survey of ICTU affiliated unions, a series of interviews with union leaders, officials and activists, and an analysis of a broad range of materials including policy documents, submissions, press releases, annual reports, information resources, consultancy reports and published statements and speeches.

BACKGROUND

Ireland in the 1990s become a 'social laboratory' for the study of migration due, in particular, to the combination of economic buoyancy and the subsequent crash, and the speed of transition from being a country of mass emigration to being one of immigration (Barrett and Duffy 2007; Fanning and Munck 2011). Historically, Ireland, like Gramsci's Italy, was a country of emigration and one colonised and ruled by Britain for a long period of its history. Its economy, up to the late twentieth century, could not provide sufficient employment for its people, who were forced to emigrate in large numbers throughout the nineteenth and most of the twentieth centuries. Thus, as a relatively poor peripheral European country with a history of sustained emigration and limited employment opportunities, it never saw any significant level of immigration.

The mid-1990s saw the birth of the 'Celtic Tiger'. During this time the Irish economy underwent a significant transformation and Ireland began to experience the highest growth rate (over 8 per cent) in the OECD area. Unemployment fell, population outflows were reversed and net inflows began. This, combined with the opening up of the Eastern European labour market, led to Ireland changing from being a country of net outward migration to becoming one of net inward migration at a speed that was unprecedented. In the decade 1991–2000 almost half a million new jobs were added to the Irish economy, an expansion of 43 per cent in the total labour force, creating a need for new labour that could not be filled from the indigenous labour force (Mac Éinrí 2005; Barrett and Duffy 2007). In an extraordinarily short time frame, Ireland moved from being Britain's ex-colony on the European periphery to being perceived by many as the epitome of neoliberal globalisation (Castles 2011).

THE CHALLENGE

The emergence of large-scale labour migration to Ireland in the 1990s came at a time when the trade union movement in Ireland, as elsewhere, was facing major new challenges never experienced before. These included European economic integration; internationalisation of financial and product markets; dominance of the neoliberal economic model; the changing structures of employment with a growth in individualisation, feminisation and informalisation; the shift from manufacturing to services; expansion of the small-firm sector and increased competitive pressure in product markets, both nationally and internationally (Hyman 2001; Frege and Kelly 2003; Munck 2011).

In the Irish case, as elsewhere, chief among the issues for the trade unions was decline in union density coupled with the reduction in bargaining coverage. But there was also the erosion of structures of interest representation. These included the decline of workplace and branch committees; the loss of mobilisation capacity, contributing to the erosion of industrial power; the decrease in resources, financial and human (linked to the drop in membership), making it more difficult to implement corrective strategies; the problems of interest definition as a result of increased membership; and heterogeneity and the loss of political influence as the majority of private-sector workplaces became non-union.

NEW APPROACHES

There was a gradual but growing recognition among elements within the trade union movement, as labour migration reached its peak in the mid-2000s, that the corporatist model involving an established social partnership arrangement[1] combined with a workplace-centred service approach, which had operated in Ireland since the late 1980s, was not sufficient to meet the needs of a potential new membership within the migrant workforce. But it was not this recognition in and of itself that prompted unions to consider new approaches. Nor was it any groundswell of voices within the trade union movement against the 'collusion' of corporatism, though there was some of that. Rather it was a confluence of circumstances that led to internal debates and subsequently to a refocusing. Unions were in decline, seeing a decrease in membership, participation and political influence. Migrants were arriving in large numbers, primarily working in non-unionised sectors. They were low-paid and they were open to exploitation. Any union revitalisation strategies had to take account of migrant workers and recognise the difficulty in reaching them through traditional union organising strategies with their focus on workplaces and employers.

Janice Fine refers to the 'mismatch between traditional union models and the structure of low-wage work' and suggests that the craft and industrial union models characteristic of the nineteenth and twentieth centuries are no longer appropriate as workers lack the long-term relationship to an occupation that lies at the core of craft unionism; and they often lack the long-term relationship to a firm or industry that lies at the core of industrial unionism (Fine 2005: 158). While Fine was making the argument in favour of the development of community unionism specifically, it also holds true for traditional trade unions striving to reinvent themselves. In line with the Gramscian view of trade unions as social institutions, they are shaped, and shape, the context in which they exist (Gramsci 1977). Unions must develop additional and alternative, more participatory, types of collective activity if they are to appeal to an increasingly diverse constituency with cultural backgrounds very different from those of the traditional trade union member (Frege and Kelly 2003; Hyman 2004; Donaghey and Teague 2006).

There is a growing literature on trade union revitalisation which points up advances in the strategic areas of organising new sectors, greater political actions, reform of trade union structures, coalition building and international solidarity. Daryl D'Art and Thomas Turner (2005) see the crisis in trade unionism as having positive elements, in that it presents opportunities for unions to engage in new strategies such as the organisation of new constituencies, while Paul Teague and Jimmy Donaghey (2009) outline what they consider the six central strategies for potential union revitalisation – organising, social partnership, political action, coalition building, union restructuring and international linkages. While revitalisation debates inevitably focus on new models of trade unionism, union revitalisation does not necessarily lead to new models, but is a specific debate about the labour movement and the need for, and possibilities of, renewal. Paul Johnson makes the point that trade union renewal, social movement unionism, community unionism, labour as a citizenship movement, and organising versus servicing are all contested concepts (2001: 35). Trade unionism is fluid and union movements adopt and adapt as they see fit. Recruiting, organising and mobilising migrant workers can have an impact in terms of integrating the migrants in society, but also increasingly serve to revitalise the trade unions.

As the revitalisation debates took place within the Irish trade union movement, a variety of perspectives emerged, with the ICTU opposed to the organising model, and member unions SIPTU (Services, Industrial, Professional and Technical Union) and Mandate (Retail, Bar and Administrative Workers' Union) favouring a proactive organisational approach which involved making community links, cooperating with non-governmental organisations (NGOs) and connecting with workers (particularly low-skilled ones) across occupations as the way forward. ICTU endeavoured to provide leadership both in the debates and in the forging of links with civil society and with government, but the focus was largely a policy-based one around awareness raising and the promotion of anti-racism. Many within the union movement were doubtful about ICTUs ability to lead in terms of bringing unions together to organise and to mobilise low-paid workers.

SIPTU had, for its part, been trying to build dedicated organising capacity since 2004 and, according to its general president, Jack O'Connor, 'making a lot of mistakes in doing so' (interview, 2012). It looked to the Services Employees International Union (SEIU) in the United States in the first instance with many of its staff spending time training and working in SEIU local branches there. It developed relations globally with unions that were trying to introduce change, particularly the SEIU and the LHMU in Australia (now United Voice). In 2006 it established a commission on trade union renewal which led to a process of rule change, leading eventually to the implementation of a radical new structure in 2010. SIPTU now operates on the basis of divisions and sectors rather than regions and branches, with all industrial staff described as organisers. It has a strategic organising department which is charged with 'the design and implementation of strategic organising campaigns across specific sectors and to work with shop stewards, activists and members in building union organisation and strength' (SIPTU 2011: 23).

SIPTU'S MUSHROOM CAMPAIGN

Subsequent to the resolution in 2005 of a high-profile case of mush-room-worker exploitation taken by the NGO, Migrant Rights' Centre Ireland (MRCI), and in light of the existence of extensive evidence of abuse of mushroom pickers in other parts of the country, SIPTU put together a special group of full-time organisers from all over the country to coordinate efforts to improve pay and working conditions in the mushroom-picking industry. In 2009 it embarked on a collabo-rative project with the MRCI and ran an information, recruitment and lobbying campaign in the sector. During the early stages of the campaign some claimed that it could not effect any substantial change because (a) it did not put in sufficient resources to support meaningful recruitment and organising at local level and (b) it continued to focus primarily on making changes and improving conditions through negotiation and lobbying of state agencies and government and employers' organisations (Allen 2010; Arqueros-Fernandez 2009). In fact, the joint campaign was ultimately successful. It attracted the support of the Irish Farmers' Association (IFA), which was unhappy at the reputational damage being done to the industry through the exploitative practices of some firms. It resulted in the creation of a Joint Labour Committee[2] (JLC) for the mushroom industry, in SIPTU and MRCI being given access to workers in mushroom farms all over the country, in the recruitment by SIPTU of 1,700 mushroom farm workers and in the almost total eradication of employment rights abuses in the sector. The mushroom industry campaign was subsequently used by SIPTU as a model of good practice and formed the basis for a focused sectoral approach which was rolled out more widely in other sectors – hospitality, the meat industry and contract cleaning. Indeed, the sectoral approach followed here defined the union's subsequent restructuring and set the tone for a new era of trade union engagement with migrant workers. SIPTU senior organiser 1 described the approach in general:

> I identify which company we're going after and from there then we could have six or seven sites located all over the country and we plan it like a military operation. Each campaign is different depending on what the target is but the basic principles of campaign planning should theoretically be the same. (Interview, 2013)

MIGRANTS AS ORGANISERS

The recruitment of migrants as organisers has become a feature of many unions that operate in sectors where migrants are strongly represented, such as agriculture, meat processing, hospitality and nursing. John Wrench and Satnam Virdee (1996) refer to this as 'like for like' recruitment, or recruitment through shared identities. It involves using an organiser with similar characteristics to those he or she is trying to recruit in terms of, for example, ethnicity, languages spoken, religion, social class, age, gender or sexual orientation. This, it is argued, is likely to have a positive effect on membership because the union may be perceived as under-standing, and better able to represent, their specific interests. It also brings the practical benefit of overcoming language barriers.

At an early stage SIPTU had toyed with the idea of setting up a dedicated Migrant Unit, but this encountered opposition from those who were active on migrant issues. The view was that this would marginalise migrant workers and that the approach to take was to employ foreign nationals as organisers within sections and integrate the workers into union branches. In 2005 it appointed two specialist organisers with a range of language skills, including Polish, Russian and Lithuanian. These appointments were considered crucial in building contacts with migrant workers through social networks as well as through workplaces and encouraging membership. The following year it formed a special group of full-time organisers to coordinate the union's efforts to improve pay and working conditions in the mushroom industry described above (Turner, D'Art and Cross 2008). It now has a stand-alone organising department which employs 20 full-time staff. A number of other unions have also moved in the direction of employing migrant organisers, though, to date, in much smaller numbers. These include the Irish Nurses and Midwives Organisation (INMO), Unite and Mandate.

COOPERATION AND COLLABORATION

A central element in new organisational approaches and in the overall logic of trade union renewal is broad-based coalition building (Heery 1998; Tarrow 1998; Wills 2001; Frege and Kelly 2004). Coalition building with other social movements and relevant NGOs such as MRCI and migrant representative groups can help unions gain access to individuals and networks within specific communities who are able to contribute to union organising campaigns (Frege and Kelly 2003). Such links can serve to broaden the range of interests and the agendas that unions seek to represent, and thus enhance their appeal to poorly represented segments of the labour force, such as migrants. However, in many cases unions have proved reluctant to collaborate with social movements and other such bodies and often consider themselves as the true representatives of civil society, particularly in areas that have direct implications for workers. Richard Hyman (2001) suggests that it is only when unions have been forced to come to terms with the decline in their autonomous influence that they are prepared to contemplate broader alliances.

In general Irish trade union collaborative initiatives seem to fit this pattern, though there was some cooperation on a policy level between the ICTU, its constituent unions and partnership bodies and NGOs in support of migrant workers from early on in the migration cycle. From this engagement, initiatives such as an Anti-Racist Workplace campaign and a joint initiative with employer organisations to draw up guidelines for the employment of migrant workers were developed. ICTU also actively engaged with migrant-support NGOs such as the National Consultative Committee on Racism and Interculturalism (NCCRI) on which it was represented and had bi-lateral relations with the MRCI and the Immigrant Council of Ireland (ICI). However, a number of interviewees were critical of ICTU on the issue of collaboration and felt it adopted an unhelpful superior position:

If I went to ICTU I'd say don't worry that working with small groups and NGOs might undermine your position. It won't. Work with them as equals and when you all sit down together you'll be first among equals. Now collaboration is not easy, it's very difficult when you've got lots of groups represented to get agreement on stuff but you know democracy means a lot of meetings, it means a lot of debate; a lot of arguments. If you don't want that, then don't claim to be engaged in democracy. (Interview, Unite Officer, 2013)

At a union affiliate level, Irish unions have increasingly been engaged in cooperative and collaborative initiatives as the challenges around migrant labour grew. As far back as 2004, SIPTU joined with ICTU and the MRCI to campaign for a Joint Labour Committee for domestic workers that would formally set out terms and conditions for this previously unregulated sector (ICTU, 2005; MRCI, 2004). The joint activity resulted in the introduction in 2007 of a Department of Enterprise, Trade and Employment Code of Practice, which set out minimum standards for the employment of domestic workers. SIPTU also took a similar cooperative approach in relation to mushroom workers, as outlined earlier:

We cooperated with migrant workers, we cooperated with FLAC, with the Law Society, with NCCRI, with African women's groups in County Louth. We were constantly looking for people that we could link up with at all levels, local regional and national. I shared platforms with everyone and anyone ... We would do anything to try and make as many inroads into the migrant community as we possibly could and that included people who were not active in the workforce. (Interview, former SIPTU regional secretary, 2013)

At an organising level, representatives from individual unions and from NGOs have collaborated on joint campaigns and, in some cases have undertaken joint training and organising initiatives. For example SIPTU and Unite worked closely together over a period on a joint campaign in the meat industry with SIPTU providing training to Unite organisers and SIPTU and Unite staff subsequently working side by side: 'There's still a lot of scepticism about dealing with them [Unite] within this organisation but I disagree with those attitudes. They're hangovers from the past but we have to park them and move on' (SIPTU senior organiser 2).

The heads of organising from a number of unions came together in 2011 to form an organising group of unions. This included representatives of SIPTU, Mandate, the Communication Workers Union

(CWU), the Technical Engineering and Electrical Union (TEEU) and the public service union, Impact who come together several times a year. The purpose is cooperation, sharing of information, undertaking joint training, all with a view to spreading strategic organisational capacity and skills. The group has relationships with the international organisation Change-to-Win, which provides assistance to unions going through a change process. It also has ongoing relationships with the SEIU in the United States, UNI Global Union and Global Alliance. Representatives of a number of unions and NGOs also work closely together and support one another in the 'coalition to protect the lowest-paid', a campaign which consists of SIPTU, Mandate, Unite, MRCI, the National Women's Council and Community Platform. There is also an ethical trade initiative which involves a similar grouping. When asked about the perspective of MRCI on these types of collaboration, Siobhan O'Donoghue, MRCI's director, was very clear:

> We have to think about the long term. We're MRCI, an NGO, where are we going, are we going to exist in a couple of years? I don't really know. But also the issues are important and they should be the future burning issues for the labour movement in Ireland. It's not about us developing expertise and being precious and being separate from everything else. Success really is working with trade unions so that these are the issues that they're also concerned with. (Interview, 2012)

SIPTU has a memorandum of understanding with MRCI, which sets out an undertaking to work and collaborate on areas that are of mutual concern, to support each other's policy positions where relevant and to meet on a regular basis to agree strategic issues and actions. On a day-to-day basis the two collaborate on a restaurant and catering forum and an agricultural forum as well as supporting each other in their various campaigns.

MIGRANT WORKER UNION ENGAGEMENT

With regard to migrant worker engagement with the unions, the low level of representation of migrants in elected positions within the structures is a particular problem. In a survey carried out for this research it was identified as an issue, though views on the reasons for this varied. Some saw the problem as a lack of willingness on the part of migrants to get involved, either through lack of interest or because employers placed barriers (such as open hostility or unwillingness to allow time off) in the way of union activity. Other perceived difficulties were the nature of union structures, colleague hostility, fear and uncertainty about immigration status, language barriers, lack of access to information, and the general fluidity of the migrant workforce.

At the time of the survey in 2010, only three unions had migrant worker representation on their national executives, six had some representation on branch committees, 73 per cent had migrants as delegates to annual conferences, though in most cases the level of representation was as low as one or two individuals, and many did not know the level of migrant representation. As a Mandate senior organiser pointed out: 'If there are 40 per cent migrant members as in the case of Mandate, then there should be 40 per cent migrant workers at our conference and there's not' (interview, 2013). He surmised that there are in fact only on average four or five individuals attending.

Of the unions surveyed, 13 have some migrant shop stewards, particularly in the sectors which have been the focus of intensive organisation campaigns. However, these tend only to emerge in workplaces where the vast majority of the workforce is non-Irish. For example, Mandate has around eight non-Irish shop stewards, mainly Polish, mirroring the fact that a large proportion of its migrant worker membership is Polish. The CWU and Unite each have fewer than ten, while BATU has only ever had one non-Irish shop steward. While SIPTU has more than 20, this is still a very small proportion. Jack O'Connor commented on the issue of representation:

> I think we were correct, albeit that it wasn't so much a conscious decision, not to create sectarian groups (migrant workers sectors) but I don't think that we have done enough to cultivate leaders among them, but that's attributable to this culture problem that exists, that's not just about migrants. It's about our whole inadequacies in the organising field generally. You know we're not any more successful organising Irish workers than we are organising workers from abroad. (Interview, 2012)

MIGRANTS AND THE NEW MODEL UNIONISM

What is abundantly clear from this research is that Irish trade unions' recognition of the potential of migrants as a new constituency has had an impact on the nature of Irish trade unionism. While the language deployed may have been about low pay, trade union revitalisation has effectively been driven by the presence of migrants in the labour force. Through their engagement with migrant workers, Irish unions have increasingly seen the benefits of cooperation and collaboration with other unions and with NGOs. This willingness to collaborate is doubtless born out of a recognition of the weakening trade union position described by Hyman (2001), but nonetheless its manifestation is noteworthy. Though not all unions are engaging with new organising models, almost all have adapted their approach to unionisation in ways that, at least, accommodate this new constituency. This in itself has acted as a barrier to the development of xenophobic tendencies and may partly explain why Ireland, perhaps uniquely in Western Europe, does not have an anti-immigration party.[3] Trade unions as part of civil society have an important role to play in terms of promoting hegemony of different discourses and the forging of a popular common sense.

The Irish model of organising that emerged in the period studied is different from other international models, though it shares many characteristics. It is union-led, it is employment-focused and it is research-based. The dynamic drive has not been external to the unions, through pressure from faith-based organisations or NGOs, for example. Rather it has been an intra-union dynamic led, in the first instance, by committed activists and developed with the support of union leaderships. It has taken place within the existing structures of unions, which may well be making links with communities, but are themselves directing the work. While it cannot be described as community unionism in that it is not community-based, and while it has moved beyond the workplace and beyond standard trade union modalities, the trade unionists interviewed for this research would say that, though engagement at community level is very much a feature of their work, it is not a free choice, but one driven by an inability to access the workplace. Thus the approach could be termed a community-oriented organising approach.

Our study shows an 'Irish solution to an Irish problem'. While there have been many studies of migrant workers and the problems they face, there have been very few focused on migrant workers as potential constituencies for trade unions facing decline and seeking means to revitalise their situation. Irish trade unions rose to the occasion in their unplanned, sometimes patchy, yet eventually effective engagement with the migrant worker population. In doing so they played a leading role in shifting the national discourse on migration towards inclusivity, against xenophobic tendencies undoubtedly present that could have intensified had the unions not taken such a stance. While effectively blocking a xenophobic reaction through their inclusive discourse and practice, the unions also began to revitalise their own democratic structures, mount an energetic organisational drive and create a coherent post-corporatist political orientation.

CONCLUSION

Trade unions in Ireland, as elsewhere, had options when faced with the new reality of mass inward migration during the Celtic Tiger boom years. Various tipping points emerged, such as the blatant exploitation of migrants in the mushroom industry discussed earlier, when the unions might have reacted differently. A number of union organisers and activists, many of whom had been migrants themselves working in Britain and elsewhere during the pre-Celtic Tiger years, addressed this crisis in a dynamic way, forging alliances with NGOs that often emerged from a faith-based tradition of care for others. As Gramsci might have pointed out, neither trade union identity nor that of migrant workers was pre-given; they were mutually constitutive, forged during the course of these struggles. Unions can change, as we have seen, and the identity of migrant workers too was forged during the process of integration into the broad working-class movement in Ireland. From the Southern Gramsci we learn the pivotal importance of the migrant in the making of the working class and in the building of working-class identities.

NOTES

1. From 1987, the Irish trade union movement operated within a corporatist political model, based in part on the German model and characterised by a social partnership arrangement involving the government, unions and employers and, to a lesser extent, other interest groups.
2. Joint Labour Committees are statutory bodies established under the Industrial Relations Acts, 1946 and 1990 to provide machinery for the fixing of minimum rates of remuneration and the regulation of conditions of employment in certain sectors of employment.
3. There have been some attempts to establish anti-immigration political movements (Immigration Control Platform in 2002, Irish National Party in 2010, National Independent Party in 2014) but these have singularly failed with the voting public and have never won a single seat at national, European or local level.

REFERENCES

Ackers, P. 2014. 'Gramsci and the Miners' Strike: Remembering the 1984–1985 Euro-communist Alternative Industrial Relations Strategy'. *Labor History* 55(2) (May): 151–72.

Allen, K. 2010. 'The Trade Unions: From Partnership to Crisis'. *Irish Journal of Sociology* 18(2): 22–37.

Annunziato, F. 2011. 'Gramsci's Theory of Trade Unionism' In M. Green (ed.). *Rethinking Gramsci*. London: Routledge.

Arqueros-Fernández, F. 2009. 'Contrasts and Contradictions in Union Organizing: The Irish Mushroom Industry'. In G. Gall (ed.) *The Future of Union Organizing: Building for Tomorrow*. Hampshire: Palgrave Macmillan.

Barrett, A. and Duffy, D. 2007. *Are Ireland's Immigrants Integrating into its Labour Market?* Discussion Paper No 2838, Institute for the Study of Labour (IZA).

Capuzzo, P. and Mezzadra, S. 2012. 'Provincializing the Italian Reading of Gramsci'. In N. Srivastava and B. Bhattacharya (eds). *The Postcolonial Gramsci.* London: Routledge.

Castles, S. 2011. 'Foreword: Diversity and Post-Tiger Ireland'. In Fanning and Munck 2011.

D'Art, D. and Turner, T. 2005. 'Union Recognition and Partnership at Work: A New Legitimacy for Irish Trade Unions?' *Industrial Relations Journal* 36(2): 121–39.

Donaghey, J. and Teague, P. 2006. 'The Free Movement of Workers and Social Europe: Maintaining the European Ideal'. *Industrial Relations Journal* 37(6): 652–66.

Ebbinghaus, B. and Visser, J. 1999. 'When Institutions Matter: Union Growth and Decline in Western Europe 1950–1995'. *European Sociological Review* 15(2): 135–58.

Fanning, B. and Munck, R. 2011. *Globalization, Migration and Social Transformation: Ireland in Europe and the World.* Farnham: Ashgate.

Fine, J. 2005. 'Community Unionism and the Revival of the American Labor Movement'. *Politics and Society* 33(1): 153–99.

Frege, C. and Kelly, J. 2003. 'Union Revitalization Strategies in Comparative Perspective', *European Journal of Industrial Relations* 9(1): 7–24.

—— —— (eds). 2004. *Varieties of Unionism: Strategies for Union Revitalisation in a Globalising Economy.* Oxford: Oxford University Press.

Gramsci, A. 1977. *Selections from Political Writings, 1910–1920,* ed. Q. Hoare, trans. J. Matthews. London: Lawrence and Wishart.

—— 1978. *Selections from Political Writings, 1921–1926,* ed. and trans. Q. Hoare. London: Lawrence and Wishart.

—— 1985. *Selections from Cultural Writings,* ed. D. Forgacs and G. Nowell-Smith, trans. W.Q. Boelhower. London: Lawrence and Wishart.

Heery, E. 1998. 'The Relaunch of the Trades Union Congress'. *British Journal of Industrial Relations* 36(3): 339–50.

Hyman, R. 2001. *Understanding European Trade Unionism: Between Market, Class and Society.* London: SAGE.

—— 2004. 'An Emerging Agenda for Trade Unions?' In R. Munck (ed.) *Labour and Globalisation: Results and Prospects.* Liverpool: Liverpool University Press.

ICTU 2005. *Migration Policy and the Rights of Workers.* Dublin: ICTU.

Johnson, P. 2001. 'Organize for What? The Resurgence of Labor as a Citizenship Movement'. In L. Turner, H.C. Katz and R.W. Hurd (eds). *Rekindling the Movement: Labor's Quest for Relevance in the 21st Century.* Ithaca, NY: Cornell University Press.

Laclau, E. 1996. *Emancipation(s).* London: Verso.

Mac Éinrí, P. 2005. 'Ireland: Country Report'. In J. Niessen, Y. Schibel and C. Thompson (eds). *Current Immigration Debates in Europe.* Brussels: Migration Policy Group.

MRCI. 2004. *Private Homes: A Public Concern, the Experience of Twenty Migrant Women Employed in the Private Home in Ireland.* Migrant Rights Centre Ireland.

Munck, R. 2011. 'Unions, Globalisation and Internationalism: Results and Prospects'. In G. Gall, R. Hurd and A. Wilkinnon (eds). *International Handbook on Labour Unions.* London: Elgar.

SIPTU. 2011. *Submission to the Commission on the Irish Trade Union Movement.* Dublin: SIPTU.

Tarrow, S. 1998. *Power in Movement* (2nd edn). Cambridge: Cambridge University Press.

Teague, P. and Donaghey, J. 2009. 'Why Has Irish Social Partnership Survived?' *British Journal of Industrial Relations* 47(1): 55–78.

Turner, T., D'Art, D. and Cross C. 2008. 'Polish Workers in Ireland: A Contented Proletariat?' *Labour Studies Journal* 34(1): 112–16.

Williams, G.A. 1975. *Proletarian Order: Antonio Gramsci, Factory Councils and the Origins of Italian Communism in Italy, 1911–1921*. London: Pluto Press.

Wills, J. 2001. 'Community Unionism and Trade Union Renewal in the UK: Moving Beyond the Fragments'. *Transactions of the Institute of British Geographers* 26(4): 465–83.

Wrench, J. and Virdee, S. 1996. 'Organising the Unorganised: "Race", Poor Work and Trade Unions'. In P. Ackers, C. Smith and P. Smith (eds). *The New Workplace and Trade Unionism: Critical Perspectives on Work and Organisation*. London: Routledge.

7

The Southern Question and the Irish Question: A Social Movement Perspective[1]

Laurence Cox

This chapter draws on Antonio Gramsci to theorise the specificities of Irish social movements, focusing on migration *out of* Ireland; the role of 'outsiders' to the local community within Irish activism; and the recent upsurge in international migration to Ireland. Gramsci offers a powerful point of reference, not as decontextualised theorist, but as the leader of a severely repressed party several leading members of which were being persecuted on the brink of clandestinity, deeply concerned with regional and national particularity in order to organise more effectively; theorising intellectual activity to explore the classed development of social movements; concerned with hegemony not simply to understand but also to overthrow; and laying the groundwork for the cross-class alliances of the anti-fascist Resistance.

THINKING SOCIAL MOVEMENT LANDSCAPES

The question of how to characterise a particular movement landscape should be fundamental, but much research on Irish movements sidelines it, whether out of provincialism or on the assumption that Ireland is fundamentally similar to the core countries where most research and theory is produced. Such analyses ignore Ireland's unusual status as an island where peasant struggles succeeded in producing a land reform which transformed rural class relationships and land ownership; the Republic's situation as a west European state founded by an anti-colonial movement; or the North's shaping by four decades of social movement conflict. The Republic is one of very few states where popular movements successfully defeated nuclear power, and the impact of women's, GLBTQ and survivor movements on religious power is equally striking globally (Cox 2010a). The Rossport struggle against Shell's pipeline stands out for its 15-year resistance to one of the world's largest companies, while popular resistance to water charges is the latest in a series of substantial challenges to EU politics.

More formally, the concept of a social movement landscape indicates underlying features of *how social movements work* in a particular context, whether city-level (Vester et al.1993), regional, national or wider (Flesher Fominaya and Cox 2013), in the sense

1. that movements cannot fully be understood in isolation, but must be seen within a system of characteristic alliances and oppositions – linking different 'movement families', but also involving typical alliances *between* these (solidarity) and with movements from above (collusion). In capitalist societies, *some* degree of the latter is a normal part of hegemony, and crisis consists at least in part of movements disrupting such alliances;
2. that as with Seymour M. Lipset and Stein Rokkan's (1967) cleavage structures, which in part reflect these and act back on them, movement landscapes are relatively long lasting, defining the 'business as usual' context within which movements and their opponents operate; only in moments of crisis, when social groups move from passivity to mobilisation, detach themselves from previous alliances and form new ones, are these cards substantially shuffled;
3. that understanding movement landscapes requires attention both to prior movement history and to present-day power relationships across the whole society.

EXISTING ANALYSES

While parallels have been drawn between Irish movements and Mediterranean (Tovey 2007) or Latin American movements, the only sustained analysis of the specificities of Irish social movements is the Marxist tradition initiated by James Connolly (1910) in terms of 'labour and nation', socialism and republicanism, etc. Such analyses of movements in terms of ethnicity and empire have long been central to Marxist writing on Ireland.

This approach explains much about Northern Irish politics and the relationship between southern movements and Irish Catholic identity; these dimensions are key to the best analysis of the Irish women's movement (Coulter 1993) as well as to Hilary Tovey's (1993) and Robert Allen's (2004) accounts of rural struggles over industrial development – all identifying tensions of social class and ethno-cultural identity. Nonetheless, there is much that this approach does not tell us.

Because of the historical matrix of Connolly's original formulation and the centrality of the Northern Irish conflict to state-oriented political thought, far less attention has been given to understanding the characteristics of the Republic and southern Catholicism as 'ethnic' (rather than religious) identity (Cox 2013). Postcolonial writing does enable recognising that society in the South is in important ways a once-subaltern social movement which has produced a state, a dominant ethnicity, and other key social institutions (a situation common in the majority world) – but has far less to say about contemporary movements.

UNDERSTANDING MOVEMENT SUCCESS,
DEFEAT AND SUBORDINATION

My 'Gramsci in Mayo' (2011) attempted a critique of 'labour and nation' accounts from the perspective of the losers in the construction of present-day Ireland (subsistence farmers, landless labourers, 'relatives assisting', and so on), noting the subordination of the labour and women's movement to Catholic nationalism; the breadth of popular mobilisation until the 1950s in support of the new state and Catholic supremacy, paralleling aspects of the continental fascism admired by De Valera and Blueshirts alike; the use of national-developmentalism to construct hegemonic relationships, paralleling other postcolonial contexts; and the extent of collusion with the vast carceral complex and political conservatism of 'Dev's Ireland'.

In cleavage terms, the new state was defined by movements representing the pre-independence 'periphery' vis-à-vis those identifying with the one-time 'core'. Irish movement history is not simply postcolonial history: it is also shaped by popular collusion with authoritarian cultural nationalism. Connolly's last-instance loyalty to church and nation mirrors this, and offers few resources for breaking with a hegemony grounded in 'Irish, Catholic, nationalist' identities and deeply embedded in popular culture.

In terms of (partial and very ambiguous) movement success, we lack serious studies of this first process of movement institutionalisation, the frequent postcolonial outcome of 'movement-become-state' (Cox and Nilsen 2014). A Gramscian analysis would ask how the remarkable levels of self-organisation visible in the Land War, the cultural nationalist project and the dual-power structures of the War of Independence were channelled, contained and ultimately demobilised during the long Irish Revolution (say 1879–1924), and how rural and urban workers, women and small farmers in the 1910s were split by nationalism and the First

World War, used as foot soldiers for the nationalist cause and by the mid-1920s put firmly back into their various boxes.

A key element here would be exploring the 'armour of coercion' which protects hegemonic relationships (Gramsci 1971: 262–3, Q6§88). In the Irish context this means the way in which carceral Catholicism and anti-Republicanism policed the boundaries of acceptability. Anti-republicanism, together with anti-communism and attacks on atheists, etc., worked well for much of the twentieth century to contain popular movements within a broad framework of loyalty to the established order (including self-policing even while protesting; Ní Dhorchaigh and Cox 2011); while carceral Catholicism traumatised those who broke with ethnic norms and rewarded respectability.

GRAMSCI IN MAYO

Understanding the national and regional peculiarities of movement organising was central to Gramsci's thought. As a radical organiser during the revolutionary years 1919–20 and party leader in a period of European and national defeat and Stalinisation in Russia (Daniele 1999), many questions arose. Why did the revolutionary years produce a socialist state in Russia, a nationalist one in southern Ireland, the fall of the Kaiserreich – but also so many defeats? How should the Italian party respond to rising fascism and repeated insurrectionary failure in Germany? How should its leadership argue their national case in the Comintern's internal struggles?

Regionally, Gramsci (who had started as a Sardinian nationalist, opposed Northern racism against Southern migrants and argued for alliances between Northern workers and Southern peasants) was interested in the potential for a *nationally* hegemonic party connecting regional and national specificities; the *Prison Notebooks* pay great attention to specificity. In this respect, Gramsci is a more robust thinker than Connolly, who preferred to dismiss these differences (and, perhaps, ultimately fell victim to them).[2]

ANTONU SU GOBBU[3]

I often explain Sardinia to Irish students as the Mayo of Italy. Gramsci's Sardinia was remote and peripheral, a land of poor tenant farmers with a largely alien ruling class (of which his father formed part until his imprisonment), from which migrant workers such as his brother travelled to the Turin factories, others found work in mining and the occasional bright boy like himself could escape on a scholarship. The

South bore a similar relationship to the North as did Ireland to Britain, and his analysis of Southern politics is directly relevant to theorising Irish movements.

Gramsci constantly attempts to understand the 'South and islands', for example, in his analysis of Italian unification in terms of the extension of Northern political and economic power. His analysis of clientelist power relationships and the ability of 'traditional' intellectuals such as the village priest, doctor, lawyer, etc. to represent local peasant needs bears directly on Chris Curtin and Tony Varley's (1995) analysis of 'consensual' community development in rural Ireland, where local notables are identified with the 'community'.[4]

Again unlike Connolly (but both arguing against the mainstream of a core-based, uncritically modernist labour movement), Gramsci does not exclude a *critique* of peasant culture, local particularism and cross-class nationalism in his struggle to build alliances between peripheral peasants and metropolitan workers. In this analogy, the equivalent to Turin would not be Dublin but Liverpool, Manchester, Glasgow, Boston, New York or Chicago. What in Gramsci are internal politics would then be mutually critical and supportive international solidarity, as his wider European politics were.

In the broadest sense, a Gramscian analysis should grasp the peculiarity of Ireland as simultaneously 'conservative province' – like Bavaria or northeast Italy, a party system skewed far to the right and rooted in religious and rural conservatism – but also capable of the destruction of an aristocratic land-holding system by popular direct action; the breaking-apart of the core state of the world's then-largest empire; and the defeat of nuclear power. It would do so by showing how the hegemonic relations constructed in the independence process were not simply repressive but involved co-optation through (partially) meeting some of the needs expressed by movements.

THE SOUTHERN QUESTION

Characteristically, the *Lyons Theses* (adopted at a Party congress in exile just prior to full-blown fascist dictatorship) and 'Some Aspects of the Southern Question', which Gramsci was working on up to his arrest, tackle these theoretical and strategic issues through concrete proposals and examples (Gramsci 1978).[5]

Two of these, in the 'Southern Question', concern the politics of migrant Sardinian workers in Turin. In one case communists scuppered the attempts of emigrant middle classes to lead a cultural nationalist association and won poor migrants to a socialist education circle. In the other, more dramatically, migrants fraternised so effectively with a Sardinian regiment sent to put down a strike that it was withdrawn under cover of darkness. While the first story sets class above nation or region, the second recognises how these combine in practical identities: the soldiers had understood the workers they came to shoot as 'gentry', and it was the strikers' Sardinian origin that led the soldiers to recognise their common situation.

Gramsci's third example highlights the developmental character of his Southern politics. Bitterly hostile to Northern racism, which saw Southern peasants and migrant workers as simply backward, he argued for building alliances of the poor, by supporting Southern peasants' efforts towards organising independently of local elites. In the face of rigged Southern elections, the Turin communists offered to elect the radical (but anti-communist) Gaetano Salvemini to their own constituency, with no strings attached, as a peasant representative. This is practical solidarity with a peripheral movement whose problems are acknowledged, but treated as something to be overcome.

The 'Southern Question' bears reading in full as Gramsci's most systematic attempt to theorise the relationship between metropolitan and peripheral *movements* in developing alliances geared towards emancipating both. If the Italian Resistance struck deep roots in rural areas and cities alike, and if the post-war left built genuine alliances of workers and peasants, this was partly due to Gramsci's earlier efforts to demolish the role of Northern workers as modernist allies of Northern capital at the expense of the Southern poor (Magri 2011).

Thus a Gramscian analysis of Ireland has to analyse 'Sardinia' (Mayo, but more broadly the then-periphery, today's Republic) in relation to 'Turin' (Birmingham or Boston, but more broadly the then-core). Irish activists often note that extraordinarily high levels of migration over the past 175 years[6] have disproportionately exported social discontent – emptying local politics of the poorest sections of society, the losers of the construction of a society dominated by small property owners.[7] These were also the groups with the most radical traditions of struggle – landless labourers (Dunne 2014), subsistence farmers and urban workers. Ireland's present-day movement landscape can hardly be explained without these (literally) absent struggles. It is no accident that one of today's anti-austerity groups is called 'We're Not Leaving'.

If one country's emigrants are another country's immigrants, we cannot read the politics of migrant groups purely in terms of their new situation. We have to ask who people are *before they migrate*: what is their politics and how have they learned to organise? As with Sardinians in Turin, the politics of the Irish diaspora have been contradictory.

Organising skills often enabled ethnic closure geared to monopolising jobs, with attendant racism (Ignatiev 1995) and right-wing religious politics. Chicago's Mayor Daley, or the NYPD, inherited the organising traditions of Catholic Emancipation. Conversely, many chose *not* to identify in these terms and rejected racism, religion and/or 'Irish' community structures (MacVeigh 1996).

At times this politics was contested in dialectically transformative ways. Irish Catholic immigrants in late nineteenth-century London held pitched battles with free-thinking English workers over the conflict between the Papal States and Italian nationalism. These conflicts were eventually resolved (after the Paris Commune ended French involvement) in joint opposition to British imperialism further afield (Cox 2010b). More broadly, Irish-identifying activists played individually radical roles on the left and in the labour movement abroad.

A PROCESSUAL THEORY OF IRISH MOVEMENTS

Central to Gramsci's historical work is exploring the changing forms of state power. Gramsci (1966) offers us some important tools here, albeit often misread. Firstly, his intellectuals are *organisers* as much as *theorists*, exercising 'directive' as well as theoretical activity (Barker and Cox 2011). Thus the organic intellectuals with whom he hoped to form the new communist party were local trade union activists, peasant leaders, and so on. The educational task of supporting this development (with Freirean overtones: Mayo 1999) was thus inseparable from organising. The traditional intellectuals of village life are the local priest, doctor or lawyer – those formed by previous social formations.

Intellectuals are *organic* in that they are formed in the making of a new class (or, as with peasants, a class finally becoming a class-for-itself). It is not about people from particular backgrounds going to college, but how far the institutions, ideas and practices organisers draw on are *of the class*, *of the movement* rather than assimilating official ways of behaving. Orienting migrant activists towards the official pieties of constitutional politics, or education for individual social mobility, does not create organic intellectuals.

Organic intellectuals, for Gramsci, are equally often the intellectuals of the newly dominant class: managers, time-and-motion men – or today, consultants, marketers, policy workers, and so on. The massive formation of a new class which *believed in* the national-developmentalist project, and forged careers in the process, is such a development – as is the subsequent construction of the new private-sector service class which has yoked Ireland to multinational corporations and international financial institutions.

Movement, then, is practically expressed by the development of new organising groups – from above and below – and their alliances with old ('traditional') leadership groups, together with the infrastructure of social classes, class fractions or other social groups coming to self-consciousness, entering into political struggle and 'making themselves'. This is the problem with the 'betrayal by leaders' theory (Allen 1997) of the Irish working class; while there were contending intellectual groups, the consistent victory after 1913 of those who spoke for subordination and practised co-option relied on popular reflexes of respectability, acceptance of the national economic project and a strong desire for 'mainstreaming' working-class institutions (Peillon 1982). The importance of the present is that not for a century has that leadership had such a fragile infrastructural base, because of state-driven austerity politics and the breakdown of partnership. However the 'ethnic' identification which underpins subalternity remains powerful.

HEGEMONY IN IRELAND

Much Irish writing reads hegemony in disabling ways that present its success as inevitable and exclude effective popular agency, whether colluding with or breaking up hegemonic relations. However, a social group only becomes hegemonic to the extent that it succeeds in leading other groups, entailing subordinating some of its own corporate (particularist) interests and (partially) meeting its allies' needs. It competes with other fractions within its own class, and employs coercion as well as consent: neither among the elite nor the wider population does it have or seek universal support. Hegemony is not permanent, but a fragile and temporary achievement measured in decades not centuries (Cox and Nilsen 2014).

Gramsci's analysis of 'common sense' as a terrain of top-down struggle against 'good sense' (grounded in practical, situated knowledge; Ytterstad 2011) is helpful here, explaining Ireland's peculiar post-independence combination of practical cooperation with local power and *sotto voce* critique – contrasting with the dramatic ruptures of the independence movement.[8]

Reading the Republic as movement-become-state – land war underpinning independence – helps understand its subsequent politics. The postcolonial state claims a popular legitimacy, initially from these struggles and subsequently from the national-developmentalist project, even replaced by neoliberalism. Radical movements struggle to be heard while significant popular groups accept this practical and intellectual leadership (and when the most visible institutions of popular self-organisation, in labour, farming, women's or environmental movements, are constantly drawn on to renew national elites).

The process of Irish independence constructed an ethnic identity deeply bound up in the state and its characteristic forms of class and gendered power, and embedded in the structures of everyday life – family and friendship, the pub and the GAA, the priest and the schoolteacher, the policeman and the local politician. This is central to understanding the historical conservatism of rural Ireland. It also explains why 'blow-ins' (outsiders) have so often played a strategic role in movement struggles – and why the autonomous organisation of migrants who do *not* identify, or seek integration within, this conservative sense of 'Irishness' holds particular political potential.[9]

The 1960s and 1970s saw a clear shift from the hegemonic alliance of 'Dev's Ireland' (national capital, large farming, and the church, with the subordinate support of small farmers, small business, organised labour and women) to the beginnings of neoliberalism: a shift to an IBEC led by multinational interests, with national capital and small business definitely subaltern; a long-term ditching of clerical power in favour of a 'liberal', modernising alliance with the new service class and women; two decades of conflict with labour and working-class communities followed by two decades of partnership. Thus even within the newer, modernising alliance there are a series of shifts: we are currently living through another one.

From below, proto-hegemony is a more Gramscian construct than counter-hegemony. A broad social alliance, around women's rights, Carnsore, more recently Rossport or water charges, is an aspect of the 'war of position': creating a social coalition which *may* be able to fight a 'war of manoeuvre' that actually shifts the main structures of power. Nuclear power was defeated and church power was at least partially dislodged. Such alliances – developing links between the working-class left, poorer rural interests and culturally radical movements – hold significant *potential* which may or may not translate further. Among the internal opponents of such moves today are elite-oriented organisational leaderships seeking professionalisation, access to policy-makers, funding, legal and media influence – but also cultural conservatives nervous about the effect on 'people' of significant challenges to everyday ethnic culture.

OUR 'LOST REVOLUTIONS'

The shift in hegemonic relations started from above, with the Lemass–Whitaker shift to foreign direct investment in the late 1950s, followed by the feminist challenge to religious and gendered power structures, union struggles and the massive local assertions of urban working-class communities in the 1970s and 1980s, along with the ecological confrontation with developmentalism at Carnsore and radical political experiments (Hanley and Millar 2009). These movements broke the localist, religious and mobilising aspects of earlier state policy – in interaction with the new hegemony.

The cultural radicalism of this period was resisted because of fears of fragmenting the broader 'national–popular' consensus on which the power of the modernisers ultimately rested, but elites were forced to abandon the alliance with the church and offer limited policy gains (and, crucially, funding) to the women's, gay and lesbian, environmental and community movements, while ex-activists took up positions of respectability in the liberal wings of mainstream political parties, state committees, academia and the media.

We need an *overall* analysis of this second wave of movement institutionalisation from the 1960s to the 1990s: how the slow retreat of church power (but not of Catholic self-identification) in the face of the women's movement, GLBTQ activism and survivor organisations worked; how EEC membership led movement elites towards strategies of legal and media activism (hence professionalisation) rather than strategies of popular struggle and alliance-building; more recent attempts to capture the capitalist high ground (the pink pound, green consumerism, fair trade and organic food); social partnership co-opting union leaderships, demobilising community struggle into state-driven service delivery and assimilating other movements; and the *rhetoric* of civil society, 'consultation', etc. (CAP 2000), in which participation became an end in itself.

Irish social partnership from the later 1980s thus seems less a late outlier from the continental pattern of *Keynesian* neo-corporatism and rather a holding pattern like the limited 'democratisations' of post-dictatorship Latin America: a national agreement not to rock the boat and to seek class harmony in the 'national interest', in some ways a 'passive revolution' taming these movements after a series of successful struggles, symbolised by the 1990 election of Mary Robinson – and the real power-holders' scramble to adapt. Now, once-radical 'outsider movements' found themselves currying favour with some of the same petty-minded, provincial bureaucrats who had always opposed them, to gain or retain funding – entailing a retreat from radical politics. While this period also saw radical movements outside this consensus, their mobilising power was constrained by the broader pattern of co-optation.

Since the mid-2000s, the state's repudiation of partnership, and subsequent austerity politics, are creating another situation. NGO and union leaderships are desperate to retain elements of the partnership they depend on. More radical forces find that the state's attack on partnership is widening discontent, but often lack the organisational capacity to make the necessary connections.

Eppur si muove; and this is the real theoretical problem: theories of movement often stop short when movements succeed, are absorbed within the state, become subaltern parts of dominant coalitions, etc. – while theories of state and society (still) minimise movements' role, even where the existence of Northern or Southern society and state can hardly be understood without movements: which are duly referenced, but not thought about. But the reality of movement finds ways to break through.

In particular, the 1970s and 1980s saw a strong development of international solidarity movements, including Cuba, South Africa, Nicaragua, Palestine and Mexico. These involved a mixture of returned migrants (often religious, radicalised in liberation theology), political refugees, long-distance nationalisms and 'blow-ins'. International solidarity is deeply complex (Aiken et al. 2014; Landy, Darcy and Gutierrez 2014; Trott 2014; Waterman and Cox 2014); in Ireland, the bases for solidarity ranged (often within groups: Landy 2014a) from a simplistic identification between 'oppressed nations' via democratic/human rights and Catholic social justice orientations to conscious support for popular revolutions.

The category of 'blow-ins' deserves particular attention. Because of intense ethnic closure, Irish community structure meant that outsiders, whether from elsewhere in Ireland or from other *Northern* societies (in a still semi-peripheral context) played a disproportionate role in most movements, NGOs and community organising. This often remains true today. Reasons include biographical availability: particularly in rural contexts, family and friendship obligations and social control placed particular constraints on 'locals', while 'blow-ins', if they did not marry in, found themselves constructing groups, events, projects and organisations of all kinds to combat isolation and make connections.

Another explanation is the strong 'taken-for-granted' characteristics of Irish social life, in which even returned migrants often leave their culturally radical experiences abroad behind them (Laoire 2007). Ireland can be like Tolkien's Shire: political and cultural adventures happen elsewhere, while 'reality' means fitting back into an everyday life defined by a closed ethnic culture. Hence those who can never fully fit in have a constant need to explore alternative possibilities and, as David

Landy (2015) puts it, import an external habitus into the field of struggle; conversely, conservatives seek to delegitimise them as 'not really Irish'.

GRAMSCI IN TURIN

The 'Southern Question' is shaped by Gramsci's own experience of chain migration to Turin and the politics of the Southern diaspora. What can we say, today, about the politics of immigrant organising in Ireland? Most immigration has taken place within the last two decades, with significant life choices for labour migrants at the start of the crisis (those who understand themselves as short-term visitors are less likely to organise). As Oliver Scharbrodt et al. observe (2015: 2), the obvious parallels are Portugal, Finland and Greece, traditionally emigrant countries which have only recently become net immigration countries (in the mid-1990s for Ireland).

As this immigration does not follow previous colonial relationships, migrant populations are extremely heterogeneous and for most individual ethnicities extremely small. Hence much effort goes towards informal support networks, community centres, Saturday language schools, religious venues, etc., while political orientations for the first generation are shaped strongly by those acquired prior to migration and long-distance nationalisms are often significant.

In this context the older history of solidarity movements revived, as a widespread if fragmented process of majority-led groups involved in anti-racism, multiculturalism/migrant support and asylum-seeker solidarity/anti-deportation, with roots in grassroots left politics, community organising, religious motives and charity (Moran 2011: 120–2). However, the landscape was also shaped by a largely Irish-dominated NGO sector providing services *for* migrants in line with state and EU funding policies (Cullen 2009), by the context of social partnership and the broader clientelist political culture. Migrant activists thus had to decide their political orientation early on: whether to tailor their demands to what mainstream political allies presented as acceptable and attainable goals in a context of widespread racism, or to test the colder waters of self-organising on their own terms, with or without 'native allies'. Similar choices were faced by majority-led migrant solidarity groups (Moran 2011: 125).

Autonomous migrant movements, then, have to be seen within a wider movement landscape – of movements in Ireland generally and the more immediate landscapes of 'blow-ins' in Irish organisations, of multicultural and anti-racist NGOs, international solidarity movements, grassroots asylum-seeker solidarity groups and migrant community networking and institution building.

The Migrant Networks Project highlighted 'lobbying, advocacy, outreach, information, training and support' as features of 436 migrant-led groups (most founded since 2001) which 'provide essential services, participate in policy debates, implement strategies of cultural adaptation and resistance, create opportunities for individual and community advancement, and provide a platform for disadvantaged segments of the population to become visible' (Lentin 2013: 77). Thus movement activity – let alone activity *not* primarily structured by state funding and seeking access to policy makers on consensual terms – is only a small part of migrants' self-organising.[10] As Landy (2014b) shows, migrant groups were deeply constrained in the form and content of their 2006–8 responses to the Immigration, Residence and Protection Bill, because they were organised in ways dictated by the need for recognition as interlocutors within 'partnership lite' (Boucher 2008).

With small absolute numbers and limited second-generation numbers, the even smaller numbers engaged politically have an uphill battle to shape political identities that can articulate themselves independently. As elsewhere, much of this involves constructing wider identities, and organisations such as AkiDwA (originally for African women but now for migrant women generally) or the migrant-led Anti-Racism Network indicate one kind of identification (Lentin 2012) in sharp contrast to the involvement of African businessmen in the clientelistic Fianna Fáil, or the construction of an 'Italian community' led by businesses with embassy support.

THE EMPIRE STRIKES BACK

In 2004 the 'racist referendum' removed the citizenship rights of children born in Ireland, creating a blood-based citizenship and causing entirely foreseen hardship; 79 per cent of the (Irish) population voted in favour, with 63 per cent of 'yes' voters understanding their vote in anti-immigrant terms. This dog-whistle politics marked the culmination of the process whereby the Irish in Ireland 'became white', a process also marked by an increasingly pro-NATO foreign policy and other signals of a 'European' identity defined against the majority world.

In this same period, however, autonomous solidarity activism outside 'social partnership' remained significant, notably Palestinian solidarity and anti-war movements, both connecting members of the majority population and migrants. The February 2003 demonstration against the Iraq war was as large as any Irish protest ever. Meanwhile, direct action against US military use of Shannon airport, while small, included a wide range of Irish-born and migrant activists. Other solidarity activism is less visible: for example, support for Asian movements among Buddhist groups in Ireland, bringing together immigrant and majority members (Cox 2013, ch. 7).

Of particular interest is the solidarity between Irish Traveller organisations and Roma/Sinti movements in Europe, with the small Traveller groups seeking legitimacy, allies and skills from their European allies and extending solidarity to Roma/Sinti in Ireland. One key organisation, Pavee Point, became a 'Traveller and Roma Centre'; in July 2007 they offered solidarity to over 80 Roma left to fend for themselves on a motorway roundabout. This highly public support earned them an instant threat to their funding, underlining the political costs of activism and the difficulty of combining funded service provision with radical politics.

In this period, migrant-led organising autonomous from the state has grown, not least in response to these constraints. Key struggles have challenged 'direct provision' (the segregation of asylum seekers in isolated accommodation with minimal autonomy) and deportation, both striking at the hard core of state racism. Significant groups include the previously mentioned Anti-Racism Network; the migrant-led Anti-Deportation Ireland, in alliance with direct provision residents (Lentin 2013: 81); and the more recent Movement of Asylum Seekers in Ireland (Flood 2014).

Ethnically and culturally outsider activists have consistently played a disproportionate role within Irish movements, and this seems set to continue. If Connolly could distribute election leaflets in Yiddish in 1902, the Ireland Palestine Solidarity Campaign has consistently played a significant role on the Irish left; Irish and Polish anarchists collaborated in the mid-2000s to produce Polish-language material; while in 2015 the radical wing of the Spanish diaspora joined Irish movements in organising a Grassroots Strategy Weekend. More generally, non-local activists (from elsewhere in the Republic, Northern Ireland, other Northern countries or the global South) continue to play a key role in most radical social movements.

GRAMSCI IN WEST DUBLIN?

Since the mid-2000s, the combination of the radical alliance politics of the anti-capitalist movement (Cox 2006) and the crisis of partnership has provoked many *simulations* of movement coalitions. Practically, these have consisted of events aimed at elites (geared to publicity, lobbying or funding) and driven by organisational leaderships committed to restoring partnership – often tied to the pro-austerity Labour Party and in at least one case with material support from the employers' organisation IBEC. Initially such events saw tables packed with bureaucrats horrified at the thought of street protests; more recently, the same basic practice has been rebranded with anti-austerity rhetoric, invocations of revolution, mentions of Latin America, etc. Since the response from elites depends on the answer to the question 'You and whose army?' it becomes important to manipulate wider movements into believing that more serious social change is sought.

However, dramatic movements are now taking place *outside* such events, as massive popular resistance to water-meter installation across working-class Dublin, rooted in local communities, places the state in crisis (Cox and Nilsen 2015, MacCionnaith 2015). In 2011, I raised the possibility of 'an Irish M-15, Icelandic or Tahrir Square experience of mass popular mobilisation against failed elites', noting that 'Labour and Fine Gael would have to lose all credibility in the way Icelandic politicians and Mubarak did'. I argued that

> something more is needed: certainly the radical-democratic experience of mass mobilisation, but also the generalisation of struggle from public space to the compartmentalised worlds of workplace and school, family and church – and a serious settling of accounts with past responsibilities for collusion in corrupt politics and abusive institutions. This may seem impossible, but Ireland is a funny place in terms of social movements. The fear of seeming strange or different means that often movements have to trundle along as minority affairs for years – until apparently all at once those who don't want to stand out jump the same way (and then often deny that they ever felt any differently). (Cox 2011)

The second large-scale water-charges protest, on 1 November 2014, tackled this problem by organising over 100 *local* protests – enabling people to see that they would not be ridiculed for participating or isolated in refusing to pay, and making visible the potential for direct resistance to meter installation. From that point, despair has increasingly turned into hope.

BEYOND THE GRIP OF 'IRISHNESS'?

In activist and conservative discourse alike, Ireland's movement landscape is often understood (justifiably) as restricting radical politics and (less plausibly) as being an eternal feature of national character. However, landscapes are not outside history – or, at times, earthquakes. As in the

Andes, direct confrontation with specific nexuses of power at Rossport proved hugely generative. It positioned an almost archetypally 'Irish' community against the destruction of farming, fishing and tourism: when individuals, families or communities are existentially threatened they can abandon what turns out to have been (long-term) conditional loyalty to 'ethnic' ways of doing politics. So too, on a much wider scale, with direct action against water charges, regularly described as 'the straw that broke the camel's back'.

Secondly, as with the complex alliances around Rossport, the water-charges movement involves a very broad social alliance – as any proto-hegemonic struggle must. By definition, this reshaping of routine alliances creates difficulties (cf. Ó Donnabháin 2014 on ethnic tensions within the Rossport Solidarity Camp), but *contra* the Irish addiction to harmony, nuclear power could be defeated with *three* competing campaigns (Dalby 1984). At the time of writing, sectarian and sectoral differences are mostly being contained in the water movement, the relationship between the working-class Dublin core and wider participation is holding, and particularism is far weaker than usual.

Third, the attempt to put Rossport outside the pale of the ethnic community, through anti-republicanism and state violence, was only partially successful, and for many provoked greater distancing from 'Irish' media and police. With the water struggle, the same combination of media hysteria and state thuggery has been experienced far more widely, and the actual state violence filmed on phones and shared on social media is readily contrasted to establishment horror at 'fascist' atrocities such as ... blocking the deputy prime minister's car or insulting the president.

All of this, finally, is happening where the state's attack on partnership, intransigent austerity politics and preference for coercive approaches has undermined 'Irish consensualism'. Organisational leaderships tied to funding, lobbying and respectability are less and less able to transmit any of these. Change *within* movements, and within organisations, is part and parcel of what is being fought over.

In the broadest perspective, the hope of challenging the 'little Ireland' that exports its poor and radicals, and grounds internal complacency in loyalty to taken-for-granted culture, must involve new forms of solidarity across differences of place and ethnicity. If allegiance to class and gender power relations is structured through an unreflected identity bound up with everyday structures of national and religious affiliation, rising migrant involvement in movements generally might offer a point of fracture for this last-instance loyalty to ethnic culture.

It may provide some of the energy needed to restore the possibility of alliance between the politically radical but culturally conservative

Irish left, and movements which challenge the socio-cultural bases of oppression and exploitation but avoid direct confrontation with the state (Epstein 1993; Thompson 1976; Rowbotham and Weeks 1977). The *loss* of state funding for social movement organisations (Lentin 2013: 82) may support more radical trends within migrant activism. As Landy (2013: 73) puts it, 'there is nothing inevitable about the current channelling of migrant groups into being service providers', and they have the potential to move outside a restrictive 'migrant field' and challenge power relations within the wider society. As with Gramsci's Sardinian workers in Turin, this is not just about 'migrant' movements but equally about the emancipation of 'majority' movements from Irishness, remaking the movement landscape.

NOTES

1. This chapter draws on my article 'Gramsci in Mayo' (2011). I am grateful to the Finnish NGO publisher, Into, for permission to reuse some of this material, now exploring the 'outside' of the ethnic 'inside' explored there. Thanks are due to David Landy and the editors for helpful comments on earlier drafts of this chapter.
2. For biographies of Gramsci, see Fiori (1990) and Davidson (1977); for an overview of interpretations, see Liguori (1996); for some scholarly approaches, see Baratta and Liguori (1999) or Burgio and Santucci (1999).
3. Nairn's (1982) title underlines the importance of reading Gramsci as *Sardinian*.
4. Another analogy lies in how the rural middle classes colonised the national administrative apparatus.
5. This discussion concentrates on his analysis of the events, rather than on historical reconstruction.
6. For example, in 1891 a full 39 per cent of those born in Ireland were living elsewhere.
7. Ireland is a European exception in that women migrants equalled or outnumbered men – understandably considering the sexual politics involved (Hall and Malcolm 2008).
8. This is often explained by fear – but the scale of practical repression in Ireland has been far *less* than in most west European countries; the real fear has been of stepping outside clientelist relationships and the narrow bounds of tolerance, ceasing to be part of the 'community' as conservatively defined; Cox 2014.
9. One of the main responses from church and state is the attempt, prominent in both state multiculturalism and 'interfaith' work, to construct an 'immigrant community', a 'Buddhist community' (Cox 2013), an 'African community', etc. which would adapt itself to a parallel form of this.
10. I share Landy's (2013: 67) scepticism about overly broad celebrations of all migrant activity as by definition resistance even when attempting to integrate on mainstream terms.

REFERENCES

Aiken, M. et al. 2014. 'Activist experiences of solidarity work', *Interface* 6(2): 216–23.
Allen, K. 1997. *Fianna Fáil and Irish labour*. London: Pluto Press.

Allen, R. 2004. *No Global: The People of Ireland versus the Multinationals.* London: Pluto Press.

Baratta, G. and Liguori, P. 1999. *Gramsci da un secolo all'altro.* Rome: Riuniti.

Barker, C. and Cox, L. 2011. 'What Have the Romans Ever Done for Us?' Helsinki: into-ebooks.

Boucher, G. 2008. 'Ireland's Lack of a Coherent Integration Policy'. *Translocations* 3(1): 1–24.

Burgio, A. and Santucci, A. 1999. *Gramsci e la rivoluzione in Occidente.* Rome: Riuniti.

CAP [Community Action Project]. 2000. *On the Balcony.* Ballymun: self-published.

Coulter, C. 1993. *The Hidden Tradition.* Cork: CUP.

Cox, L. 2006. 'News from Nowhere'. In N. Hourigan and L. Connolly (eds). *Social Movements and Ireland.* Manchester: Manchester University Press: 210–29.

—— 2010a. 'Another World is under Construction?' www.irishleftreview.org/2010/05/17/world-construction-social-movement-responses-inequality-crisis/

—— 2010b. 'Dhammaloka as social movement organiser'. *Contemporary Buddhism* 11(2): 173–227.

—— 2011. 'Gramsci in Mayo'. Helsinki: Into.

—— 2013. *Buddhism and Ireland.* Sheffield: Equinox.

—— 2014. 'Community, history, power'. Talk to People's Forum, Erris.

—— and Nilsen, A. 2014. *We Make Our Own History.* London: Pluto Press.

—— —— 2015. 'First we take Athens, then we take Berlin?' *Ceasefire.* https://ceasefiremagazine.co.uk/athens-berlin-syrizas-victory-twilight-neoliberalism/

Cullen, P. 2009. 'Irish Pro-Migrant NGOs'. *Voluntas* 20(2): 99–128.

Curtin, C. and Varley, T. 1995. 'Community Action and the State'. In P. Clancy et al. (eds). *Irish Society.* Dublin: IPA.

Dalby, S. 1984. *The Nuclear Syndrome.* Belfast: Dawn Train. www.innatenonviolence.org/pamphlets/nuclearsyndrome.rtf

Daniele, C. 1999. *Gramsci a Roma, Togliatti a Mosca.* Turin: Einaudi.

Davidson, A. 1977. *Antonio Gramsci.* London: Merlin.

Dunne, T. 2014. *Cultures of Resistance in Pre-Famine Ireland.* Ph.D. thesis. National University of Ireland Maynooth.

Epstein, B. 1993. *Political Protest and Cultural Revolution.* Berkeley: University of California Press.

Fiori, G. 1990. *Antonio Gramsci.* London: Verso.

Flesher Fominaya, C. and Cox, L. 2013. *Understanding European Movements.* London: Routledge.

Flood, A. 2014. 'MASI'. www.wsm.ie/c/masi-movement-asylum-seekers-ireland

Gramsci, A. 1966. *Il materialismo storico e la filosofia di Benedetto Croce.* Turin: Einaudi

—— 1971. *Selections from the Prison Notebooks*, ed. and trans. Q. Hoare and G. Nowell-Smith. London: Lawrence and Wishart.

—— 1978. *Selections from Political Writings, 1921–1926*, ed. and trans. Q. Hoare. London: Lawrence and Wishart.

Hall, D. and Malcolm, E. 2008. 'Diaspora, Gender and the Irish'. *Australasian Journal of Irish Studies* 8: 3–29.

Hanley, B. and Millar, S. 2009. *The Lost Revolution.* London: Penguin.

Ignatiev, N. 1995. *How the Irish Became White.* London: Routledge.

Landy, D. 2013. 'Negotiating Power'. In L. Brennan (ed.). *Enacting Globalization.* Basingstoke: Palgrave.

—— 2014a 'We don't get involved in the internal affairs of Palestinians', *Interface* Vol. 6(2): 130–142.

—— 2014b 'Challengers in the Migrant Field'. *Ethnic and Racial Studies* 38(6): 927–42.

—— 2015. 'Bringing the Outside In'. *Social Movement Studies* 14(3): 255–69.

—— Darcy, H. and Gutierrez, J. 2014. 'Exploring the Problems of Solidarity'. *Interface* 6(2): 26–34.

Lentin, R. 2012. 'Migrant Women's Networking'. In G. Bhattacharyya (ed.). *Ethnicities in a Changing World.* Farnham: Ashgate.

—— 2013. 'Migrant-Led Activism and Integration from Below in Recession Ireland'. In L. Brennan (ed.). *Enacting Globalization.* Basingstoke: Palgrave.

Liguori, P. 1996. *Gramsci conteso.* Rome: Riuniti.

Lipset, S. and Rokkan, S. (eds). 1967. *Party Systems and Voter Alignments.* New York: Free Press.

MacCionnaith, C. 2015. *They Say Cutbacks, We Say Fightback.* MA thesis. Department of Sociology, Maynooth University.

MacVeigh, R. 1996. *The Racialization of Irishness.* Belfast: Centre for Research and Documentation.

Magri, L. 2011. *The Tailor of Ulm.* London: Verso.

Mayo, P. 1999. *Gramsci, Freire and Adult Education.* London: Zed Books.

Moran, N. 2011. *The Grassroots Pro-Asylum Seeker Movement in the Republic of Ireland.* Ph.D. thesis. National University of Ireland Maynooth. http://eprints.nuim.ie/2893/

Nairn, T. 1982. 'Antonu su gobbu'. In Anne Showstack Sassoon (ed.). *Approaches to Gramsci.* London: Writers and Readers: 159–79.

Ní Dhorchaigh, E. and Cox, L. 2011. 'When Is an Assembly Riotous, and Who Decides?' In Sheehan, W. and Cronin, M. (eds). *Riotous Assemblies.* Cork: Mercier.

Ní Laoire, C. 2007. 'Reflections on Narratives of Migration and Return Project'. Paper for Sociological Association of Ireland conference, Limerick.

Ó Donnabháin, S. 2014. *Ideological Diversity and Alliance Building across Difference in Social Movements.* MA thesis. National University of Ireland Maynooth.

Peillon, M. 1982. *Contemporary Irish Society.* Dublin: Gill & Macmillan.

Rowbotham, S. and Weeks, J. 1977. *Socialism and the New Life.* London: Pluto Press.

Scharbrodt, O. et al. 2015. *Muslims in Ireland.* Edinburgh: EUP.

Thompson, E.P. 1976. *William Morris.* New York: Pantheon.

Tovey, H. 1993. 'Environmentalism in Ireland'. *International Sociology* 8(4) (December): 413–30.

—— 2007. *Environmentalism in Ireland.* Dublin: IPA.

Trott, B. 2014. 'A Spinozist Sort of Solidarity'. *Interface* 6(2): 224–9.

Vester, M. et al. 1993. *Soziale Milieus im gesellschaftlichen Strukturwandel.* Cologne: Bund.

Waterman, P. and Cox, L. 2014. 'Movement Internationalism/s'. *Interface* 6(2): 1–12.

Ytterstad, A. 2011. *Norwegian Climate Change Politics and the Media.* Ph.D. thesis. University of Oslo.

Part III
Avoiding Misplaced Alliances

8

Hegemony, Migration and Misplaced Alliances: Lessons from Gramsci

Peter Mayo

The spectre of colonialism is returning to haunt Europe with a vengeance. The old continent's former colonies and protectorates are points of origin for several migration flows. They are mainly directed to this continent which is viewed as the colonial El Dorado, the constructed outlet for 'the good life.' Migration has become the principal concern in the Mediterranean region, the pathway by sea to the heart of the old continent. Migration provides cause for grave concern because of the tragedies occurring there. These tragedies are turning the surrounding sea into a 'graveyard.' This partly results from the barriers erected by the same 'old continent' through its fortress and nationalistic policies that serve to pit workers against workers on the basis of ethnicity and national origins, despite the right to asylum affirmed by the 1951 Geneva Convention. The Geneva Convention also allows for possible instances of 'irregularity' in recognition of situations that lead to 'forced migration.' This necessitates a call for policies that should be international rather than national (so much for the 'receding' of the nation state in a time of intensified globalisation), since we are dealing with international, global phenomena.

Concerns with and fears of waves of immigration often lead to misplaced alliances between people on the basis of an ideology that obfuscates the reality that both immigrants and 'autochthonous' workers are members of an international class exploited by international capital and the international ruling class that benefits from it. This ideology induces people to engage in strange alliances involving those whose class interests are economically opposed. They engage in the belief that the interests of the dominating class are very much their own class interests. As the history of the First World War indicates, nationalism is not to be underestimated as a powerful force in creating alliances that pit worker against worker on the grounds of country affiliation, irrespective of the contradictory class interests involved. Many are those who wrote and struggled against this, notably Rosa Luxemburg. Antonio Gramsci is another. He expressed such concerns in the wake of a nationalistic politics within a migratory Mediterranean context, in his case an 'internal' national migratory context (South to North, island to mainland or *il continente*). I argue in this chapter that his writings on the Italian migratory contexts of his time, and the strange alliances to which these migrations gave way, have relevance for the present context of migration across the Mediterranean. I submit that one has to unveil the prevailing ideology that obfuscates the underlying power dynamics marking these alliances to be able to confront issues of racism and labour-market segregation on ethnic and national grounds that threaten the very bases of democracy, industrial or more generally. Gramsci argued along these lines within the context of a nation state characterised by regional inequality generating internal migration. In this chapter I develop a similar argument, with a focus on global regional inequality having its effect on demographic changes and the nature of the labour force within different national states through cross-border migratory waves.

EXCHANGE IN HISTORICAL AND CONTEMPORARY CONTEXTS

The French historian Fernand Braudel (1992) declared that 'exchange' was, for a long historical period, a prominent feature of life in and around the Mediterranean basin – the *longue durée* (long term). Despite different wars and national and international antagonism, before the onset of Western colonialism all manners of goods and services were exchanged. People bartered and traded in one large regional souk – or, perhaps more accurately, networks of souks. The nature of the exchange is however different these days. As far as people are concerned, it is not an exchange of and among equals. This applies to migrant's crossing over to Europe from and through North Africa, after having negotiated the Sahara and Libya itself (the 'Tijuana of the Mediterranean') where all sorts of hazards are encountered. These are described by Derek Lutterbeck (2012) who, through interviews with Somali immigrants, tracked the movement of Somalis from Mogadishu via the Sahara and Libya to Malta. His account certainly captures a sense of the tragedy surrounding the plight of migrants from sub-Saharan Africa (SSA).

He provides vivid accounts not only of the hazards encountered when crossing the desert or contending with rough seas in rickety boats but also of the callousness of people along the way. Included here are people, either acting alone or through smuggling organisations, on both sides of the North–South Mediterranean divide, who traffic in human misery, hardly valuing human life.

FORTRESS POLICIES AND 'SECURITY'

The European Union's fortress policy with respect to denial of visas and travel opportunities is compelling immigrants from SSA and more lately from Egypt and Syria, and other countries facing the scourge of religious persecution, to pursue some of the most hazardous routes to flee their country and reach Europe.

The EU, through its 'fortress' politics, centring on the notion of 'security', is the target of current protests regarding this human tragedy. Parallels with the Mexico–USA border situation are invited. While people from South and Central America use sewers to cross over to the USA (see the 1980s film *El Norte*[1]), people from Africa are risking their lives by selling all their possessions to make the journey, in the case of SSA migrants across the Sahara to Libya, and then across the sea in the hands of unscrupulous coyotes, perceived as not caring a toss about human lives. They (or rather their boats) are now the declared targets of a recent EU effort in the wake of the April 2015 tragedies.[2]

RESPONSIBILITY SHARING

These situations are rendered more desperate by the failure of the fellow EU partners of frontier countries or islands such as the Canary Islands, Lampedusa and Malta to assist in responsibility sharing. These islands are left to cope with the disproportionate demands (regarding size and population density) placed on them as first port of call for migrants who cross over from North Africa with a view to reaching Italy or other places in Europe. Alison Gatt (2014) calls for a comprehensive responsibility-sharing mechanism among the EU member states in general. This is a global situation which requires international and not national solutions, a point underlined in several chapters of Peter Xuereb (2013). Possible solutions, as suggested by the Maltese lawyer–activist Neil Falzon in a newspaper interview, include issuing international humanitarian visas to ensure that people can safely exercise their right to asylum. Constant reference is made, throughout the various chapters, to the Dublin II Regulation according to which immigrants are to have their asylum-seeking application evaluated by the state through which they first entered the EU – hence the pressure on a small island such as Malta, a frontier country with respect to North Africa. This raises the question regarding the EU and its 'Fortress Europe' politics: where is the much-spoken-of (in EU discourse) 'solidarity'? (Mallia 2012).

IMPERIALISM AND FORCED MOVEMENT

It is goods that generally circulate freely; but even here some qualification is necessary. It is goods from certain countries and within certain regional arrangements (e.g. the EU) which transfer smoothly. Ask Palestinians, who cannot carry goods from one part of Palestine to the other as they negotiate checkpoints. Those who carry goods which are not Israeli products but Palestinian, from say their parents' home, may well have them confiscated at checkpoints. This is part and parcel of settler colonialism within this Mediterranean country. It is part of a global imperial system as a result of which some people are accorded the right to move freely and exchange their goods in the process while others are left stranded or forced to risk life and limb as victims of what Zygmunt Bauman (2006) calls the 'human waste-disposal industry'. *The Guardian* reported in 2013 that no less than 20,000 people had drowned in the Mediterranean during the then preceding two decades. At the time of writing (April 2015), in not more than a week, around 1,100 people, including children and toddlers, have drowned off the Libyan coast in what has been dubbed the biggest tragedy in the Mediterranean since the Second World War – people who are thus eliminated from the index of human concerns.

The reasons which compel people, primarily from SSA and the Middle East and North Africa (MENA) regions, to leave their homelands are many. These would include the effects of neoliberal structural adjustment programmes; civil wars fuelled by a Western-based arms industry, involving the sale of conventional weapons, especially during the post-Cold War period; exacerbation of tribal conflicts, often involving rape, with the female victims being disowned by their families; women's attempts to avoid female genital mutilation; evading religious fundamentalism, which has taken on sinister forms with the emergence of first Al-Qaeda, and then Boko Haram, Shabab and Isis, the latter recently displaying their ruthless hand in the 'transit' country of Libya. These circumstances will lead to even greater migrations from SSA and MENA in the forthcoming years, since little intervention takes place to protect the thousands of victims involved – unless one can trade 'blood for oil', with Nigeria's oil wells offering sickening possibilities here.[3] There are also the negative effects that subsidies for farmers in Europe and North America can have on African farming; climate change and its negative ramifications; the spread of fatal diseases such as Ebola that decimate families, tribes and communities; an impoverished environment (the ransacking of Africa); a colonial ideology whereby the West is presented as 'the Best'; the quest for better employment opportunities ... and one can go on, perhaps falling prey to Western stereotypes and constructions of 'Africa' (see Wright 2012). Life in and throughout Africa and among Africans is much more complex than any set of ideas would make us believe, prone as people are to essentialising. Handel Kashope Wright's (2012) title from *Macbeth*'s 'dagger scene', 'Is this an African I see before me?' appears very apt in this context.

POTENTIAL 'RESERVE ARMY' AND THE 'CARCERAL STATE'

There is however one major global reason that cannot be discounted, no matter how simplistic or complex the argument is made. The economies of highly industrialised countries register shortages in the amount of labour power that is required, and this has to be 'imported', often at a cost which can undercut any claims for high remuneration by locally based workers and their representatives on the basis of national or regional 'demand and supply' politics (Apitzsch 1995: 68). This kind of politics can be undermined by a greater 'reserve army' pool available through the process of uneven levels of global industrial development endemic to the capitalist mode of production. This plays into the hands of unscrupulous employers, and also governments, on the lookout for ways and means of depressing local wages. It is this quest on the part of capitalism itself and its representatives to depress wages that renders members of the autochthonous working class vulnerable, rather than the spectre of immigrant labour. This is crucial for any discussion concerning alliances between capital and labour in the present historical conjuncture.

Couched differently, the main reason for massive migration from South to North and East to West is the quest for low-cost labour by corporations and other businesses alike that serves as a 'push-and-pull factor'. As David Bacon (2008) argues, hegemonic globalisation makes migration necessary.[4] Meanwhile, the victims of this process are rendered 'illegal' and criminalised for responding to this necessity, victims of the 'carceral state'. By 'carceral state', a term adopted by Henry A. Giroux and adapted from Foucault's notion of the 'carceral society', I mean the state that places excessive emphasis on its repressive apparatus to 'control' those who suffer from the excesses of the global neoliberal polices it accommodates (Mayo, in Simicevic 2013). It is part of the process whereby the state organises, regulates, 'educates' (the ethical state), creates and sustains markets, provides surveillance, evaluates (Gentili 2005), forges networks and represses. One should underscore the role of the repressive factor as manifest by the state during this period. Behind the whole facade of consent lurks naked power which, in Mao's famous words, 'grows out of the barrel of a gun.' Giroux uses the term 'carceral state' mainly with regard to schooling, with reference to 'the school-to-prison-pipeline' that 'has come to represent an appendage of the carceral state' (Giroux 2015).

The state also provides a policing force for what can easily be regarded as the victims of neoliberal policies as well as related 'structural adjustment programmes' in the majority world. The migrants from SSA knocking on the doors of 'Fortress Europe' and who are contained in veritable prisons referred to as detention centres are among these victims. They live within the carceral framework which has been characterising the life of many immigrants on Mediterranean shores of late, most notably in the aforementioned frontier islands.

The shifting of Southern populations against their will has been standard European imperialist policy.[5] Politics of this kind occur throughout history, repeating themselves over and over again, ending in tragedies.[6] Southern and oppressed populations can be moved at will to suit imperial interests. It happened with Africans during the slave trade periods; with the 1948 Nakba (Masalha, in Gargour 2009; Masalha 2012) and later (Palestinians uprooted from their homeland); it happened during 'operation bootstrap' involving the uprooting and dislocation of Puerto Ricans (Darder, in Borg and Mayo, 2007); it certainly happens with people from sub-Saharan and North Africa today. All are pawns in a game of chess played by predominantly Western powers, conditioned by the long-term and deep-rooted legacies of their carefully engineered colonial, pre-independence and postcolonial moves.

This legacy of colonialism and its effect on the migratory movements from South to North across the Mediterranean and beyond reflects the similar colonial situation discussed by Gramsci. In his case, the colonial situation was of an 'internal' nature. Italy's North colonially dominated the country's Southern regions and islands. Gramsci discussed this in his writings on the Southern question and his prison notes on Italian history. He calls for solidarity among subaltern people on both sides of the North–South divide.

Equally relevant, in this context, is Gramsci's concept of 'national–popular.' What is 'national' reflects the culture of hegemonic ethnic groups. It plays a key role in the structure of hegemony and its apparatuses. Hegemony is the key concept used by Gramsci throughout the prison notes.[7] And yet one would be hard-pressed to discover any systematic exposition of the concept by Gramsci (Borg, Buttigieg and Mayo 2002: 1). I would interpret this concept as referring to a situation in which most arrangements, constituting a particular social reality, are conditioned by and tend to support the interests of a particular class or social grouping.[8] Hegemony incorporates not only processes of ideological influence and contestation but, as Raymond Williams (1976: 205; 1977) argues, a 'whole body of practices and expectations'.

Concepts such as 'national identity' and 'national culture' are thus challenged, to negotiate relations of hegemony. This entails the renegotiation of relations among different groups within a single nation state. Subaltern groups, such as the proletariat and peasants, in Gramsci's time, needed to form a firmly entrenched and deep rooted *historical bloc* (this is not to be confused with a simple alliance, which can be ephemeral) in order to challenge the absolutising concept of 'national'. They would thus transform the hegemonic relations embodied in this unitary concept. One therefore had to challenge misplaced alliances that occur as a result of the obfuscation of these hegemonic relations and the interests they serve, specific interests made to look universal in order to acquire popular consent. When considering the impact of ideology and its underlying contradictions, however, they turn out to be very partial. The alliances help to retain the status quo in the interest of the dominant hegemonic groups.

Gramsci makes reference, in his Southern question piece, to a proposed alliance involving the exploited Sardinian peasants and their offspring on the island and the mainland[9] and the offspring of the exploiting Sardinian landowning class, regarded by Gramsci as the Sardinian overseers of capitalist exploitation. In this regard, he refers, in 'Some Aspects of the Southern Question', to the efforts he describes of eight communists to thwart attempts at forming the Giovane Sardegna, a sort of all-embracing movement of Sardinians, irrespective of different and opposing social-class interests. Landowners and peasants are thus lumped together in what would have been a false alliance buttressed by the ideology of regionalism or Sardism. This disruptive effort proved successful, causing the postponement *sine die* of the coming into being of the proposed organisation.

Then we have the episode involving the Brigata Sassari (the Sassari Brigade) and its engagement to quell industrial strife in the North. Gramsci touches on the issue of cultural and ethnic hybridisation. He felt that solidarity between proletariat and peasants can be facilitated by an important relation that exists between the two. The proletariat consists, for the most part, of descendants of the latter, given that much of the industrialisation in Italy's North depended on internal migration from the South. Gramsci argues that bonding between the soldiers and strikers, resulting from conversations, led to a change in consciousness or perspective transformation. They were both members of the same exploited subaltern class. The brigade returned to Sassari. The themes of solidarity therefore and the struggle against misplaced alliances feature prominently in Gramsci's ruminations concerning the South, which he never romanticises, highlighting its unsavoury and wayward aspects (Germino 1990). 'Some Aspects of the Southern Question' contains these kinds of ruminations. I have argued (Mayo 2015) that they have great resonance with respect to the present day Southern question, viewed in the larger context of North–South/South–North relations. I am writing about conceptualising the Southern question on a regional and trans-continental scale. In short, while Gramsci wrote about North–South relations in the context of a single nation state, I am discussing these relations in a larger context, that of the Mediterranean and European–African relations.

RENEGOTIATING HEGEMONY AND THE NATIONAL–POPULAR

Gramsci argued that the North was an octopus that enriched itself at the expense of the South. (Gramsci 1975: 47). The same can be applied to Europe and its colonial centres vis-à-vis the larger South. Migrants from sub-Saharan Africa attempt to reach the centres of Europe and often end up on the continent's periphery. The intermeshing of cultures that this brings about leads to hegemonic contestation, depending on how strong and well developed the lobbies representing migrants are. Old hegemonic arrangements are questioned. The concept of 'national–popular' develops a new meaning in this context. Concepts such as 'national identity' and 'national culture' are called into question by those who derive their inspiration from Gramsci and others (the latter would include Said, who draws on Gramsci's 'Some Aspects of the Southern Question' in his work; see Said 1994: 56–9). The greater the presence of multi-ethnic groups and the stronger their lobby, the greater is the challenge they pose to the established hegemonic arrangements. In short, migrants who establish themselves and hone their lobbying skills as an ethnic group or specific community would, in the long term, demand certain rights which can be obtained following a lengthy process of renegotiation, persuasion and activism. In doing so they would be challenging established hegemonic relations. One can refer to the right to build mosques, secured by Muslims, or synagogues, secured by Jews, alongside the historically hegemonic Catholic churches in Southern European countries such as Italy and Spain.

Gramsci insisted that Turin's communists had the task of bringing the Southern question to the attention of the workers' vanguard. He went so far as to regard this as a key task for the proletariat (Gramsci 1977: 181; 182). Furthermore, the national–popular alliance of Italian workers and peasants he advocated, echoed in this regard by Piero Gobetti (ibid.:

204), assumes a broader and global North–South significance at a time of South to North mass migration. Bringing the Southern issue to the forefront of political debates is a key task for genuine contemporary socialist politics.

NORTH–SOUTH SOLIDARITY

This is necessary to strengthen global working-class solidarity. It is also intended for the avoidance of misplaced alliances, often detrimental in the long run to subaltern-class interests. One can include as examples much-called-for alliances between 'labour' and 'management' against 'the competition'. Hegemonic neoliberal globalisation has engendered misplaced alliances involving and exacerbating racist labour-market segmentation. Workers are segregated on ethnic, national and religious lines, and on the bases of being refugees, black, asylum seekers, Muslim, Arab, 'economic migrants' or, worse, 'illegal migrants'.[10] They are otherised, with the local autochthonous workers said to assume, in their regard, 'positional superiority', in Edward Said's (1978; 1994) terms. In this respect, especially where Arabs and Muslims are concerned, Egyptian writer Nawal El Saadawi states:

> Perhaps the problem of the world has always been the 'objectification', the nullification, of the 'other'. For the West or the North, the South is the other which exists only as an object to be exploited and oppressed. Christianity or Western culture sees Islam and Arab culture as the other. And in all religions, all that does not belong to God is seen as emanating from the devil. The problem of our world is to ignore, to dismiss, to destroy the other. To do this, the other must be satanised. (El Saadawi 1992: 137)

I would argue that an educational anti-racist programme, in concert with other types of action (education is not an independent variable), can only be effective when grounded in political economy and an understanding of colonialism. Gramsci sought to infuse his analysis of the Italian Southern question with these elements. He combined political economy with a historical understanding of Italy's process of North–South 'internal colonialism'. This is most evident in 'Some Aspects of the Southern Question' and the notes concerning Italy's post-Risorgimento state (see Notebook 1 of the *Prison Notebooks*, Gramsci 1975). In these works he gives both economic and cultural historical reasons for the subordination of the South. Economic historians such as Luigi De Rosa (2004) support this view. Gramsci mentions the Northern economic protectionist strategies undermining the Southern economy. De Rosa (2004) mentions the process of de-industrialisation of Southern economies such as that surrounding Naples, famous for the production of locomotives among other things. The protectionist strategies include the Tariff wars with France that impacted negatively on southern Italian agricultural life (Gramsci 1975: 45). Furthermore, a point made earlier, economic power blocs such as the EU adopt economic and agrarian 'closure' policies that are detrimental to the economic development of Africa and other 'tricontinental' regions. Almost daily, wealthy countries provide billion-dollar subsidies to their farmers, while Southern agricultural workers find it hard to survive and maintain their families. They simply cannot compete and feed their children and rest of the family. Migration therefore appears to provide the only way out, often at terrible human costs.[11]

Inter-ethnic solidarity necessitates work of an educational nature to contribute towards improving the situation. Providing effective anti-racist education, predicated on an understanding of colonialism and neo-colonialism, and grounded in both cultural understanding and political economy, is one of the greatest challenges facing those committed to a socialist, anti-neoliberal politics in the Mediterranean and elsewhere. This work is as broadly educational as was the work in which Gramsci was engaged when attempting to generate a revolutionary working-class consciousness in his country. In Gramsci's view, education is central to the workings of hegemony (Borg, Buttigieg and Mayo 2002: 8). And the kind of educational work in which one must engage, in the contemporary context, is a lengthy one. Without an educational strategy of this sort, working-class people, living in a state of precariousness, are likely to be attracted to the populist right-wing and often neo-fascist discourse that plays on their fears (see Hall 1987a; 1987b). This situation would alas lead to greater segmentation among workers on ethnic lines. Once again, misplaced alliances facilitate this and serve to mystify even further the common fate shared by workers of different ethnicity: being subaltern and victims of a ruthless process of 'racialisation', a callous form of *divide et impera*. One-time socialist or Labour parties have been accused of having done nothing over the years to broaden the meaning of international as opposed to national solidarity, since 'socialism', the appropriate word in this context, has become passé in the discourse of these parties. If anything the target of any anger, where vulnerable working-class employees are concerned, should be those unscrupulous employers who prey on a destitute 'reserve army' to considerably cut down labour costs. According to hearsay, they often completely do away with these costs, at best paying the migrant a pittance.

These aspects of the migration issue need to be tackled systematically in a manner backed by robust research. They need to be addressed especially by those who historically served as leaders of the working class. What is required for this purpose is a sustained and inclusive workers' education programme spanning different media and settings. Unless this wide-ranging educational process is engaged in, we are more likely to see a swing toward the right. And by this, I mean not only the emergence of right-wing parties, but also former leftist parties veering towards right of centre.

Few if any attempts have been made, over the years, to raise consciousness in the rank and file regarding the pitfalls of racism and to foster a comprehensively inclusive, including gender-inclusive, notion of workers' solidarity. The term 'working class' has also become passé despite the presence of whole swathes of societies worldwide suffering from precarious living conditions rendering many sectors déclassé. With many members of what I would call the new working class (including those déclassé sectors) feeling vulnerable in this age of constant layoffs and downsizing and economic meltdowns, it is likely that they will misguidedly pursue the route of xenophobia and racism.

It is not surprising to see that racism toward people of colour and Arabs, as well as the Roma, is rife in Europe. The swing to the right is typical of many countries worldwide, large or small, in the context of increasing immigrant labour, including the *Gastarbeiter* (guest worker). It is certainly writ large in small frontier countries with respect to North Africa, which are the first port of call for many SSA and MENA migrants. A classic example is provided by the island of Malta, the country in which I live, which has a small land mass and around 400,000 inhabitants. The criminalisation[12] of immigrants serves to fan the flames of racism and xenophobia. The marginalisation of immigrants with no access to citizenship rights and social benefits, especially rejected asylum seekers, leads them to eke out a living at the very margins of society, in the 'underworld' if need be. This furthers the construction of irregular migrants as given to criminality, promiscuity, etc. rather than as being victims of a systemic oppressive and ultimately racist structure that encourages abuse of their vulnerability.

How often do we see one-time socialist parties shunning their responsibility of fostering inter-ethnic solidarity among workers? They are often accused of acting in this way because they fear losing electoral votes. I have argued that this situation highlights the limits of bourgeois democracy in generating a genuinely socialist politics involving workers' solidarity across different identities, including ethnic ones (see Mayo 2007: 105). The lengthy process of consciousness-raising required exceeds the usual five-year term of office of a government period. Five years are a long time in bourgeois representative democratic politics.

While hope springs eternal with regard to political parties' involvement in anti-racist education, focused on the quest for international workers' solidarity (Gramsci himself had a party, a Modern Prince, at the heart of his political strategy), there is a greater chance that this work will be carried out, in the present scenario, by other agencies. I would include here progressive social movements, or alliances of these movements, which have been making their presence felt in the various rallies taking place in, say, England against UKIP and the BNP with regard to UK and European elections, actions such as ¡Democracia Real Ya! and *indignados* rallies in Spain and 'Debtocracy' manifestations in Greece, the Occupy activities in various international cities, the occupation of Gezi Park in Istanbul (Gezgin, Inal and Hill 2014; see Chapter 3) and such forums as the World Social Forum, where Gramsci is a constant source of reference. There seems to be greater potential for progressive change in these grassroots movements than in certain 'socialist' parties of yore. It might well be argued that, in the words of Mark Fisher (2009), these parties have easily adapted to and accommodated 'capitalist realism', operating within the bourgeois consensus politics framework marked by a swing to centrist or right-of-centre politics. One should however not tar all parties with the same brush in this context, as there have been powerful voices for inter-ethnic solidarity among the SNP, Plaid Cymru and the Green Party in the 2015 UK elections' televised debates and also among a variety of emerging progressive parties in Greece and elsewhere. It remains to be seen to what extent these parties can and will provide educational platforms and projects to combat misplaced alliances that exacerbate workers' or prospective workers' segregation on ethnic, racist lines.

NOTES

1. www.youtube.com/watch?v=tiuRrsgMoME
2. www.bbc.com/news/world-europe-32776669; www.dw.com/en/eu-defense-foreign-ministers-approve-military-mission-targeting-smuggler-boats/a-18457439; www.theguardian.com/world/2015/apr/20/eu-launch-military-operations-libya-migrant-smugglers-mediterranean
3. www.rt.com/news/223575-boko-haram-nigeria-usa/; www.theguardian.com/environment/earth-insight/2014/may/09/behind-rise-nigeria-boko-haram-climate-disaster-peak-oil-depletion
4. It also has a strong influence on identity, especially with regard to communities that have traditionally not been organised along individualist lines as has been the case with most Mediterranean and non-Western communities. Hegemonic globalisation, as with other previous modernising forces, seems to be at odds with the fundamentally religious way of life experienced in certain regions of the Mediterranean and also tends

to destroy that sense of mystery so much cherished in several non-Western societies. This fundamentally religious life can create tensions, with the influx of people holding on to their own religious beliefs with the same vehemence as that to which large swathes of the autochthonous population cling to theirs. I am indebted to Michael Grech for this point.

5. See Hrvoje Simicevic's interview with me (Simicevic, 2013). http://truth-out.org/opinion/item/20474-migration-across-the-mediterranean-how-many-deaths-will-it-take-till-europe-knows-that-too-many-people-have-died (viewed 8 August 2014).

6. And I would add: never in farce. Due apologies to Karl Marx (1907) concerning his famous comment, in a different context and on a different matter, that history repeats itself, first ending in tragedy and later in farce (*The Eighteenth Brumaire of Luis Bonaparte*).

7. It dates back as a concept to the ancient Greeks and was later used by revolutionaries such as Lenin and Plekhanov. It was also used in the linguistics debates to which Gramsci was exposed as a student in Turin where philology was his specialisation in the old broad-based Italian *laurea* degree.

8. Because his writings contained in the *Prison Notebooks* are notes for a future work, are fragmentary and would probably have been subject to eventual revision, expansion and re-organisation had Gramsci lived longer to bring this work to fruition, one comes across ambiguities regarding 'hegemony.' The ambiguities concern whether hegemony refers solely to the consensual aspect of power or also combines this aspect with the coercive element involved. These inconsistencies have given rise to different uses of this term by different writers and commentators. In short, hegemony is often said to refer to either one of the heads (consent) or both twin heads (coercion and consent) of Macchiavelli's Centaur: force (coercion) + consent or else force + hegemony (consent). I personally favour the more comprehensive conception of hegemony, i.e. consent + coercion / force, since it is very much in keeping with Gramsci's notion of the 'integral state' (Gramsci 1971: 239, Q22§1), an all-encompassing state which combines aspects of consent and repression at the same time. This separation is delineated by Gramsci for simply heuristic purposes. In reality one cannot separate the two since there is no 100 per cent repressive apparatus and no 100 per cent ideological apparatus, as Althusser would point out. Schools for instance may appear prima facie to be ideological but they are also repressive at the same time, the degree of repression varying from state to state.

9. 'Il continente' (the continent), as Sardinians refer to the Italian mainland.

10. Maria Pisani (2012) points out that 'illegal immigrant' is a non-existent term in international law. It is bandied about by politicians to justify 'illegal legalities', that is to say the trampling over human rights: basic ones at that (a person's right to asylum). It has unfortunately become part of the popular doxa.

11. I am indebted to the late Professor M. Kazim Bacchus, professor emeritus of the University of Alberta, Canada, for this point.

12. In the majority of cases, we have bona fide breathing human subjects being criminalised for sins not of their making – sins for which Europe itself has a lot to answer. All this attests to the legacies of colonialism in Africa and the Middle East and the Western powers' collusion in the creation of situations characterised by the presence of client tyrannical regimes.

REFERENCES

Apitzsch, U. 1995. 'Razzismo ed Atteggiamenti Verso gli Immigrati Stranieri: Il Caso della Repubblica Federale Tedesca', *Quaderni dei Nuovi Annali* 33: 67–76.

Bacon, D. 2008. *Illegal People: How Globalization Creates Migration and Criminalizes Immigrants*. New York: Beacon Press.

Bauman, Z. 2006. 'The Crisis of the Human Waste Disposal Industry'. In D. Macedo and P. Gounari (eds). *The Globalization of Racism*. Boulder, CO: Paradigm Publishers.

Borg, C. and Mayo, P. 2007. *Public Intellectuals, Radical Democracy and Social Movements: A Book of Interviews*. New York, Frankfurt, Berne, Vienna: Peter Lang.

—— Buttigieg, J.A. and Mayo, P. (eds). 2002. 'Gramsci and Education: A Holistic Approach'. In C. Borg, J.A. Buttigieg and P. Mayo (eds). *Gramsci and Education*. Lanham, MD: Rowman & Littlefield.

Braudel, F. 1992. *The Mediterranean and the Mediterranean World in the Age of Philip II*, vol.i. London: HarperCollins.

De Rosa, L. 2004. *La provincia Subordinata: Saggio sulla Questione Meridionale*. Bari: Laterza.

El Saadawi, N. 1992. *The Nawal El Saadawi Reader*. London and New York: Zed Books.

Fisher, M. 2009. *Capitalist Realism: Is There No Alternative?* Winchester: Zero Books.

Gargour, M. 2009. *The Land Speaks Arabic*. Video documentary. www.youtube.com/watch?v=nY3v-yht_6g

Gatt, A. 2014. 'Fair Sharing of Asylum Responsibility within the EU: Addressing Malta's Scenario'. In Xuereb 2014.

Gentili, P. 2005. *La Falsificazione del Consenso: Simulacro e Imposizione nella Riforma Educativa del Neoliberalismo*. Pisa: Edizioni ETS.

Germino, D. 1990. *Antonio Gramsci: Architect of a New Politics*. Baton Rouge, LA: Louisiana State University Press.

Gezgin, U.B., Inal, K. and Hill, D. (eds). 2014. *The Gezi Revolt: People's Revolutionary Resistance against Neoliberal Capitalism in Turkey*. Brighton: Institute for Education Policy Studies.

Giroux, H.A. 2015. *Neoliberalism's War on Higher Education*. Chicago: Haymarket Books.

Gramsci, A. 1971. *Selections from the Prison Notebooks*, trans. Hoare, Q and Nowell-Smith, G (eds). New York: International Publishers.

—— 1975. *Quaderni del Carcere: Edizione Critica dell'Instituto Gramsci*, ed. V. Gerratana (4 vols). Turin: Einaudi.

—— 1977. *Selections from Political Writings, 1910–1920*, ed. Q. Hoare, trans. J. Matthews. New York: International Publishers.

Hall, S. 1987a. 'Gramsci and Us'. *Marxism Today* (June): 16–21. www.unz.org/Pub/MarxismToday-1987jun-00016

—— 1987b. 'Blue Election, Election Blue'. *Marxism Today* (July): 30–5. www.unz.org/Pub/MarxismToday-1987jul-00030

Lutterbeck, D. 2012. 'From Malta to Mogadishu: Travel Experiences of Somali Migrants'. In Xuereb 2014.

Mallia, P. 2012. 'The Disembarkation of Migrants Rescued at Sea: Where Is the "Solidarity"?' In Xuereb 2014.

Marx, K. 1907. *The Eighteenth Brumaire of Louis Bonaparte*. Chicago, IL.: Charles H. Kerr.

Masalha, N. 2012. *The Palestine Nakba: Decolonising History, Narrating the Subaltern, Reclaiming Memory*. London and New York: Zed Books.

Mayo, P. 2007. 'Gramsci, the Southern Question and the Mediterranean', in *Mediterranean Journal of Educational Studies* 12(2): 1–17.

Mayo, P. 2015. *Hegemony and Education under Neoliberalism. Insights from Gramsci*. New York City and London: Routledge.

Pisani, M. 2014. 'The Elephant in the Room: A Look at How Policies Impact the Lives of Female Sub-Saharan African Rejected Asylum Seekers Living in Malta'. In Xuereb 2014.

Said, E. 1978. *Orientalism*. New York: Random House.

—— 1994. *Culture and Imperialism*. London: Vintage.

Simicevic, H. 2013. 'Migration across the Mediterranean: When Will Europe See That Too Many People Have Died?' (Interview with Peter Mayo). *Truthout*. 9 December. http://truth-out.org/opinion/item/20474-migration-across-the-mediterranean-how-many-deaths-will-it-take-till-europe-knows-that-too-many-people-have-died

Williams, R. 1976. 'Base and Superstructure in Marxist Cultural Theory'. In R. Dale, G. Esland and M. Macdonald (eds). *Schooling and Capitalism: A Sociological Reader*. London: Routledge & Kegan Paul.

—— 1977. *Marxism and Literature*. Oxford: Oxford University Press.

Wright, H.K. 2012. 'Is This an African I See Before Me? Black/African Identity and the Politics of (Western, Academic) Knowledge'. In H.K. Wright and A.A. Abdi (eds). *The Dialectics of African Education and Western Discourses: Counter-Hegemonic Perspectives*. New York, Bern, Berlin, Brussels, Frankfurt, Oxford and Vienna: Peter Lang.

Xuereb, P. (ed.). 2014. *Migration and Asylum in Malta and the European Union*. Malta: Malta University Press.

9

For the Sake of Workers
but Not Immigrant Workers?
Social Dumping and Free Movement

Óscar García Agustín and Martin Bak Jørgensen

In August 2013 two Danish construction workers were waiting to begin a blockade against the company Trevi which was working on the metro in Copenhagen. Both workers had been fired by the company and replaced. As they waited in silence for the moment of action to begin, one of them said: 'There are Polish, Italians, Germans and Portuguese [workers].' This might have been an acknowledgement of the national diversity in their job sector and of cooperation between nationalities, but it was not. The construction worker continued: 'If one looks at that from the perspective of Unicon [a cement producer] employees, then there are no Danes at all. This is completely crazy. We should be there constructing the metro for our country, and not the foreigners.' He concluded that it is not only about jobs: 'Have you ever thought that this could just be the beginning? They have already taken our jobs from us; soon they will take the entire country' (in Mathiassen and Jensen 2014: 8).

This situation illustrates some of the problems that workers, both native and migrant, are facing: the increasing perception of foreign workers as undermining the rights of national workers, and more generally of foreigners as a threat. To put it simply, the national struggle is predominant and the international dimension of class exploitation is being ignored. There is a risk that native workers perceive foreign workers in terms of national rights without being aware of the international dynamic of capital (and its capacity for fragmentation). We are witnessing how a national bloc has been established with the alliance of trade unions and political parties (from left and right), making the emergence of other alliances among workers difficult. The confrontation between the national (labour) model and the foreign labour force (due to international mobility) impedes alliances across nationalities and the identification of global neoliberalism as the main source of conflict (and those who exploit the labour force as the 'real' enemy) (Robinson and Harris 2000).

The neoliberal restructuration of economy, labour markets and welfare states has had pronounced effects on life conditions for people living in different states of precariousness. Capital has been strengthened and labour weakened. Globalisation and neoliberal restructuration have increased the level of precariousness and expanded the groups constituting this part of society. It has led to segmentation, segregation and antagonisms along cultural, ethnic and racial lines, creating new social and political divisions in society and strengthening processes of exclusion. It has spurred claims for national protectionism and national homogeneity, blurring the commonalities and shared fate of people in precarious positions. States have prioritised bailing out financial institutions, but have left it to the workers and precarious groups to pay the bill. All across Europe austerity measures and programmes have been the main tool used to address the economic crises – without having the desired effect (Seymour, 2014). Finally, the global crisis has put the labour movement under pressure (Bieler, 2014). Trade unions are losing their capacity to represent the interests of the working class, which cannot be reduced to those who have a permanent job, and the left-wing parties are not the only ones that channel the discontent of the more precarious parts of the population or of those who feel rejected by the political system.

Antonio Gramsci emphasised the danger of what Peter Mayo (2008) has termed 'misplaced alliances' in 'Some Aspects of the Southern Question' and outlined how solidarity was generated between North and South. This chapter looks into the construction and dynamics of misplaced alliances in a Danish context. Denmark's universalist and social democratic welfare-state model combined with a historically strong tradition for solidarity and a market economy turned 'competition state'[1] makes it an interesting case for analysing misplaced alliances. The chapter examines the position of populist parties on the Left and Right and in particular trade unions and social partners and analyses how relations between migration, the nation state, the welfare state, the European Union and protectionism constitute a misplaced alliance that strengthens divisions in society and thereby also processes of marginalisation, segregation and xenophobia. We consider the emergence of new activism and organisations as possible alternative means for opposing and changing this tendency. We discuss how transnational solidarity may reveal and disturb misplaced alliances, but first we outline how a Gramscian approach can be used to analyse the problem at hand.

NATIONALISING SOLIDARITY

In this chapter, we focus on the alliances that are detrimental for solidarity among immigrants, and especially the working class and in a broader sense the precarious groups in society. In 'Some Aspects of the Southern Question', Gramsci explains how the bourgeoisie in Northern Italy produced essentialist and stereotypical images of the Southerners, which blurred and disguised the commonalities in terms of capitalist exploitation between the workers in the North and the peasants in the South.[2] The 'mystification' (in Michael Burawoy's reading of Pierre Bourdieu) of common conditions exists today between natives and migrants.

This misrecognition of commonalities exists not only in practices of social and political struggles but also as an overriding principle in social science theories. Andreas Wimmer and Nina Glick Schiller (2002) have described the latter as methodological nationalism. The implications of this perspective include: normalising the status quo, i.e. constructing distinctions between 'the migrants/foreigners' and natives; obscuring transnational local/global interpenetration in the past and the present; homogenising national culture by depicting the migrant as a source of disorder, difference and disintegration; and homogenising migrants into ethnic or ethno-religious groups that are believed to share essential differences.

These claims parallel what Gramsci analysed in the propaganda of the bourgeoisie and what we identify in political debates today – for instance, the way in which the Greeks are represented (Agustín and Jørgensen 2013). Moreover, it sets up limits for political strategy. Political explanations for unemployment rates, budget deficits and challenges to the welfare state are found in the disturbing elements coming from outside the nation, and solutions are found in the framework of the nation state, e.g. national protection of the labour markets. Daniel Chernilo sums it up as 'the all-pervasive assumption that the nation-state is the natural and necessary form of society in modernity; the nation-state is taken as the organising principle of modernity' (2006: 5–6). This perspective assumes that national borders define the unit of study and analysis; it equates society with the nation state, and it conflates national interests with the purpose and central topics of social science. We might ask: What kind of political space does this leave for solidarity beyond borders? The consequence is a continued and deepening fragmentation of social groups.

Mayo and Guy Standing have analysed these tendencies from different perspectives. Mayo argues that globalisation has given rise to misplaced alliances based on racist, labour-market segmentation strategies. He argues: 'Workers continue to be otherised and segregated on ethnic, national and religious lines, as well as on such lines as those of being refugees, asylum seekers or "economic migrants"' (2008: 9). Standing's analysis is similar. He identifies increased fragmentation, retrenchment of social rights and growth of insecurities caused by the liberalisation underpinning globalisation and argues that a new group – the 'precariat' – is emerging. Leaving aside the critique of Standing's concept (see Jørgensen 2015; Seymour 2012), the precariat carries with it a turn to populism, xenophobia and exclusion, to which Mayo also refers.

Mayo employs the notion of 'misplaced alliances' based on antagonism between for instance national workers and foreign workers. He claims that socialist parties have traditionally shunned the responsibility of fostering inter-ethnic solidarities among workers. The explanation is the risk of losing votes. The subtitle of Standing's book on the precariat (2011) is 'The New Dangerous Class'. The danger is not the precariat itself but its ways of organising and searching for solutions. According to Standing, the lack of political alternatives and being stuck in the precarity trap make the precariat easy prey for populist politicians, who play on their fears and insecurities to lure them 'onto the rocks of neo-fascism'. He focuses on parties like the True Finns, the Sweden Democrats and the French National Front – parties with natural allies in the US Tea Party, the English Defence League and Berlusconi's neo-fascist supporters. The political message of the populists is to blame the immigrants for all evil.

The economic crisis has had severe consequences in the field of immigration. Governmental policies are constrained by the politics of austerity. Immigrants have experienced higher levels of unemployment than before, the flows of migration have been drastically reduced, and in the political sphere radical right-wing parties are gaining terrain in national parliaments on a platform of blaming integration models and even immigrants for the crisis (Agustín and Jørgensen 2013). Distinctions between deserving and undeserving groups are being strengthened and rearticulated across Europe. At the political level, this can be seen as a response from governments to appease immigrant-sceptical voters. David Cameron's response was to favour those who work hard, by 'stopping our benefits system from being such a soft touch; by making entitlement to our key public services something migrants earn, not an automatic right; and by bringing the full force of government together to crack down on illegal working' (Cameron 2013).

What is important here is that the diagnosis as such, i.e. that the immigrants are the cause of the problems, is reified among national workers. Blaming the immigrants is not a new phenomenon of course.

The slogan 'National jobs for national workers' has a long history in different countries. As early as 1967, the Danish tabloid *Ekstra-Bladet* was asking its readers, 'Why should we let more immigrants into the country when Danes are unemployed?' in the context of discussions about allowing especially Turkish and ex-Yugoslavian workers to take up jobs in Denmark (Jørgensen and Thomsen 2012). Similar discussions have taken place all over Europe since then, and attitudes towards migrants and refugees have become harsher.

Gramsci would not have been surprised. He describes the tendency of the trade union to be 'nothing other than a commercial company, of a purely capitalist type', working to secure maximum price for the commodity labour and to 'establish monopoly of this commodity in the national and international fields' (Gramsci 1978: 76). In this sense, the internationalism has been nationalised and creates its own logic of exclusion and xenophobia, often drawing on cultural stereotypes that delegitimise the identity and qualifications of foreign workers. They are not only bad for the national economy and the labour market on a structural level, they are also 'bad' workers. They are perceived as lacking solidarity, causing downward wage pressure, impeding security measures at the workplace and provoking stagnation of technological developments (Jørgensen and Thomsen 2012). The result is as described above and the consequences are ever increasing segmentation, which does not improve matters either for national or foreign workers. What is the alternative, we ask again? We return to Gramsci and his ideas on regional solidarity to consider whether they can be expanded to apply to a solidarity transgressing national borders.

As discussed in the introduction to this volume we, like Bob Jessop, Adam David Morton and Edward Said, read Gramsci as a spatial thinker. Although his own work is placed within the Italian context, his work on regional solidarities and insistence that territory and space are socially contested allow us to think beyond national borders. 'Some Aspects of the Southern Question' offers reflections on how to disturb the common sense that legitimises the continued segmentation of natives and immigrants. The following passage is from an especially compelling and often quoted encounter between a member of the Sassari Brigade sent in to control industrial unrest in Turin and a tannery worker, both originating from Sardinia:

> I approached a bivouac on X Square (in the first days, the Sardinian soldiers bivouacked in the squares as if in a conquered city) and I spoke with a young peasant, who had welcomed me warmly because I was from Sassari like him. 'What have you come to do in Turin?'

'We have come to shoot the gentry who are on strike.' 'But it is not the gentry who are on strike, it is the workers and they are poor.' 'They're all gentry here: they have collars and ties; they earn 30 lire a day. I know poor people and I know how they are dressed, yes indeed, in Sassari there are lots of poor people; all of us "diggers" are poor and we earn 1.5 lire a day.' 'But I am a worker too and I am poor.' 'You're poor because you're a Sardinian.' 'But if I go on strike with the others, will you shoot me?' The soldier reflected a bit, then put a hand on my shoulder: 'Listen, when you go on strike with the others, stay at home!' (Gramsci 1978: 448)

Here Gramsci identifies the practices through which solidarities are forged. As David Featherstone has argued (2013), Gramsci differs from Lenin in the understanding of alliances. Rather than being instrumental for a vanguard party in Lenin's terms, they are, in Gramsci's understanding, more integral to the formation of a collective will. Understanding Gramsci is about understanding practice. In his *Prison Notebooks*, he states that 'a philosophy of praxis ... must be a criticism of "common sense"' not in terms of introducing a form of philosophical thought into the life of the individual, but a matter of 'renovating and making "critical" an already existing activity' (Gramsci 1971: 330–1, Q11§12). In the last part of the chapter, we speculate about the conditions required to change practices and challenge the common sense. How can misplaced alliances be exposed, and what does it take to overcome fragmentation? Gramsci comes up with a partial answer in 'Some Aspects of the Southern Question':

[I]t is necessary – in order to win the trust and consent of the peasants and of some semiproletarian urban categories – to overcome certain prejudices and conquer certain forms of egoism which can and do subsist within the working class as such, even when craft particularism has disappeared. The metalworker, the joiner, the building-worker, etc., must not only think as proletarians, and no longer as metalworker, joiner, building-worker, etc.; they must also take a further step. They must think as workers who are members of a class which aims to lead the peasants and intellectuals. (Gramsci 1978: 448–9)

Basically, they have to develop political consciousness. Whereas the common sense reifies hegemony and tell us how things are supposed to be and how we are supposed to act (Cox and Nilsen 2014), Gramsci used the notion 'good sense' to distil what is good in the common sense (Gramsci 1978). Good sense is the practical consciousness, which can be a platform for subaltern resistance. It can lead to a 'practical transformation of the world' (Gramsci 1978: 333), and good sense therefore is necessary to challenge misplaced alliances. When the factory occupations in Turin failed in 1919–1920, it was not because the workers used the good sense within the common sense but because the working-class institutions – the trade unions and the socialist party – were 'wedded to capitalism', as Burawoy (2012: 10) describes it. In recent years, other scholars writing from a Marxist perspective like David Harvey (2012) have argued that the category of the proletariat must be expanded and new collective identities allowed to emerge. This would entail that precarious groups begin to realise what they share instead of drawing mental borders. In what follows, we show how misplaced alliances have been shaped by trade unions and political parties by creating a rigid distinction between nationals and migrants through a combination of labour and migration policies. This has negative consequences for immigrants, who are perceived as posing a threat to the welfare system, and for the potential for shaping an alliance that reveals the functioning of exploitation. We illustrate this dynamic with the issue of social dumping and conclude with some perspectives on how the hegemonic order can be challenged and new alliances can emerge.

SOCIAL DUMPING:
FOREIGN WORKERS OR NATIONAL WAGES?

The European Parliament elections in Denmark in May 2014 had very little focus on EU politics of austerity, whereas social dumping became the major topic of the electoral campaign.[3] This implies that the critique of the neoliberal model and its dominant role in Europe was displaced by critique of the EU principle of free movement, which was perceived as a risk for the Danish welfare state (or the so-called 'flexicurity' model) and Danish workers' rights and decent wages. It gave the far-right Danish People's Party (*Dansk Folkeparti*) an opportunity to target the debate about the threat represented by Eastern European immigrant workers (Johansen 2014). It made it difficult for left-wing parties to offer a genuine alternative that was not based on the underlying idea that immigrants are welcome as long as they work under Danish labour-market conditions. We consider that the predominance of social dumping in this sense illustrates the conformation of a *national* bloc, which avoids social alliances between natives and migrants. Two dimensions are at stake: an economic dimension related to the free market and internationalisation of capital, and a national dimension in which foreign workers are considered mainly as immigrants and as subject to immigration and integration policies.

The common sense around the Danish model legitimises the division between natives and immigrants and blames immigrants for being willing to work in unfavourable conditions which undermine national labour conditions. Migrants, particularly undocumented migrants, experience what Sandro Mezzadra and Brett Neilson (2008) call 'differential inclusion', since they are not excluded from the labour market but included as 'illegal', and thus experience both exploitation as workers and control as 'illegal'. The *national* common sense makes workers organise themselves in trade unions and react against material conditions that harm their rights. They identify an 'illegal' workforce as a problem for native workers, instead of finding a common framework against exploitation that affects immigrant and native workers alike. In their fight against social dumping, unions and left-wing political parties have difficulty challenging this expanded common sense, and the struggle for Danish labour rights may therefore result in the rejection of foreign workers or increased control of undocumented migrants. In the next section we show how domination is expanded through welfare agencies as the extension of the state (Burawoy 2003: 215), but with an important particularity in the Danish case: the unions' autonomy in regulating labour-market conditions gives them an essential role.

Trade Unions: Labour Rights as National Rights

Social dumping consists of two contradictory elements: capital's search for increasing competitiveness and a cheaper workforce, and workers' quest for more security and wealth (Lind 2012). This creates two scales: the global one, in which the logic of capital is dominant, and the national one, where the nation state tries to impose its rules and norms. We do not claim that one scale is beneficial and the other prejudicial (migration is after all a global phenomenon), but prefer to address the contradictions emerging from the intersection of these scales. We see social dumping as the encounter of different actors (migrants, national workers and politicians) and interests (competitiveness and wealth). The relation between actors is not necessarily conflictual, and alliances can indeed be envisaged, but the role played by the state (and its actors) contributes to social divisions as if they were the solution to (or the cause of) social uncertainty and exploitation of the labour force.

Ensuring equal pay and working conditions for foreign and Danish workers is a maxim that is accepted by all actors in the debate on social dumping. This affects both foreign companies and foreign workers and usually there is consensus on pointing out the responsibility of employers, rather than employees. However, the underlying idea of equalising the conditions of foreign and Danish workers reveals what Étienne Balibar (2004) calls the double function (social and national) of the state. The social state created the conditions under which the social conflict is abandoned and assumed by the state and its representatives (both trade unions and political parties). Thus the state assumes workers' interests as mainly national interests. The state assures employment (or at least wealth) to its citizens, and citizens are expected to be workers. Being part of the wage relation became a condition *sine qua non* to 'the right to have rights' (Cocco 2003) which was attributed to representative organisations of workers (trade unions) and business men (employers' organisations).

The Danish system even gives trade unions and employers' organisations autonomy to negotiate and regulate labour-market relations without interference by the government. With the division of tasks between the state and the social and economic partners, the labour-market model relies on two main principles: collective bargaining and self-regulation (Jørgensen 2006). Besides this deciding role in negotiations, unions have strong and expanded membership rights, and this strengthens their position in negotiations. However, collective bargaining as the main instrument of unions has been gradually decentralised (Hansen 2007). When the minimum pay is fixed, conditions must then be negotiated at the local level and with employers. As a consequence, the 'battlefield' against social dumping is the negotiation and application of collective agreements with companies, because there is no legislative regulation.

Within this labour and legal framework, unions plan their actions to watch out for foreign or national companies they suspect of hiring 'illegal' workers and disregarding the collective agreements. The defence of the social state, as carried out by unions, becomes inseparable from the defence of the national state, meaning of course national labour conditions, but also who have or do not have rights as citizens and not only as workers. This is clear when we look at the means of action deployed by unions. Danish unions made over 300 blockades between 2004 and 2009 against Danish and foreign companies in the construction sector. In comparison, Norwegian unionists refuse to take action against work places with foreign workers because this creates a division between 'us' and 'them' (Andersen 2009). This division implies that one group has rights and the other does not.

This tactic can be considered symbolic, but must be seen as embedded within a larger strategy whereby the Danish unions, particularly 3F (United Federation of Danish Workers),[4] report illegal actions by employers but also those of the foreign workers to the authorities. Unions like 3F have also fought against so-called 'pirate driving' as an illegal practice against cabotage driving. The principle applied is similar to that of social dumping: 'Foreign lorry drivers are welcome on the Danish market as long as they register and drive according to our rules' (Ankerstjerne 2012). The drivers are accused of staying in Denmark longer than allowed and selling goods at dumping prices. 3F cooperates with the police and reports drivers who do not respect the rules and proposes increased border control and surveillance of lorries with foreign license plates.

In the cases of both social dumping and 'pirate driving', legislation and political action are considered insufficient, and unions feel obliged to monitor the proper functioning of the labour market, which in this case also means making decisions related to migration policies. Jakob Mathiassen (2014) reflects on how the fight against social dumping, especially through blockades in the construction sector, changed the functions taken on by unions: 'In my opinion this strategy [of blockades] changed the basic role of building trade unions, when it is about East European workers. The unions ended up looking more and more like an authority than a movement'. Mathiassen compares this function to a sort of 'work police' responsible for enforcing collective agreements vis-à-vis East European workers.

Although unions highlight the fact that employers take advantage of foreign workers' ignorance about the Danish labour market, the conflictual and control-oriented strategies explain why a possible alliance among workers, regardless of their nationality, is impossible. Without trying to generalise, workers, principally in certain sectors, perceive foreign workers as posing a threat because they are willing to work for low wages and thus undermine the Danish model, and because they are 'stealing' their jobs, understood as a national right associated with citizenship. Therefore we talk about the existence of a national bloc that makes worker alliances difficult. The unions play an essential role due to their capacity to negotiate, but to protect their interests they seek alliances mainly with political parties. When collective agreements cannot solve the problems derived from social dumping, unions support tightened legislation in terms of control and surveillance. It is no surprise that social dumping became the key theme in the 2014 European parliamentary elections campaign or that all political parties want to fight it when it is presented as a challenge to national rights. When the issue becomes part of the political field, the connection with migration policies is even more evident.

Political Parties: National Rights as Voters' Rights

A few weeks before the general elections in June 2015, the Social Democratic Party launched its new proposal 'Danish wages for Danish work' (Socialdemokraterne 2015) to counteract social dumping. If the name of the document is not significant enough, the Social Democratic Party does not hide its intention to intervene in order to maintain the Danish model. The measures are aimed at employers who expand unfair labour conditions, but also at the 'illegal workforce'. A couple of years before, the government (a coalition between the Social Democratic and Social Liberal parties) had reached an agreement with the other left-wing parties (the Socialist People's Party and the Red–Green Alliance) to increase the measures against social dumping. The agreement reflected some of the main concerns exposed by the unions.

It shows how the unions had moved towards the political arena and found alliances beyond the concrete negotiations within the labour market. They expanded the issue of social dumping beyond their own field of action with a focus on companies abusing the 'illegal' labour force. The leader of the Danish Confederation of Trade Unions, Harald Børsting, points directly at 'illegal' work as the main problem: 'It often happens under miserable conditions far away from collective bargains; society is missing out on taxes, and wages are lowered to the point of harming the Danish employees' (in Borg and Johansen 2014). Social dumping is not limited to the labour market but expands towards the field of migration. The social democratic Mette Frederiksen, then minister of justice, proposed intensifying the national function of the state through police control of borders: 'Illegal migration may potentially undermine our entire society model' (in Borg and Johansen 2014). Social dumping linked to 'illegal' migration is ultimately a social problem and affects all Danes, not only workers.

The liberal and conservative parties barely challenge the efforts to fight social dumping and ensure fair conditions for Danish workers. The defence of the Danish model as a defence of Danish society prevails. The adhesion of the radical right-wing party to this bloc further emphasises the national dimension. The only exception to this consensus was the ultra-liberal Liberal Alliance Party, which finds it natural to hire foreign labour to increase competitiveness. Although the party does not dare reject the common sense on social dumping and the promise to do everything possible to keep Danish jobs, it takes sides on the needs of companies and is critical of the unions' social-dumping agenda. Left-wing parties have trouble finding an alternative to the national consensus without being perceived as protecting the rights of native workers against foreign ones. They hardly ever introduce discussions on the public agenda that highlight the contradictions between labour and capital or the exploitation of workers across countries.

During the national election campaign in 2015 the debate between the candidates for prime minister, the social democratic Helle Thorning-Schmidt and the liberal Lars Løkke Rasmussen, proved how hegemonic the national discourse had become and how the defence of the Danish labour-market model, and more generally the Danish social model, relies on an efficient migration policy. Thorning denounced Løkke's migration programme and said in relation to social dumping:

> With your migration policy you want to invite half of the world to come to Denmark to work here for a very low wage. At the same time, you reject everything we have done in relation to social dumping and even say that you want to revoke it. (*Ritzau*, 2015)

She referred to the liberal party's document 'Denmark: For Those Who Can and Want to', which indeed aimed to tighten migration policies against foreigners 'who do not want to contribute to Danish society or respect Danish essential values' (Venstre 2014: 3). The hard-line approach to migration is maintained even though the proposal shows a relatively open attitude towards highly qualified workers from a select group of countries. In addition to the electoral campaign, what is at stake here is the reinforcement of the interwoven dynamic between migration policies and social dumping. However, the national formation is so dominant that the neoliberal formation cannot enter this space if it clashes with it.

The national formation is not a homogenous space though. Subsuming class struggle to national interests enables the radical right-wing party to appropriate the fight against social dumping as its own by including it in their anti-migration policies. The ambiguities of the national bloc disappear completely in the case of the Danish People's Party, which blames EU interference in Danish politics and an abundance of foreigners. The sense of nation thus consists of preserving national interests against the foreign threat – either a supranational entity like the EU or the migrant labour force. This greatly increases the risk of misplaced alliances, particularly of workers who see migrants as enemies and do not consider the Social Democratic Party's discourse strong enough in this field.

In the national election in June 2015, the Danish People's Party demonstrated its ability to compete against the Social Democratic Party when it became the largest party in the liberal–conservative bloc, and the second largest party in parliament. Party leader Kristian Thulesen Dahl wants to put Eastern European workers on the political agenda. He sees the free movement of labour fostered by the EU and Denmark as the problem and holds Eastern European workers responsible for social dumping. Thulesen Dahl (2015) appeals to national interests: 'It is problematic and paradoxical that we look for labour force outside while Danes are unemployed. And that many Eastern workers cause lower wages and social dumping.' The solution would not be to control construction sites, as suggested by the unions or the Social Democratic Party, but to limit access to the Danish labour market and welfare system, in line with the proposal formulated by David Cameron. This completes the closure of the national formation and fixes its exclusionary character against all Eastern European migrants, who are denied rights because they are not native Danes.

A vast share of voters has accepted the hard line on migration, and practically no political parties are capable of challenging the national bloc. Associating 'illegal' migration with social dumping makes this possibility even smaller. The electoral competition (and the competition over who leads the national bloc) between the Social Democratic Party and the Danish People's Party makes the national identification the only option for the voters, while solidarity based on class or ethnicity is cast aside. It creates the paradox of working and precarious classes supporting the radical right-wing party, which passes measures proposed by the liberal government against their own rights. The misplaced alliance shows that other precarious workers (like East Europeans) are perceived as enemies, on the one hand, and that working classes emphasising their national identity endorse policies against their own class interests, on the other.

SHAPING SOLIDARITIES

Let us return to the dialogue between the two unionists who were waiting for the imminent blockage. After the comments of his colleague, another worker clearly disagrees:

'He was right in a certain way but I did not see those guys [the undocumented workers] as enemies. I saw them as colleagues who were forced to abandon their families to find a job. For me the enemy was the ones we could not see. The enemy flies over our heads in their private jets.' (Mathiassen and Jensen 2014: 8)

This is surely the most important step: identifying a common enemy that enhances the possibility of solidarity without borders instead of exclusion within them. In other words, knowing the enemy's identity is a prerequisite for expanding solidarity across the precarious classes without it being a matter of nationality. It requires a double organisational effort: at the national level, to undo the separation between nationals as those who have rights and migrant workers as those who do not; and at the international level, to focus on social dumping as a problem derived from the conflict between international capital and wages, and not from international mobility. Furthermore, social alliances must be capable of reorienting the public debate and moving political parties, or at least some of them, beyond the national bloc and its negative effect on migrant workers perceived as a threat against the welfare system.

There can be no ambiguity in identifying the enemy, not as foreign employees, but as the employers who violate labour standards agreed by the unions. This point is not always clearly explained. However, the main labour victories have been the ones where unions have targeted companies and their abuses, as in the cases of airlines (e.g. Ryanair) or construction companies (e.g. CIPA). Reflecting on the ruling that condemned CIPA's social dumping practices, John Ekebjærg Jakobsen (2015) emphasises that 'the fight against social dumping is not about sending illegal workers out of Denmark but about stopping corrupt employers who are willing to do everything possible to destroy the Danish model'. Understanding equality in terms of labour rights and not national rights is essential for forging new alliances.

However, the main challenge is organising, which has diverse ramifications. First, unions must be open to migrant workers rather than controlling them, fostering dialogue and facilitating organisation. An example concerns 120 Polish construction workers in Amager Bakke, Copenhagen (Ott 2014), employed by two Polish cement companies. Half of them decided to join the union. They claimed better salaries and reached collective awareness on the matter through their meetings in the 'Polish club'. Some of them had previous union experience from Poland and now they had their own 'union representative'. This represents a considerable shift from informing or monitoring them to including them in organisation through different means: being in contact with other organisations, taking other languages into consideration, and acknowledging them as group. This openness can identify common interests and undo the divisions of a labour conflict based on nationality.

At the international level, the task is huge, because the formation of a national bloc impeding solidarity beyond borders must be prevented. International organisation between unions and social movements must be enhanced and the goal must be the same as at the national level: to point out austerity policies as responsible for the deteriorating welfare state models and to claim the right to migrate. The European Trade Union Confederation's campaign 'Free movement, yes! Social dumping, no!' (ETUC 2015) shows the path. According to the campaign, migrants are not abusing free movement (and are consequently not a risk); businesses abuse free movement by treating workers as commodities. Thus social dumping is not an undesirable consequence of free movement, since it is caused by precarisation of work conditions and by the promotion of unfair competitiveness. The solution cannot be national, but must be sought within a common European framework to protect collective agreements (Braemer 2009). What is at stake here is the constitution of a social Europe in times when neoliberal policies are undermining social policies inherited from welfare states. Migrants are consequently necessary allies in the attempt to build the social dimension that Europe is lacking. Otherwise, inequality and exclusion will increase.

NOTES

1. A competition state is a state that is in international competition with other states to achieve the greatest possible economic growth (Cerny 1997; Pedersen 2011 for a Danish analysis).
2. Burawoy argues that mystification is not part of Gramsci's 'theoretical toolkit' (Burawoy, 2012). It is, however, a well-known concept in Marx's writing. We introduce the notion of mystification as it holds the potential to explain the mechanisms which form misplaced alliances. We use the notion of mystification to describe the mechanisms at stake in the construction of misplaced alliances. However, we do not claim that Gramsci used the notion of mystification.
3. Social dumping is a practice in which an employer makes use of a cheaper labour force than would otherwise be possible, e.g. by employing foreign labourers at lower wages and in worse working conditions than would be possible with the regulated national labour force.
4. 3F is the largest Danish labour Union.

REFERENCES

Agustín, Ó.G. and Jørgensen M.B. 2013. 'Immigrants and Civil Society. New ways of democratic transformation', *Migration Letters* 10(3): 271–6.

Andersen, N.T. 2009. 'Er den papirløse kollega fjende eller kammerat?' *Information*. 28 March.

Ankerstjerne, M.V. (ed.). 2012. *Cabotagekørsel i Danmark: En rapport om et samfundsproblem.* Copenhagen: Advice A/S.

Balibar, È. 2004. *We, the People of Europe? Reflections on Transnational Citizenship.* Princeton: Princeton University Press.

Bieler, A. 2014. 'Transnational Labour Solidarity in (the) Crisis'. *Global Labour Journal* 5(2): 114–33.

Borg, O. and Johansen, M. 2014. 'Antallet af illegal indvandrere i Danmark mere end fordoblet'. *Jyllands Posten.* 8 December.

Braemer, M. 2009. 'Social dumping udfordrer fagbevægelsen'. *Ugebrevet A4.* 5 October. www. ugebreveta4.dk/social-dumping-udfordrer-fagbevaegelsen_18982.aspx

Burawoy, M. 2003. 'For a Sociological Marxism: The Complementary Convergence of Antonio Gramsci and Karl Polanyi'. *Politics and Society* 31(2), 193–261.

—— 2012. 'The Roots of Domination: Beyond Bourdieu and Gramsci'. *Sociology* 46(2): 187–206.

Cameron, D. 2013. 'David Cameron's Immigration Speech'. Prime Minister's Office, 10 Downing Street. 25 March. www.number10.gov.uk/news/david-camerons-immigration-speech/

Cerny, P.G. 1997. 'Paradoxes of the Competition State: The Dynamics of Political Globalization'. *Government and Opposition* 32(2): 251–74.

Chernilo, D. 2006. 'Social Theory's Methodological Nationalism: Myth and Reality'. *European Journal of Social Theory* 9(1): 5–22.

Cocco, G. 2003. *Trabajo y ciudadanía.* Xàtiva: Dialogos.

Cox, L. and Nilsen, A.G. 2014. *We Make Our Own History: Marxism and Social Movements in the Twilight of Neoliberalism.* London: Pluto Press.

ETUC. 2015. *Free Movement, Yes! Social Dumping, No! Workers in Europe Are Suffering from Social Dumping.* 26 February. www.etuc.org/sites/www.etuc.org/files/publication/files/flyer_social_dumping_en_06.pdf

Featherstone, D. 2013. 'Gramsci in Action'. In M. Ekers, G. Hart, S. Kipfer and A. Loftus (eds). *Gramsci: Space, Nature, Politics.* Oxford: Wiley-Blackwell.

Gramsci, A. 1971. *Selections from the Prison Notebooks,* ed. and trans. Q. Hoare and G. Nowell-Smith. London: Lawrence and Wishart.

—— 1978. *Selections from Political Writings, 1921–1926,* ed. and trans. Q. Hoare. New York: International.

Hansen, L.L. 2007. 'From Flexicurity to Flexicarity? Gendered Perspectives on the Danish Model'. *Journal of Social Sciences* 3(2): 88–93.

Harvey, D. 2012. *Rebel Cities: From the Right to the City to Urban Revolution.* London: Verso.

Jakobsen, J.E. 2015. 'Den danske model gav historisk dom mod social dumping i metroen'. *Modkraft.* 17 March.

Johansen, I.V. 2014. 'Social Dumping Takes Centre Stage as the Eurosceptics Look to Gain Power'. *Transform.* www.transform-network.net/cs/ohnisko/die-europawahlen-aus-linker-perspektive/news/detail/Programm/social-dumping-takes-centre-stage-as-the-eurosceptics-look-to-gain-power.html

Jørgensen, H. 2006. *Arbejdsmarkedspolitikkens fornyelse: innovation eller trussel mod dansk flexicurity?* Copenhagen: LO/FTF.

Jørgensen, M.B. 2015. 'Precarity: What It Is and Isn't: Towards a Dynamic Understanding of What It Does'. *Critical Sociology* OnlineFirst, published on 15 October 2015. DOI: 10.1177/0896920515608925.

—— and Thomsen, T.L. 2012. 'Crises Now and Then: Comparing Integration Policy Frameworks and Immigrant Target Groups in Denmark in the 1970s and 2000s'. *Journal of International Migration and Integration* 14(2): 245–62.

Lind, J. 2012. 'Det danske arbejdsmarked og social dumping'. *Kritisk Debat.* 15 April. http://kritiskdebat.dk/articles.php?article_id=1125

Mathiassen, J. 2014. 'Fagbevægelsen og østarbejdere: et dilemma'. *Arbejderen.* 28 February.

—— and Jensen, K.B. 2014. *Kamppladser: Østarbejdere og social dumping i byggeriet.* Copenhagen: Information Forlag.

Mayo, P. 2008. 'Antonio Gramsci and his Relevance for the Education of Adults'. *Educational Philosophy and Theory* 40(3): 418–35.

Mezzadra, S. and Neilson, B. 2008. 'Border as Method, or, the Multiplication of Labor'. EIPCP. http://eipcp.net/transversal/0608/mezzadraneilson/en

Ott, L. 2014. 'Polakker organiserer sig'. *3F.* 28 March. www.3f.dk/bjmf/aktuelt/nyheder/polakker-organiserer-sig

Pedersen, O.K. 2011. *Konkurrencestaten.* Copenhagen: Hans Reitzel.

Ritzau. 2015. 'Thorning: Løkke inviterer lavtlønnede udlændinge til Danmark'. *Ekstra Bladet.* 8 June.

Robinson, W.I. and Harris, J. 2000. 'Towards a Global Ruling Class? Globalization and the Transnational Capitalist Class'. *Science and Society* 64(1): 11–54.

Seymour, R. 2012. 'We Are All Precarious: On the Concept of the "Precariat" and its Misuses'. *New Left Project.* 10 February.

Seymour, R. 2014. *Against Austerity.* London: Pluto Press.

Socialdemokraterne. 2015. *Dansk løn for dansk arbejde.* www.socialdemokraterne.dk/da/nyhedsarkiv/2015/6/dansk-loen-for-dansk-arbejde/

Standing, G. 2011. *The Precariat: The New Dangerous Class.* London: Bloomsbury Academic.

Thulesen Dahl, K. 2015. 'Østarbejdere og social dumping skal på dagsorden'. 1 June. www.danskfolkeparti.dk/%C3%98starbejdere_og_social_dumping_skal_p%C3%A5_dagsordenen

Venstre. 2014. *Politisk oplæg: Ny udlændingepolitik. Danmark for dem der vil og kan.* www.venstre.dk/_Resources/Persistent/4689b69077e55e9c209b150c5727ef7ce1c850b1/Udlaendingepolitik---Danmark-for-dem-der-kan-og-vil---aug-2014.pdf

Wimmer, A. and Glick Schiller, N. 2002. 'Methodological Nationalism and Beyond: Nation-State Building, Migration and the Social Sciences'. *Global Networks* 2(4), 301–34.

Part IV

Spaces of Resistance

10

Politicising the Crisis: The Southern Question, Uneven Geographies and the Construction of Solidarity

David Featherstone

On 26 March 2015 tens of thousands of protesters marched in Dublin against the Irish government's water charges, which have come to symbolise the unequal character of that country's austerity programme. Many in the crowd, as a *Guardian* report of the demonstration noted, were 'holding Greek flags to show solidarity with the stricken eurozone member'.[1] Such displays of solidarity between different actors struggling against austerity have been an important aspect of the post-crisis political terrain. The 'Right 2 Water' campaign in Ireland has also 'highlighted the plight of the residents of Detroit in the US' and 'brought over activists from the Detroit Water Brigade who addressed local meetings and protests' (Hearne 2015: 316). Such articulations of solidarity are a significant contrast to the divisive geographies mobilised by dominant elites in support of political projects of austerity.

Thus reacting to the election of Syriza, the German newspaper *Bild* asked, for example, referring to Alexis Tsipras's victory gesture, 'How much will that raised fist cost?' These contrasting framings of the geographies of austerity signal the importance of thinking about the struggles over the terms on which solidarities are constructed across geographical divisions and how they are articulated in political terms. In this regard, Antonio Gramsci's 'Some Aspects of the Southern Question' remains one of the most enduring, significant and perceptive attempts to think politically about the construction of solidarities and political alliances on uneven geographical terrains. In this chapter I argue that the theoretical problematic that animates his essay is of particular relevance for the contemporary conjuncture of crisis and austerity. The remainder of the chapter then draws on Stuart Hall's argument that 'race' can function as a key 'lens through which people come to perceive that a crisis is developing' and can be 'the framework through which the crisis is experienced' (Hall 1978: 31). The chapter uses this as a starting point to engage with different struggles in the past which have sought to engage with solidaristic alternatives in contexts of crisis and austerity and in opposition to racist articulations of migration.

THE SOUTHERN QUESTION, UNEVEN GEOGRAPHIES AND THE CONSTRUCTION OF SOLIDARITY

Writing in an internal Italian Communist Party document on 9 February 1924, Gramsci argued that it was necessary to 'open up a discussion, before the mass of the Party membership, on basic issues dealing not only with our internal situation but also regarding a new alignment of the groups aspiring to the leadership of the party' (Gramsci 2014: 218). His account articulated a set of different problematics facing the Italian left, and ended by addressing the failure of Communist organising to engage effectively with questions of the South, arguing:

> The Fourth and last of these problems is that of the South, which we have misunderstood just as the socialists did, believing it could be resolved in the normal course of our general political activity. I have always been of the opinion that the South would become the graveyard of fascism, but I also think that it will turn out to be the main reservoir and training ground of national and international reaction if, before the revolution, we do not study the questions adequately and are not prepared for everything. (Ibid.: 231)

Gramsci's observation that the Southern question was not one which could be resolved 'in the normal course of our general political activity' is central to his contribution on the Southern question. One of the important aspects of the text is the way that it positions space and politics as struggled over and the subject of contestation, rather than as simply a stage on which the antagonisms shaped by left politics are performed (see Sparke 2005). In this regard the way the essay frames the question of the South is to politicise it and to contest the terms on which it has been understood.

This politicisation of the Southern question in part emerges from a sharp critique of the terms on which Socialist Party intellectuals internalised constructions of 'the South' as backward. Thus Gramsci argues that the Socialist Party remained within an understanding which argues that 'if the South is backward, the fault does not lie with the capitalist system or with any other historical cause, but with Nature which has made the Southerners lazy, incapable, criminal and barbaric' (Gramsci 1978: 444). Indeed he argued that the 'Socialist Party was to a great extent the vehicle for this bourgeois ideology within the Northern proletariat'. By rejecting ways of framing the South as a problem with intrinsic causes, as evolving 'organically from its own transformations', Gramsci here politicises the question of regional inequality, rather than falling back on racialised accounts of Southerners to explain this inequality. In such accounts it becomes the region itself that is seen as a problem rather than the broader relations which produce particular regions in unequal ways (Cochrane 2013: 88). Further, in such accounts poor, marginal or exploited regions become blamed for their own poverty and the more dominant regions are not even seen as 'regional' (see also Massey 2007).

The novelty of the way in which Gramsci poses and politicises such relations in his essay can be seen by comparison with some of the mainstream regional geography of the early twentieth century, and through the ways in which other Communist writers sought to construct questions of regional inequality. Regional geography in the period Gramsci was writing was shaped by environmental determinism which delimited regions on a 'naturalistic basis' based on the 'unity of configuration, climate and vegetation' (Livingstone 1992: 280). Even the writings of other Communist intellectuals and activists on regional questions in the inter-war period tended, whilst articulating strong leftist sympathies, to remain within the terms established by dominant framings of regional issues. Thus the British Communist Wal Hannington, an activist with the National Unemployed Movement, wrote about depressed regions such as South Wales largely in terms which were constructed within the framework of a particular discourse about the 'distressed areas'.

'Some Aspects of the Southern Question' sought to critique not only Socialist Party positions on questions of regional inequality and organising, however. A key intellectual and political target was the effects of anarchist and syndicalist currents of political activity. As Carl Levy has argued, 'when Gramsci arrived in Turin as a financially embarrassed scholarship student, his politics had been little affected by Marxism', and were instead a 'mixture of Sardinian nationalism and revolutionary syndicalist rhetoric' (Levy 1999: 63). In this regard Gramsci's intellectual formation was strongly shaped by engagements with syndicalist intellectuals; 'as a devoted reader of Milan's syndicalist journal, *Il Viandante*' he 'was fully alive to the theoretical and cultural debates within the mainland's fissiparous movement' (ibid.: 64). Paradoxically, however, it was the syndicalism which Levy argues was such a formative influence on Gramsci's early intellectual development that was one of the key targets of 'Some Aspects of the Southern Question'.

Thus Levy argues that in Gramsci's 'essay on the Southern question and in the *Prison Notebooks* Gramsci's notion of subversivism, spontaneity and the peculiar weaknesses of the pre-fascist left in Italy revolved around the effects of the anarchists and syndicalists on Italian political culture' (ibid.: 228–9). Gramsci argued, for example, that the 'proletariat, in order to become capable as a class of governing, must strip itself of every residue of corporatism, every syndicalist prejudice and encrustation' (Gramsci 1977: 448). Given that, as Levy argues, the 'revolutionary syndicalists and their anti-protectionist and anti-trans-formist sentiments' were 'natural allies of southern and insular socialists' (1999: 63) it is unsurprising that their influence in constructing relations between organising in the South and North were brought into contestation in Gramsci's essay.

The terms on which Gramsci articulated the Southern question drew on his own long-standing attempts to forge connections between and share knowledge with the Southern and Northern lefts. In his journalism and editing work for *Avanti!* he sought out contributions from Sardinian leftists such as Angelo Corsi (Gramsci 2014). Thus in October 1917 he wrote to Corsi, noting that he had read one of his articles in *Avanti!* and one in Prezzolini's *Voce* and that he had 'followed through *Sardegna Socialista* your assiduous work as mayor and provincial councillor'. He enquired if he could 'write something on the political–economic movement of the Sardinian proletariat' as he argued 'it would be of great use to have the new Sardinia known in the North of Italy ... so as to better strengthen the united consciousness of the Italian proletariat' (ibid.: 98–9). This was to be a lasting political engagement. In July 1926, at the time that 'Aspects' was being drafted, Gramsci wrote to Emilio Lussu, the Sardinian parliamentary deputy, soliciting Lussu's views on many issues including the attitude of Sardinian peasants to the Russian Revolution and asking 'with what [mainland] social and political forces does the S[ardinian] A[ction] P[arty] think it necessary to ally' (ibid.: 363).

One of the major contributions of 'Some Aspects of the Southern Question' is to treat such connections and solidarities as generative. In this regard the essay traces interrelations which shaped, and reshaped, the terms of left political activity and organising. Thus Gramsci discusses accounts of Sardinian soldiers from the Sassari Brigade who were sent to Turin, in their words to 'shoot the gentry who are on strike'. He recounts a conversation between a Sardinian tannery worker from Sassari and a soldier from the brigade bivouacked on the X square in Turin. The 'tannery worker' had approached a young peasant 'who had welcomed him warmly because I was from Sassari like him'. He managed to convince the peasant soldier that despite their dress the strikers were far from being members of the gentry. Gramsci's account gives a strong sense of the ongoing connections that developed between veterans of the Sassari brigade and militants in Turin. He argues: 'Did these events have no consequences? On the contrary, they have had results which still subsist to this day and continue to work in the depths of the popular masses' (Gramsci 1978: 448).

Gramsci here foregrounds the practices through which the veterans of the Sassari brigade and the *Avanti!* editorial offices were connected. He notes the importance of the letters, and notes the significance of their collectively signed character, which linked Sassari brigade veterans in Sardinia with militants in Turin. These mark and foreground the ongoing work of making such political connections and solidarities. For Gramsci such connections matter. The 'brains' of the soldiers were marked by their experiences, and were 'radically modified'. As Gramsci notes 'their songs, though still songs of war, no longer had the same content as those they sang on their arrival' (ibid.). Further, in writing of the three hundred carabinieri from the Cagliari Legion who were sent to Turin he notes that 'by uncontrolled and uncontrollable paths, the political attitude we supported was disseminated'. Through drawing attention to such dynamic and generative paths of political activity and attitude Gramsci stresses the ways in which different subaltern geographies of connection could shape the production of political trajectories, solidarities and alliances.

Gramsci's essay, then, does not just critique dominant framings of the Southern question. He also situates such geographies of solidarity in relation to the geographies of connection that shaped the South, analysing the ways in which remittances from migrants to the United States were used to entrench rather than challenge regional inequalities. This prefigures the ways in which uneven geographies are now thought of in 'relational' terms whereby such unevenness is the product of contested relations, rather than an inevitable outcome. Thus Gramsci critiques the expectation of 'liberal economists' when 'remittances began to flood in from America' that the result would be a 'silent revolution ... under way in the South' which would 'change the entire economic and social structure of the country' (ibid.: 459). Instead Gramsci charts how the 'emigrants and their families were transformed from agents of the silent revolution into agents for giving the State the financial means to subsidise the parasitic industries of the North' (ibid.). Further Gramsci notes how the collapse of the *Banca Italiana di Sconto* in December 1921 disproportionately impacted on Southern savers.

This opens up important ways of accounting for the dynamic geographies of subaltern political activity. Such an approach in turn shaped Gramsci's engagement with the challenges of anti-fascist exile and migration which were beginning to have a significant impact on the

PCI in the mid-1920s. Thus he notes that 'the Communist Party of Italy has up to now sought to send abroad only those comrades who, after receiving heavy sentences or having very serious accusations pending, could not possibly remain in Italy' (Gramsci 2014: 142–3). He noted, however, that 'various workers, given they have found themselves in such pitiful conditions that they have had to choose between dying of hunger and submitting to the fascist yoke, have made their own decision to emigrate, wandering aimlessly without any guide, and with their revolutionary spirit totally downcast' (ibid.).

Gramsci suggested as a result that it would be necessary to 'keep a closer eye on the flow of emigrants abroad and their life there, check their identity as refugees, know where to send them, and where work can more easily be found for them; who and how they can be used for propaganda and Party work and who should go back to Italy' (Gramsci 2014: 143). This engagement with trajectories of migration and exile shaped Gramsci's thought in significant ways; though one also detects here something of Gramsci as Comintern functionary wishing to maintain surveillance on the activities of Italian Communists abroad (see Saccarelli 2008). Most importantly an engagement with such forms of unequal mobility shaped his engagement with forms of 'subaltern cosmopolitanism' (Gramsci 1985; Chatterjee 2011). He argues that the Italian people are the people with the greatest 'national' interest in a 'modern form of cosmopolitanism', which he uses in a way that is akin to 'proletarian internationalism'.

What is significant in Gramsci's account here is a sense of the significance of forms of cosmopolitanism and internationalism being produced through practices such as labour mobility. He develops an understanding of such cosmopolitan experiences directly in relation to practices of labour and experiences of labour migration. He treats as productive such connections between Italian workers and the non-Italian world that they are connected to through the relations they have produced through their labour (Gramsci 1985: 247, Q8§72). In this way Gramsci's work is of far more relevance to debates on questions of 'race' and migration than is often recognised. As Hall notes, the 'emphasis, stemming from the historical experience of Italy … led Gramsci to give considerable weight to *national* characteristics, as an important level of determination, and to *regional* unevenness' (Hall 1996: 435, emphasis in original). In this regard Gramsci's work enables an understanding of the ways in which '[r]acism and racist practices and structures frequently occur in some but not all sectors of the social formation; their impact is penetrative but uneven; and their very unevenness of impact may help to deepen and exacerbate these contradictory sectoral antagonisms' (ibid.). The next section draws in depth on Hall's work to think about the relations between 'race', racism and contested articulations of crisis.

CRISIS, 'RACE' AND THE CONTESTED POLITICS OF PLACE

In his 1978 essay 'Racism and Reaction' Hall comments that 'race' can function as a key 'lens through which people come to perceive that a crisis is developing' and can be 'the framework through which the crisis is experienced' (Hall 1978: 31). A detailed articulation of this argument was central to the Gramscian-inflected analysis he developed with his co-authors in *Policing the Crisis*. As the authors argue, the book is 'about a society which is slipping into a certain kind of *crisis*' and examines 'why and how the themes of *race, crime* and *youth* – condensed into the image of "mugging" – come to serve as the articulator of the crisis, as its ideological conductor' (Hall et al. 1978: viii, emphasis in original). These different 'dimensions of the "crisis" came finally to be appropriated – by governments in office, the repressive apparatuses of the state, the media and some articulate sectors of public opinion – as an interlocking set of planned or organized *conspiracies*' set 'against "the British way of life"' (ibid.: 309, emphasis in original).

What is significant in this analysis, for the purposes of the current discussion, is the way such an approach enables a focus on how crises are constructed, envisioned and imagined through particular geographies and through particular racialised narratives. This is a central contribution both of Hall's work and of Gramsci's articulation of understandings of fascism and crisis. In this regard, as in the 1970s, a key way in which the 2008 crisis moment and its aftermath has been understood in Britain and in Europe more generally is through the lens of 'race' and in relation to discourses around migration. As Doreen Massey and Mike Rustin have argued, 'more potent than the rise of these new formations of the left', most significantly parties such as Podemos and Syriza, has been 'the upsurge of nationalist and xenophobic movements of the right in many countries' (Massey and Rustin 2015: 193).

Such 'nationed' responses are central to the geographical terrain on which the 'crisis' is being articulated and politicised. The term 'nationed geographies of crisis' is used here to suggest 'ways in which the nation is reasserted as the primary locus through which grievances are articulated and envisioned' (Featherstone 2015: 21). As Josep Antentas has argued, 'resistance to austerity has followed national dynamics and its rhythms have been dependant on the vicissitudes of national politics' (Antentas 2015: 10). Antentas's attention to the ways in which resistance to austerity has been articulated and confined within national dynamics emphasises that such nationed responses are not solely the terrain of the political right. Such imaginaries have also been important in shaping the terms of some labour-movement responses to situations of crisis in different contexts. Further, it is important to recognise that such contestation has taken place in contexts such as the United Kingdom, where migrants 'are stratified into a "hierarchy of rights" defined by distinctions in skill and origin' (Reid-Musson, Buckley and Anderson 2015: 6).

The ways in which grievances around labour conditions and hiring practices became powerfully mobilised around the demand for 'British jobs for British workers' in 2009 emphasises how such antagonisms can become racialised (see Ince et al. 2015). Wildcat disputes in the engineering construction industry mobilised around this slogan, which had been used by Gordon Brown at the previous year's Labour Party Conference. The strikes began on 28 January 2009; 800 British engineering construction workers walked off a construction project at the Lindsey Oil Refinery and action quickly spread to other sites across the United Kingdom. The disputes were occasioned by the employment of approximately 200 Italian and Portuguese workers by the Italian contractor IREM, which engineering construction workers engaged in existing contracts at the Lindsey plant saw as a violation of existing national agreements (Ince et al. 2015; Gall 2012).

As Reid-Musson notes, 'there are signs that the integrity of the NAECI [National Agreement for the Engineering Construction Industry] collective agreement is being undermined by industry practices which have pitted unionised British engineers against non-union, lower wage "posted workers" from elsewhere in the EU on British worksites' (Reid-Musson, Buckley and Anderson 2015: 17). During the dispute, the terms on which such antagonisms were challenged were contested and there was some attempt to position the dispute in relation to more solidaristic discourses (see Ince et al. 2015). Central to the dispute was the ways in which the European Posted Workers Directive (PWD) was implemented in the United Kingdom. While this was 'designed to provide "posted" migrant workers with standards of employment equal to those that apply to host country citizen-workers ... UK lawmakers have looked to minimum legal standards as a baseline for migrants' wages and conditions rather than the voluntary standards established under collective agreements' (Reid-Musson, Buckley and Anderson 2015: 17). This is part of a broader context of neoliberalisation in relation to EU labour market regulations which in this case intersected with a UK government strategy to support flexible labour markets (Mackinnon, Cumbers and Featherstone 2015).

One of the ways in which the Lindsey disputes were framed, both by some union leaderships and in broader media discourses, was in relation to debates about the demands of an 'indigenous' 'white working class'. Derek Simpson of Unite, for example, used the term 'indigenous workers', which can be interpreted as a cipher for white, in discussions of the dispute on key UK media outlets. The term 'white working class' has been broadly mobilised as a 'trans-historical' formation in recent discourses in Britain. In this sense, it is important to see debates about a 'white working class' as one response to globalising processes that locate this formation as a product of ways of negotiating such processes, rather than that a homogenous white working class had pre-existed such processes. This speaks to a profound racialisation of discourses of class which has been taken up very uncritically in some recent Labour Party thinking, notably in relation to the ways in which One Nation Labour became associated with problematic narratives around homogenous past working-class communities (Virdee 2015).

Engaging with the histories and geographies through which discourses of whiteness and class can come to be co-articulated, however, show that such relations can be contested and struggled over, rather than being inevitable. The importance of the ways in which these can be shaped and challenged can be illustrated by looking at debates about a similar articulation of crisis and race in 1930s Britain. In the early to middle twentieth century one of the key ways in which labour struggles and organising were articulated was a white labourism which functioned as a 'common ideology' shaped by an 'imperial working class' where 'the element of the critique of exploitation and the element of racism were inextricably intermingled' (Hyslop 1999). One key institution in shaping such white-labourist discourses was the National Union of Seamen (NUS), which lobbied for various racist regulations and acts such as the Alien Coloured Order in 1925 and the Tramp Shipping Subsidy Act 1935 sought to exclude black, Asian and Arab seafarers from work in the maritime labour market in British port cities. The Tramp Shipping Subsidy Act, in particular, was a direct attempt to prioritise white seafarers at the expense of seafarers of colour, often from different British backgrounds, including diverse colonial contexts, during the depression of the 1930s.

The Act shaped exclusionary 'local labour market control regimes' which were the product of links between NUS officials, the Board of Trade and shipping companies (Jonas 1996). This drew on the longstanding embeddedness of the NUS in such relations. As Gopal Balachandran puts it, the National Seamen and Firemen's Union, which from 1926 became the National Union of Seamen, 'increasingly resembled an employment brokerage for seafarers loyal to the union, employers and the state' (Balachandran 2012: 255). If there was considerable ambiguity in the way in which the Act mobilised British citizens there was little ambiguity in the way the Act was interpreted and applied. Thus there were allegations that the 'Shipping Federation' issued a confidential circular which suggested that preference in terms of employment should be given in the order of (1) seamen of England, Scotland, Wales and Northern Ireland; (2) Southern Irish; (3) British subjects from other parts of the Empire; (4) aliens.[2] B. Fazoze Bhader, an Indian seafarer based in the port of South Shields, wrote: 'I don't know who is responsible but each time a ship signs we have been refused ... [T]he Union blames the owners and the owners blame the Union.'[3]

The Tramp Shipping Subsidy Act was contested by assertive forms of working class multicultural organising in port cities such as Cardiff, London and South Shields. The Cardiff Coloured Seamen's Committee included 'spokesmen of Malayan, Arab, Somali, West-Indian and African workers' to fight the 'proving of nationality clause' (Cardiff Coloured Seamen's Committee 1935). The Colonial Seamen's Association (CSA) was also founded in 1935 to oppose the Act. 'Led by president Chris Jones (aka Chris Braithwaite) and secretary Surat Alley, an Indian labour organiser, the association remained active in the late 1930s' (Tabili 1994: 158–9). The sense of 'working class multiculturalism' which shaped the Association can be given by reports of its first annual conference (Bressey 2014: 255), which record that it 'was attended by 51 workers – drawn from "Negroes, Arabs, Somalis, Malays and Chinese"'. It was 'addressed by Chris Braithwaite the chair of the CSA', a key pan-African seafarers' organiser from Barbados, and the secretary, the 'lascar' leader Surat Alley, 'who had links to the Textile Workers' Union in Bombay and the All-India Seamen's Federation' (Visram 2002: 219). The conference passed a motion denouncing 'the pernicious colour discrimination which is deliberately fostered by the employers and the Government in order to divide and rule the seamen of all countries in the interests of the ship owners.'[4] Indian unions also condemned the Act and drew attention to the Labour Party's role in its conception.

The organising of movements such as the CSA had significant impacts. Thus Balachandran argues that

> the principle of white-only crews proved unworkable. Some shipowners especially from South Wales complained of not being able to find full crews of white British sailors, while fears of divisions in its ranks persuaded the NUS to back away from its earlier demand for excluding all foreign seamen. At several ports its 'burgeoning

anti-Black campaign' drove activists and rank-and-file members closer to left-wing organisations. (Balachandran 2012: 193)

By contesting the exclusionary 'local labour control regimes' shaped by the NUS, the Board of Trade and Shipping Lines, organisers like Harry O'Connell in Cardiff and Surat Alley and Chris Braithwaite in London did not just challenge the terms on which maritime labour was articulated and hired. Rather, they also made a broader challenge to the racialised practices and hierarchies endorsed by the mainstream trade union movement.

The struggles against the Tramp Shipping Subsidy Act emphasise that the ways in which crisis, race and place are politicised can be challenged and brought into question. Organisations like the CSA demonstrated that white labourism was not the only, or an uncontested, way of articulating maritime organising. Further, the ways in which such movements generated translocal solidarities shaped through multi-ethnic spaces and organising also challenged the terms on which labour organisations negotiated and responded to the crisis. This signals that constructions of the 'white working class' can be mobilised in relation to crisis in ways which silence and close down important histories of forms of 'working class multiculturalism'. This also emphasises the possibilities of different more solidaristic ways of negotiating and articulating crisis. The next section explores in more depth the terms on which solidarities have been articulated in relation to the 2008 crisis and its aftermath.

AUSTERITY, UNEVEN GEOGRAPHIES AND THE CONSTRUCTION OF SOLIDARITY

In an intervention on the relations between crisis and regional development theories Costis Hadjimichalis and Ray Hudson have argued of the Eurozone crisis that Southern European 'regional economies, including those formerly seen as "success stories", together with Ireland, became the weak link in a very unstable monetary union and the old social and spatial division of labour between North and South in Europe began to be reproduced in a heightened manner' (Hadjimichalis and Hudson 2014: 211). Such socio-spatial divisions have been intensified and exacerbated through the adoption of austerity as the dominant political response to the crisis by European elites and institutions. As Massey and Rustin note: 'Across Europe the remedy very quickly adopted for the failure of the neoliberal system was to insist that it be imposed with even greater rigour on economies and societies already ruined by the crisis' (Massey and Rustin 2015: 191).

The implementation of austerity has taken place in a broader context where at an institutional level the European Union has 'made a big shift in the neoliberal direction, since the 1980s, particularly with the Maastricht treaty of 1992' (Davison and Shire 2015: 185). As Erne et al. argue 'The European marketization project is intensifying in response to the euro crisis' (2015: 127). One key way in which such a marketization project has been articulated and generated is through exploitative approaches to migrant labour. As Sally Davison and George Shire argue: 'For the existing EU member states, the new East European members were seen as offering a source of new markets, cheap labour and investment opportunities, and the pre-accession treaties made privatisation and liberalisation central to the negotiations' (Davison and Shire 2015: 185). In this regard the implementation of the PWD discussed in the previous section is a useful example of the uneven impacts of such neoliberalisation on the terrain of labour migration.

The intensification of a market-driven European project in the wake of the crisis, and crucially the use of the crisis as a political opportunity to further this project, underlines the importance of challenging the relation between austerity as a political project and the divisive geographies on which it both depends and produces. This raises important questions of how solidarities might be articulated that challenge and refuse the unequal character of such divisions. There are clear resonances here with Gramsci's project of thinking about how solidarities and alliances might be forged across the uneven terrain of Italy during the 1920s. To engage seriously with the formation of such solidarities and alliances involves dislocating some of the ways in which the crisis has been articulated by some key leadership figures of organised labour.

Thus in 2012 Berthold Huber, then general secretary of IG Metall, gave a speech which demonstrates some of the pressures on the formation of solidarities across the 'socio-spatial' divisions of contemporary Europe. For rather than challenging dominant constructions of such divisions, the logic of his speech was to intensify and deepen them. As Andreas Bieler and Roland Erne note, he first 'blamed Spanish unions for the fate of the Spanish economy. Having obtained "too high wage increases" they would be responsible for undermining the competitiveness of Spanish economies. Then he argued that the Spanish labour market should be restructured to regain competitiveness' (Bieler and Erne 2014: 163).

Bieler and Erne observe that, by 'arguing that wage formation is responsible for competitiveness and supporting labour-market deregulation, Huber placed himself within dominant understandings of the crisis and its required solution' (ibid.). Further, officials like Huber have been dismissive of organising efforts, such as the cross-European action of 14 November 2012, which *had much stronger* support in countries such as Portugal, Greece and Spain than in Northern Europe. Huber 'criticized the planned strikes in some Southern European countries for the European-wide trade union mobilisation of 14 November 2012 as "voluntaristic nonsense"'. The action of such trade union leaderships has, however, not gone uncontested. Thus Simon Dubbins, the international officer of Unite the Union, commented in a talk at the Kilburn Manifesto conference in February 2015 that Unite had been involved in seeking to exert pressure on sister unions from Germany and the Netherlands to take issues of austerity seriously. Further, he noted that austerity tended to be seen as an issue relating to Southern Europe, rather than being of broader significance. He noted, however, that the political context in Britain meant that there were deeper commonalities with Southern European contexts facing harsh austerity than with countries such as Germany and the Netherlands (Dubbins 2015).

Some left organising in Germany has also directly challenged the centrality of German politicians to the Troika (the tripartite organization of the European Commission's Eurogroup with the European Central Bank and the International Monetary Fund, which has been central to implementing policies of austerity) and in so doing have challenged official constructions of place. Thus the organisation Blockupy emerged in Frankfurt as a movement challenging the central role of the city in 'Troikapolitics' and positions itself as 'resistance in the heart of the European crisis regime'. It has since developed a focus as a more explicitly transnational focus of resistance. Thus a statement from the Blockupy Action Conference held in Frankfurt in November 2013 notes that it

> stood in a row with different meeting of European movements, networks and organizations in the fall of this year – in Barcelona, Amsterdam, Brussels and Rome. In addition to specific arrangements for Blockupy 2014, it offered the participants from many European countries the opportunity to share their experiences of a growing, increasingly disobedient opposition to the Troikapolitik. (Blockupy 2013)

In this regard, however, the transnationalising of protest in relation to austerity has been uneven and fragmentary.

There are signs, however, that such mobilisation has intensified in recent months, partly catalysed by the increasing prominence of Syriza and Podemos. The terms on which such emergent mobilisations are developing can be gleaned from the declaration of

> a broad coalition of social organisations, unions and networks, intellectuals, artists, migrant organisations and various left, green and

progressive political powers being active in Greece, propose international actions between the 20th and the 26th of June in order to create
the positive social and political environment that will support the
Greek struggle. Moreover we are willing to host an event here in Athens
on the 27th to share our experiences of mobilisations and solidarity. It
is significant to transform the European peoples from passive viewers
to active players of this story. (Greek Social Movements 2015: n.p.)

The presence of migrant organisations in forging this declaration
speaks to the importance of migrants, both as those who experience
the sharp end of austerity in terms of material conditions, and also as
scapegoats and targets of far-right repression. This addresses the issue
of engaging with the decidedly uneven, racialised, gendered and classed
impacts of such local politics (Vachelli, Kathrecha and Gyte 2015). In
line with Gramsci's discussion of the 'uncontrolled and uncontrollable
paths' through which radical ideas travelled between movements in the
North and South of Italy, various migrants have also been important in
shaping political trajectories and solidarities from below in relation to
the Eurozone crisis. This is in part linked to dislocations, e.g. of Greeks
and Spanish forced to move as a response to the crisis, especially with
regard to the impact on young people. A good example here is the ways
in which links were forged between the *indignados* movement in Spain
and London Occupy.

Thus Sam Halvorsen notes that

Occupy London had closer personal links to *indignados* than Occupy
Wall Street. During the summer of 2011, as part of a global movement
of solidarity with Spain, a small occupation was set up outside the
Spanish Embassy in West London that attracted thousands of Spaniards
living in London. Many of those who participated in that action went
on to be active organisers with Occupy London. (Halvorsen 2015: 25)

Migrants have shaped the politics of different movements struggling
against austerity in significant ways. Thus in Spain Ecuadorean migrants
have been at the forefront of struggles against evictions in the housing
movement. Such organising builds on ongoing struggles for recognition
and on their partial recognition and inclusion within the Spanish labour
movement (Lucio and Connolly 2012). As Miguel Martínez Lucio and
Heather Connolly note,

most of Spain's leading and majority trade unions have developed and
involved a series of immigrant activists. A series of leading figures have

begun to play a role within these sections, although in the national conferences and congresses of the unions the presence of immigrants is not visible to any great extent. (Lucio and Connolly 2012: 678)

This locates the role of immigrants in housing activism in relation to trajectories of organising, rather than seeing them as just reactive to a particular crisis moment. These distinctive geographies of connection have shaped the 'political opening' that Vijay Prashad associates with movements such as Occupy and the *indignados*. Thus he notes that Occupy has 'broken the idea of American exceptionalism and linked US social distress and protest to the pink tide in Latin America, the Arab Spring, and the pre-revolutionary struggles of the *indignados* of southern Europe' (Prashad 2012: 18).

CONCLUSIONS

Writing to Julia Schucht shortly before his arrest and imprisonment in 1926 Gramsci noted that he was 'finishing off a work that has taken up much time and effort and which maybe will turn out to be interesting and useful' (Gramsci 2014: 377). This modest assessment of the 'Southern question' belies the significance of the last major political and intellectual intervention he wrote under conditions of freedom. This text deserves its recognised place as one of the most important Marxist texts to deal with questions of uneven development and political solidarity. It is also one of the most significant attempts to engage with questions of space and politics. It is a text which, as I have sought to argue in various ways here, has significant contemporary resonance.

In this chapter I have sought to use Gramsci's essay as a way into thinking about political strategies in relation to the uneven and divisive geographies being generated through crisis and austerity. There are four key issues I want to signal as being particularly important in this regard. Firstly, there is the urgency of challenging the terms on which crisis is narrated through particular racialised politics, in particular through scapegoating migrants. Secondly, there is the importance of destabilising narratives of a 'white working class', which rest on a very problematic way of racialising class. Such narratives make unrepresentable important articulations of ordinary or 'working-class' multiculturalism which can offer a significant challenge to divisive geographies on which projects of austerity depend. Thirdly, I have sought to engage with the terms on which solidarities are articulated in ways which challenge arguments that contesting austerity is only an issue of some countries in Europe, rather than being integral to struggles for a different way of envisioning the relations between different parts of Europe and their broader transnational connections. Finally, the chapter has sought to suggest the importance of migrants in forging opposition to 'austerity' from below and in constituting broader trajectories of opposition. This emphasises that such subalternised mobilities can be important to shaping political alternatives which might offer alternatives to the divisive geographies of austerity and crisis.

NOTES

1. www.theguardian.com/world/2015/mar/21/tens-thousands-march-dublin-protest-water-charges March, 26th, 2015
2. British Library IOR/L/E/955, p.425.
3. BL IOR/L/E/955,p.441.
4. *Negro Worker* 7(2), February 1937: 4. On Surat Alley, see Visram 2002: 239–53.

REFERENCES

Antentas, J. 2015. 'Sliding Scale of Spaces and Dilemmas of Internationalism'. *Antipode* 47(5), 1101–20.

Balachandran, G. 2012. *Globalizing Labour? Indian Seafarers and World Shipping, c. 1870–1945.* Delhi: Oxford University Press.

Bieler, A. and Erne, R. 2014. 'Transnational Solidarity? The European Working Class in the Eurozone Crisis'. *Socialist Register 2015.* London: Merlin Press: 157–77.

Blockupy. 2013. 'Mobilization to "Day X": Blockupy wants to disturb ECB opening'. http://blockupy.org/en/2798/pr-mobilization-to-day-x/

Bressey, C. 2014. 'Geographies of Early Anti-Racist Protest in Britain'. In A. Adogame and A. Lawrence (eds). *Africa in Scotland, Scotland in Africa: Historical Legacies and Contemporary Hybridities.* Leiden: Brill.

Cardiff Coloured Seamen's Committee. 1935. 'Coloured Seamen's Struggle against De-Nationalisation Memorandum'. *Negro Worker* 5(9): 10–11.

Chatterjee, P. 2011. *Lineages of Political Society.* New York: Colombia University Press.

Cochrane, A. 2013. 'Spatial Divisions and Regional Assemblages'. In D.J. Featherstone and J.M. Painter. *Spatial Politics: Essays for Doreen Massey.* Chichester: Wiley Blackwell.

Davison, S. and Shire, G. 2015. 'Race, Migration and Neoliberalism'. In S. Hall, D. Massey and M. Rustin (eds). *After Neoliberalism? The Kilburn Manifesto.* London: Lawrence and Wishart.

Dubbins, S. 2015. 'After Neoliberalism? Wider Contexts'. Talk given at *Soundings* Conference, 'After Neoliberalism: The Kilburn Manifesto'. February. http://blog.lwbooks.co.uk/after-neoliberalism-kilburn-manifesto-conference-programme/

Erne, R. et al. 2015. 'Editorial'. *Transfer* 21(2): 127.

Featherstone, D.J. 2015. 'Thinking the Crisis Politically: Lineages of Resistance to Neoliberalism and the Politics of the Current Conjuncture'. *Space and Polity* 19(1): 12–30.

Gall, G. 2012. 'The Engineering Construction Workers Strikes in Britain, 2009'. *Capital and Class* 36(3): 411–31.

Gramsci, A. 1977. *Selections from Political Writings, 1910–1920*, ed. Q. Hoare, trans. J. Matthews. London: Lawrence and Wishart.

—— 1978. *Selections from Political Writings, 1921–1926*, ed. and trans. Q. Hoare. London: Lawrence and Wishart.

—— 1985. *Selections from Cultural Writings*, ed. D. Forgacs and G. Nowell-Smith, trans. W.Q. Boelhower. London: Lawrence and Wishart.

—— 2014. *A Great and Terrible World: The Pre-Prison Letters, 1908–1926*, ed. and trans. D. Boothman. London: Lawrence and Wishart.

Greek Social Movements. 2015. 'Call for a European bottom up mobilization, from movements of Greece: United we stand against austerity and social injustice'. Alter Summit. www.altersummit.eu/accueil/article/united-we-stand-against-austerity?lang=en

Hadjimichalis, C. and Hudson, R. 2014. 'Contemporary Crisis across Europe and the Crisis of Regional Development Theories'. *Regional Studies* 48(1): 208–18.

Hall, S. 1978. 'Racism and Reaction'. In S. Hall (ed.) *Five Reviews of Multi-Racial Britain*. Commission for Racial Equality by special arrangement with BBC Television Further Education.

—— 1996. 'Gramsci's Relevance for the Study of Race and Ethnicity', in Morley, D. and Chen, K.-H. (eds). *Stuart Hall: Critical Dialogues in Cultural Studies*. London: Routledge.

—— et al. 1978. *Policing the Crisis: Mugging, the State and Law and Order*. London: Macmillan.

Halvorsen, S. 2015. *Subverting Space in Occupy London: Rethinking Territoriality and the Geographies of Social Movement*. Unpublished Ph.D. thesis. University College London.

Hearne, R. 2015. 'The Irish Water War'. *Interface* 7(1): 309–21.

Hyslop, J. 1999. 'The Imperial Working Class Makes Itself "White": White Labourism in Britain, Australia, and South Africa before the First World War'. *Journal of Historical Sociology* 12(4): 398–421.

Ince, A. et al. 2015. 'British Jobs for British Workers? Negotiating Work, Nation and Globalisation through the Lindsey Oil Refinery Disputes'. *Antipode* 47(1): 139–57.

Jonas, A. 1996. 'Local Labour Market Control Regimes: Uneven Development and the Social Regulation of Production'. *Regional Studies* 30: 323–38.

Levy, C. 1999. *Gramsci and the Anarchists*. Oxford: Berg.

Livingstone, D. 1992. *The Geographical Tradition*. Oxford: Blackwell.

Mackinnon, D., Cumbers, A. and Featherstone, D.J. 2015. 'Local and Regional Economic Development in Britain'. In J. Green, C. Hay and P. Taylor-Gooby (eds). *The British Growth Crisis: The Search for a New Model*. London: Palgrave Macmillan.

Lucio, M.M. and Connolly, H. 2012. 'Transformation and Continuity in Urban Struggles: Urban Politics, Trade Unions and Migration in Spain'. *Urban Studies* 49: 669–84.

Massey, D. 2007. *World City*. Cambridge: Polity Press.

—— and Rustin, M. 2015. 'Displacing Neoliberalism'. In S. Hall, D. Massey and M. Rustin (eds). *After Neoliberalism? The Kilburn Manifesto*. London: Lawrence and Wishart.

Prashad, V. 2012. 'This Concerns Everyone'. In K. Khatib, M. Killjoy and M. McGuire (eds). *We Are Many: Reflections on Movement Strategy From Occupation to Liberation*. Edinburgh and Oakland: AK Press.

Reid-Musson, E., Buckley, M. and Anderson, B. 2015. 'Building Migrant Precarity: Employment, Citizenship and Skill in Toronto and London's Construction Sectors'. Working paper. www.urbanizationfrombelow.net/wp-content/uploads/2015/04/Building_Migrant_Precarity_WorkingPaper_April2015.pdf

Saccarelli, E. 2008. *Gramsci and Trotsky in the Shadow of Stalinism*. New York: Routledge.

Sparke, M. 2005. *In the Space of Theory: Postfoundational Geographies of the Nation State*. Minnesota: University of Minnesota Press.

Tabili, L. 1994. '*We Ask for British Justice': Workers and Racial Difference in Late Imperial Britain*. Ithaca, NY: Cornell University Press.

Vachelli, E., Kathrecha, P. and Gyte, N. 2015. 'Is It Really Just the Cuts? Neoliberal Tales from the Women's Voluntary and Community Sector in London'. *Feminist Review* 109: 180–9.

Virdee, S. 2015. 'Anti-Racism, Working Class Racism and the Significance of the Racialised Outsider'. New Left Project. www.newleftproject.org/index.php/site/article_comments/anti_racism_working_class_formation_and_the_significance_of_the_racialized.

Visram, R. 2002. *Asians in Britain: 400 Years of History*. London: Pluto Press.

11

Contesting Urban Management Regimes: The Rise of Urban Justice Movements in Sweden[1]

Lisa Kings, Aleksandra Ålund and Nazem Tahvilzadeh

Residential segregation in Swedish cities has increased since the 1990s and interconnects class and race as signature features, polarising the urban landscape between prosperous inner city centre and marginalised suburbia – the periphery in social, cultural and, especially, economic terms (Nordström Skans and Åslund 2009). In this chapter we discuss how urban development programmes form an integrated part of what we call 'urban management regimes', aiming at coming to grips with these conditions. One of the most important policy interventions has been the promotion of targeted programmes for marginalised neighbourhoods, with directives aimed at promoting residential participation through consultation, dialogue initiatives and trans-sectoral partnerships; however, results have been disappointing in terms of impact and large-scale effect, such as a reduction in socio-economic inequality, or democratic renewal. It is, we argue, an approach that exhibits a democratic enigma, based as it is on the difference between, on the one hand, manifest intentions claiming to advance spaces for participation of local civil society and, on the other, institutional practices. Differences between rhetoric and restrictive practices have affected spaces for residential participation, resulting in an incipient contestation with the dominant urban management regime. This chapter looks at the ideological dominance of the state and considers these aspects of urban politics in Sweden during the last few decades.

As a reaction against the increased inequality of Swedish society and especially its spatial expression in cities, we are today witnessing the emergence of a new form of grassroots activism from marginalised suburbia, mobilising in particular youth with an immigrant background. This activism displays a variety of orientations and forms of organisation, ranging from more localised initiatives and spectacular cultural events to the long-term building up of activist platforms with local, and to some extent national, ramifications. Youths have started to come together to address the issues of segregation, racism and welfare transformation. The common denominator is that these initiatives can be seen as an urban justice movement in the making – with marginalised neighbourhoods, commonly referred to as *'orten'* ('neighbourhoods' or simply 'places') as the social ground for mobilisation.

For the scattered voices of the emerging urban justice movement, the notion of *'orten'*, imagined and lived, usually represents a locus for shared identity. Place is here used as a ground for the collective mobilisation of youth to raise consciousness about social inequality, racialisation, marginalisation, segregation and stigmatisation of the urban periphery and its inhabitants. In their claims and activities these voices merge local rootedness with critical consciousness of the effects of these wider structural and institutional conditions.

Against this background, we set out in this chapter to analyse the contemporary rise of the Swedish urban justice movement in relation to political and ideological production of contemporary urban politics in Sweden and particularly urban development programs. Our discussion of Swedish civil society's options and obstacles is inspired by a neo-Gramscian perspective on the ideological hegemony of the state and its institutional apparatus – both including and subordinating civil society. We discuss a hegemonic urban policy forging unequal citizenship and at the same time, mystifying socio-economic polarisation and a racialised ethnic division of the city. We focus on the role of the locality as the place of mobilisation of its inhabitants, mostly the daughters and sons of migrants. We define space as an arena for agency; including conflicts, negotiations and interconnection between the state and civil society; struggles as well as alliances within and between different actors, and their embeddedness and expressions at different levels. We connect action with the meaning of the locality; the place – as locus of lived experience – a foundation of shared identity, mobilisation and the related creation of trans-local networks of solidarity – within and beyond the place. Inspired by David Harvey (2001) and Doreen B. Massey (2005), both of whom refer to Gramscian theoretical contributions on the connection between ideological hegemony, socio-economic development and its relation to uneven spatial development, we view space as social space. Space in this sense encloses the intersection between the political economy of the divided city and the political space for civil-society agency – the ambivalence between autonomy and control/dependence and resistance in relation to the state.

Starting from the theoretical legacy of Gramsci in the work of neo-Gramscian scholars, we discuss the durability of ideological hegemony within contemporary urban policy, expressed through mys-

188 · SOLIDARITY WITHOUT BORDERS

tification of the socio-economic polarisation of the city. On the basis
of a case study of the establishment and early development of the
organisation Megafonen (the Megaphone) in Stockholm, in the later
parts of the chapter we contextualise the organisation's early emergence
and establishment and its claims and strategies in relation to the institutional frameworks of urban government.

While this organisation has developed an extended trans-local
solidarity network among similar organisations, networks and
movements in wider Stockholm and other Swedish cities, these are still
rather small in scale, with loose organisational forms that are currently
undergoing reorganisation, and with insecure futures. Still, as discussed
in the conclusion, with their focus on place, '*orten*', they have been part
of bringing forward and merging local solidarities, thus grounding social
space of resistance in Sweden, and have positioned themselves as public
voices against the polarised development of the contemporary urban and
social landscape. In other words, an emerging urban justice movement
has contributed to questioning and to some extent demystifying the
ideological hegemony of Sweden's urban management regime, even if its
position is still marginal and the prospects for its future are still unclear.

THE SECOND FRONT OF CONFLICT,
HEGEMONY AND MYSTIFICATION

Gramsci's influence in contemporary social science cannot be overestimated. Stuart Hall (1986, for example) developed a Gramscian approach
in culture theory and underscored the importance of Gramsci in studies
of race and ethnicity. Political theorists Chantal Mouffe and Ernest
Laclau (1985, for example) elaborated a Gramscian-inspired notion
of radical democracy. Last but not least, critical planning has since
the 1970s followed in the shadow of Gramsci, criticising traditional
planning processes and working to develop more participatory methods
for planning (Ekers et al. 2013; Allmendinger and Tewdwr-Jones 2002).

This later intervention on issues of democracy in urban planning
research can be related to what Manuel Castells refer to as 'the second front
of conflict'. Governments' involvement in various forms of community
services or financial transactions has resulted in unequally distributed
benefits among the inhabitants of cities and in social conflict related to
this. Castells (1983; cf. 1996) argues that collective consumption – the
goods or services produced and consumed collectively, such as infrastructure, public transport, education, fire and medical services – are
in advanced capitalist societies to be understood as a second front
of conflict in addition to that between labour and capital (cf. Harvey

1989). With civil society generating opposition and providing a possible foundation for change, this implicates a shift in focus from the workers' union and the conflict around the first front to the development of urban movements and the second front of conflict (Castells 1983; 1996. cf. Leitner et al. 2007). Even if Castells underestimated the continuing importance of workers' unions in the early 1980s when he proclaimed the shift from the factory to the neighbourhood, his analyses are important contributions for the understanding of emerging urban conflicts. This argument does not imply a rejection of class in the struggle for social change; on the contrary it rather underscores the need for taking the heterogeneity of new political actors and differing scales into consideration.

In this chapter the main theoretical inspiration is Michael Burawoy's (1979; later developments in 2003 and 2012) reading and development of Gramscian analysis, since it includes arguments and nuances necessary to classify frameworks for analyses of durability of hegemony within the second front of conflict. Based, amongst other things, on his ethnographic studies of exploitation as an objective condition, and its expression in subjective experiences among industrial workers in Hungary and the United States, Burawoy aimed to show how exploitation is concealed and more or less stable in different systems. As for many Marxist-influenced ethnographic studies of the 1960s and 1970s, the factory was the primary micro-cosmos for Burawoy. If at that time theories of the state were situated on the factory floor, we propose that for a more contemporary approach, the neighbourhood has become a base for solidarity and a potential space of resistance.

Following Burawoy, this includes problematising the original conceptualisation of hegemony as based on a rational, cognitive basis of consent. For the specific aim of this chapter, the neo-Gramscian concepts of mystification and management regimes are of importance. They apply to the organisation and practice of certain aspects of urban politics in Sweden that implicate particular conditions for the possibilities and obstacles of an emerging urban justice movement. Referring to what Marx termed 'mystification', Burawoy (2012: 189) re-uses the concept and argues that though mystification is not part of Gramsci's theoretical toolkit, the concept can be fruitful in extending Gramsci's analysis when applied to contemporary capitalism and the power relations between the state and civil society.

Another contribution of Burawoy – in his analysis of the stable foundation of hegemony in advanced capitalism – is the term 'management regime'. Inspired by Burawoy, we argue that mystification is working through different forms of management regime which tend to lead to the durability of hegemony rather than contestation of its domination. The management regime stands in contrast with the despotic regime common during early capitalism. In advanced capitalism, a management regime endeavours to create an environment that produces some sort of consent rather than coercion (direct force) as under a despotic regime. Burawoy (2012) introduces 'managing a game' as a central aspect of hegemony. For the game to produce consent, the application of coercion only functions under well-defined circumstances. At the same time, the game has to include sufficient aspects of uncertainty to attract the players; but it also has to give the player some control over the result.

Burawoy develops these analytical concepts primarily with the help of his empirical studies in factories. While the management regime for Burawoy embraced social and institutional conditions amongst the managerial staff of the factory, we are here applying this idea to marginalised neighbourhoods and the participatory aspect of urban politics. A comparison can be made between the factory, portrayed as a relatively autonomous arena in which labour is marked by a balance of certainty and uncertainty, and urban development programmes. Through development programmes, an urban management regime promotes the investment of participation; this can be conceived as a game in which residents are constructed as individual players and coordinated in favour of the hegemony of urban management regimes.

Constituting urban politics as a game under a management regime also creates specific circumstances for the merging of the objective existence of exploitation and its subjective experience. For Burawoy this means that hegemony is not only based on a rational, cognitive basis of consent. Mystification for Burawoy 'rests on individuals being inserted into specific social relations. It is the necessary condition for a stable hegemony, that is, for the organization of consent to domination' (2012: 198). The rhetoric and practice of the compensatory and participatory orientation of urban policies in marginalised neighbourhoods can give the residents a sense of extended freedom and symbolic rewards to individuals, but it also tends to produce a mystification of the tensions in the contemporary city that obscures the subjective experience of the underlying and intensified polarisation and domination. With that background we now address the ambivalent position and related options for civil society actors.

THE AMBIVALENCE OF CIVIL SOCIETY

Critical of the dominant Marxist trends of his time, Gramsci offers a complex and to some extent pessimistic account of the future of opposition and social change. Criticising the common failure of scholars to recognize the autonomous and progressive role of civil society, Burawoy (2003) argues that Gramsci helps us to understand that state and civil society are inseparable. Burawoy discusses the complex meaning of the force embedded in hegemony, arguing that it is not disappearing but it 'recedes in visibility'. Still, for Gramsci, civil society has a liberating potential. For example, societal crises offer the opportunity for the public exposure of the hegemonic ideology; furthermore, despite the circumstances, the best condition for spontaneous radicalism is always to be found among the subalterns, who have nothing to lose (Burawoy 2003).

Gramsci's theorisation of social change is not so well developed, but he underlines the importance of 'historical legacies, balance of class forces in organic crises and national models as carried by intellectuals' (ibid.: 213). The breakdown of hegemony is in the struggle essential for a successful result. Here domination is also seen as twofold, and by virtue of position it always contains the seeds of criticism, the so-called 'good sense', which is the opposite of 'common sense', that springs from the contemporary order. The emancipatory potential in Gramsci's 'good sense' represents the heart or theorisation of the lived experiences of the oppressed (ibid.). If Swedish urban politics produces mystification by the notion of common sense, the position of the subaltern in the urban periphery also provides a base for a possible good sense. This brings us to the issue of resistance.

The seeds of resistance can be developed through dialogue between organic and traditional intellectuals and thus can become a part of the 'war of position' – another central concept for Gramsci and his theory of social change and political strategy (Gramsci 1971). The central distinction Gramsci is making here is that between 'war of manoeuvre' (classic revolution) and 'war of position' (cultural struggle). The war of position is about civil society's efforts to gain positions of influence within the state. Emphasising the importance of dominance over ideas and culture, war of position is a more suitable strategy in advanced capitalism, where the focus has shifted away from the political economy towards superstructures and hegemony. The strategy of war of position is to 'slowly conquer the "trenches" of civil society before seizing state power' (Burawoy 2003: 215). But the war of position involves enormous efforts and sacrifices; patience is a much needed virtue when a successful outcome can never be guaranteed.

Of particular importance for our exploration of the emerging urban justice movement in Sweden is the Gramscian understanding of how forces of hegemony within the state apparatus continue to subordinate civil society. As Burawoy summarises this problem: 'In being harnessed to the state, civil society becomes a vehicle of domination as well as a terrain of contestation' (ibid.: 248). This development includes resistance in terms of an oppositional movement of civil society, still acting within and subordinate to the state, but also challenging it.

THE URBAN MANAGEMENT REGIME AND THE ORGANISATION OF CIVIL SOCIETY IN THE URBAN PERIPHERY

The increased polarisation in Swedish cities constitutes in Gramscian terms the objective 'exploitation' or, in Castells' wording, the second front of conflict. Focusing here on the development of resistance, we nonetheless need to understand the specific form of domination that frames the way in which the subjective and collective experiences are shaped. Following what Burawoy (2012) conceptualises as domination through the social structure, contemporary urban politics has to a large extent become a regular feature of Swedish cities.

Central features of contemporary Swedish urban politics are targeted policy interventions, including specific directives and earmarked economic funding directed at demarcated urban neighbourhoods (Elander 2002). Even though some of the contemporary urban peripheral areas have been exposed to area-based interventions more or less since they were built during the post-war period that was marked by economic and population growth, it is possible to identify a shift in focus since the 1990s. This shift is along a combination of social, economic and physical dimensions and, in particular, these programmes have deployed a post-radical language of the late 1960s and 1970s by emphasising the importance of developing neighbourhoods through empowerment, bottom-up perspectives and participation (Tahvilzadeh 2015). The trend towards new forms of politics and steering are not limited to the urban periphery, but it is here that it is possible to observe its most far-reaching attempts.

Underlying this ideational and factual development is the notion of changed relations between the state, the market and civil society. In Sweden, the withdrawal and marketisation of the welfare state has forced civil society to 'take over', on a voluntary base or as contract work, services and activities formally undertaken by the public sector (Wijkström and Lundström 2002). This tendency has been enhanced by the directive on democracy development and governance renewal, which calls for the more frequent solution of societal problems through cooperation between the public sector, civil society and private actors (Regeringskansliet 2008). In Sweden, the implications so far have been a move towards a more professionalised and service-oriented civil society. Wijkström (2012) concludes that these developments should be understood as an active endeavour and an ideological dislocation, which in the end remodels the relations between the state, civil society and the market in Sweden and has increasingly come to support civil society's role as a welfare producer rather than a mobilising force for political influence.

An important aspect of mystification produced by the urban management regime is illuminated when these more or less permanently ad hoc based activities of the urban development programmes are related to the local civil society. Interventions from above, together with a strong tradition of social movement in Sweden, have contributed to create a vigorous community life primarily engaged in producing social welfare to meet the large needs of marginalised neighbourhoods (Kings 2011). This kind of civil society engagement with general welfare is closely connected with the new urban management regime: this regime is dependent on the residents, through local civil-society work, for maintaining social services. In this way, and through the 'NGO-isation' of civil society (including primarily state funding) a dependency between the associations and management and politicians, along with local and central government and their funding authorities, has been created (Dahlstedt 2009; Ålund and Reichel 2007). This sort of dependency has so far undermined the conditions for creating stronger alliances between different local civil-society associations as well as their cooperation around more radical visions concerning issues of democratic participation (Ålund et al. 2013; Kings 2011).

THE RISE OF AN URBAN JUSTICE MOVEMENT

In contrast to and as a reaction against dependency on the traditional associations described above, we have during the last years witnessed a new form of grassroots mobilisation in the urban periphery. This mobilisation has developed in a range of collective initiatives – beyond place-bound struggles – that together have managed to become an articulated voice of marginalised suburbia in the public and political debate. For the larger Swedish (and international) public this form of mobilisation became renowned during the violent uprisings in Stockholm and other Swedish cities in May 2013. Megafonen in Husby, the neighbourhood where the riots started, arranged a press conference that was broadcast on state television, in which events during the riots were viewed from a wider structural perspective and police brutality was criticised. If the 2013 riots were and still are a critical event in the history of the newly emerging urban justice movement in Sweden (see Schierup, Ålund and Kings 2014), the initial rise and development of their different organisations, networks and actors must be analysed in relation to specific local experiences and related to the overall political context of urban development.

Focusing on Stockholm, Megafonen is the obvious case for applying this analysis since this organisation has been one of the most visible examples in terms of mobilisation, activities and public interface. Megafonen originated in the neighbourhood of Husby, in Järvafältet in the north-west of Stockholm. Since its beginning at the end of 2008, the organisation has expanded in numbers of sympathisers, activists and participants and geographically to new areas and since 2013 has been established in Alby in Botkyrka, a municipality to the south of Stockholm. According to its political programme, Megafonen's overall aim is to mobilise youth in the suburbs to work for social justice and a society free from 'racism, sexism and class oppression'. The strategies and methods of this joint work are defined as 'all that the situation allows and calls for' (Megafonen 2013; our translation). Furthermore, with its slogan 'A united suburb cannot be defeated'[2] Megafonen proclaims itself a foundation of identity and citizenship based on the idea of justice, with suburbia as the locus for its organisation and mobilisation that stretches beyond the local context (Megafonen 2013, our translation).

THE ESTABLISHMENT AND DEVELOPMENT
OF MEGAFONEN, HUSBY

During its rather short history, Megafonen has developed from a small-scale journal produced by a group of friends in Husby into a broad coalition acting in various arenas on issues that go beyond the local neighbourhood. The new orientation and further mobilisation developed through their early experience of the latest urban development programme, Järvalyftet, in Husby, Stockholm municipality. Järvalyftet, started in 2007, with the aim of creating, through citizen participation and cross-sectoral partnerships, a positive social and economic development whereby Järvafältet would become a hub for the development in the Stockholm region (Stockholms stads kommunfullmäktige 2007; cf. Stockholm stads kommunfullmäktige 2009).

Järvalyftet was among other things criticised for its lack of citizen participation and as a way of meeting this criticism Megafonen suggested to public officials that Järvalyftet should begin a dialogue with the youth in the area. As part of this, they conducted an interview study and presented their findings in a public report, 'Att vara ung i Husby' ('To Be

Young in Husby') (Megafonen 2010). A quotation from the introduction to the report sheds light on the positive spirit of the time, showing that Megafonen intended to collaborate with the city and the local housing company: 'We invite municipal, public and private actors to participate jointly with us, so that together we can realise the good ideas for the areas of Husby and Järva that are presented in this report' (Megafonen 2010:1; our translation).

Soon after Megafonen launched this report, the cooperation with Järvalyftet came to an abrupt end. From Megafonen's perspective, the work they had done was not taken into consideration when the aims and future investments in Järvalyftet in Husby were being determined. All the work that Megafonen had put into the dialogue and the views of youth they had collected and compiled, which underscored the need for social measures, were neglected in favour of what Megafonen saw as too great a focus on physical renewal. They were frustrated and disappointed with this treatment of their dialogue with the citizens of Husby.

For Megafonen, both as an organisation and as individuals living in the area, their legitimate existence was at stake. Taking part in the dialogue and putting their reputation at risk were according to Megafonen necessary for the youth to participate. For Megafonen not to be written off by the youth they needed to raise a critical voice within the local work of Järvalyftet:

We criticised them [politicians and public officials] for saying one thing, but doing another. People who had taken part in various forums and dialogues needed to know what was happening with their suggestions and ideas. For us [Megafonen] it was things like that, which started it, but we had not yet broken free. (Megafonen interviewee 1; our translation)

The tense relationship between Megafonen and politicians, local administrators and authorities at the publicly owned housing company became even more intense when Megafonen together with other local organisations and networks arranged the demonstration Vredens dag: från Tahrir till Husby (The Day of Anger: From Tahrir to Husby). This protest at the planned closure of the health centre in Husby, deriving its inspiration from the concurrent protests in Egypt, was one of the first public political events for Megafonen. It was followed by the occupation of a community centre in Husby in January 2012, in which Megafonen was one of the principal actors. The community centre, which functioned as a venue for social and cultural events, was under threat of being relocated to a smaller and, from the perspective of the residents, less suitable place. Together with the network Järvas framtid (The future of Järva) Megafonen mobilised local residents of all ages and organisational backgrounds during the two-week occupation. The nonviolent occupation was to be seen according to Megafonen as a protest against the two-faced politics that on the one hand articulated the aim of investing in the urban periphery through programmes such as Järvalyftet, and on the other was responsible for the loss by neighbourhoods like Husby of schools, health centres and administrative and other important public services for the residents.

This was the beginning of a new orientation for Megafonen especially evident during 2012 and 2013. This included locally based awareness strategies and protest actions, complemented by direct outreach pursuits. Besides taking part in public demonstrations and acting as a watchdog and pressure group with regard to political and administrative decisions at local and regional levels, Megafonen functioned as a critical voice in the mass media. Its role in the media of setting local issues within a broader context had started in 2012. In background articles in the regional and national media they heavily criticised Swedish urban politics, especially area-based projects launched to combat segregation. Megafonen's activities were not just broadened in the sense of becoming more outward-oriented, embracing aspects other than those directly or indirectly related to their essential analysis of place and the intersection of social and spatial inequality. With regard to their more direct continuous community work, a seminar series named Harakat,[3] for example, along with movie seminars, was basic to their work during this period.

It was also during the violent uprisings in 2013 that Megafonen became known to the general public through the mainstream national media, when they addressed the need to discuss structural inequalities. During the same period they also participated in another nationally recognised struggle against the sale to a private company of 1,300 public rental apartments at Albyberget in Botkyrka municipality (Tahvilzadeh and Kings 2015). Their role in both old and new media during these turbulent times should not be overestimated, but it made Megafonen one of a number of familiar voices in the news and media (Schierup, Ålund and Kings 2014).

In the aftermath of the 2013 riots and the Albyberget struggle, Megafonen has adopted a low profile. Their rapid expansion with local organisations in a number of neighbourhoods, early expectations, and especially the pressure of standing in the public line of fire during two nationally debated events, have led to a new orientation of organisational introspection. Currently the organisation does not engage in public events or debates, and the various local organisations work primarily behind closed doors. Even though no distinct future plan has been revealed, the aim is through introspection to develop a more stable and grounded organisation moving in a somewhat different direction:

> After everything that has happened, we now have to focus inwards. For now it is as if we have said what we want to say to the media and it is time for a restart. Our activities must be based on the needs of the neighbourhoods, and we need to create new relationships, and maintain existing ones, in the neighbourhoods. We need to keep our feet on the ground. (Megafonen interviewee 2; our translation)

DEMYSTIFICATION: THE EXIT STRATEGY AND THE CREATION OF PARTIAL AUTONOMY

With its focus on the rise of the Swedish urban justice movement, Megafonen illustrates the uniting element of early and negative experiences of different forms of participatory initiative that are directly or indirectly related to urban development programmes and new forms of urban governance (Tahvilzadeh and Kings 2015). In contrast to most of the traditional civil society actors in the urban periphery it early on distanced itself from the zero-sum game of silence in relation to the urban management regime. As mentioned, Megafonen started out as a partner in the latest urban renewal programme, though for its activists, the participatory practices of urban politics resulted in disappointment. Conflicts arose early and affected the future establishment, aims and claims of Megafonen when the inherent contradictions within the urban management regime came into the open.

The mismatch between the young activists' expectations of participatory democracy within the frame of the contemporary urban management regime and its reality in practice have led them to develop a Gramscian good sense and to question the overall partnership arrangement legitimised by the common sense of the hegemonic order. Megafonen is of course not the first to question the continuous urban development programmes and the actually existing participatory methods. This has constantly been addressed within the mainstream local civil society for years (see Kings 2011). However, in contrast to the traditional local associations that are usually engaged in producing different forms of welfare services to the locality, Megafonen has not been dependent on external funding. This may be one reason why the strategy of distancing itself from new forms of partnership within local governance became a plausible alternative.

Understanding the withdrawal from the urban management regime as a central act in the albeit rather short history of Megafonen indicates the importance of recognising the alternative of such an exit. Following Davis (2007), the exit strategy is to be understood as a possible alternative for groups that are unable to secure full democratic inclusion, resulting in frustration, dissolution and effective subordination in a depoliticised partnership, regardless of outcome. If Megafonen's own negative experience contributed to questioning the practice of the contemporary urban development programme, the distancing strategy also facilitated the possibility of demystifying the contemporary urban management regime as a whole (Burawoy 2012). Even though it is far from being an easy option, the exit strategy made it possible for Megafonen to search for an independent space in which to elaborate and test their own ways of defining problems and solutions (Davis 2007). This included the establishment of new sections in other parts of Stockholm, illustrating how Husby has become an important example in the emergence of a more general struggle.

Furthermore, an internal policy of partial autonomy later crystallised within Megafonen. Besides the ties and personal relations between the activists of Megafonen and other similar networks and organisations, such as Pantrarna (The Panthers) in the city of Gothenburg or Hassela ungdomsrörelse (Hassela youth movement) in Malmö, autonomy in relation to party politics, other civil society organisations (especially traditional ones) and the state was seen as essential, both in terms of legitimacy and of the actual capacity for defining independent agendas. Yet, as this quotation illustrates, Megafonen's desire for autonomy is not perceived as isolation.

> We do cooperate, but the cooperation cannot restrict us in what we want to create and what we do not what to create, that is the most important thing. Reinfelt [the name of the conservative prime minister at the time] can of course give us 3 million SEK, but not if the money comes with conditions. (Megafonen interviewee 3; our translation)

This indicates an openness towards accepting public financial support and towards entering into partnership with other organisations and movements as long as Megafonen's independence is not thereby undermined. Megafonen has, for example, collaborated with other organisations on both local and national levels. During the first years of Megafonen's formation, their collaboration partners were primarily other local associations in Husby and the surrounding area in relation to various actions. These included political parties (usually on the left), networks and more traditional social movement organisations such as Folkets Hus och parker (The People's Houses and Parks), PRO (The National Organisation of Pensioners), and to a lesser extent local migrant associations. For example, Rädda barnen (Save the Children) co-organised the seminar series Harakt. Even though Megafonen still considers organisations such as these as potential allies, it also sees the need for distancing itself from them, underscoring in the quotation below the problem of 'misplaced alliances' with regard to local migrant associations (Mayo 2007).

They [the local migrant associations] work with their own youth, we have a different strategy. Many of these associations are of course important for the neighbourhood, but they are held back by being dependant financially.... Sometimes they also [the local migrant associations] tend to become alibis for the municipality.... For us that means that they are friends with those in power. (Megafonen interviewee 3; our translation)

The strategy of exit or partial autonomy has been a successful one for subalterns who at different times and in other contexts have acted for greater rights and against discrimination (Burawoy 2003). But with regard to the persistence of an organisation, network or movement and the affirmation of its political orientation, this strategy can place it in rather a precarious position. For Megafonen, this includes the challenge of conducting a more stable form. The challenge for Megafonen is that of achieving stability and gaining acceptance and legitimacy for its vision and activism. Furthermore, as a new form of organisation that in a short period of time has achieved a high degree of public visibility it has been subject to different expectations and contradictory representations – by some praised as future saviours and by others condemned as terrorists in disguise. For Megafonen's young activists, it is not easy to navigate in a landscape that includes the risk of being smothered by well-meaning attention as well as that of prosecution – based on stereotyped perceptions of their actual intentions.

CONCLUDING DISCUSSION

In this chapter we have analysed the emergence of the contemporary Swedish urban justice movement in relation, firstly, to their negative experience of – and later active revulsion from – having participated in activities and issues related to the urban management regime. For the activists of the organisation Megafonen, their lack of trust and frustration in relation to the local participatory practices of urban politics resulted in a strategy of exit from the partnerships of local urban politics. We argue that this experience and their later proclaimed partial autonomy have been decisive factors in their development and that of the broader urban justice movement as political subjects and their success so far in at least destabilising the hegemonic order of subordination and de-politicisation of civil society. This is very far from having automatically led to their stability or to wider acceptance of the movement, but it is at least a more rewarding outcome for those involved than the widespread cynicism and frustration that has characterised local civil society acting within the urban management regime.

The struggle, focusing on the interconnection of place-based livelihoods, emerging modes of civic agency and their wider structural–institutional conditionality, has in other words created a wider space and a new space of resistance for a critical position wherein urban politics are questioned and publically promoted within the national mass media and social media. Using place as the base for social mobilisation highlights, following Chris Pickvance (2003), both symbolic and material aspects in which the struggle for daily livelihood is connected with the need to influence political processes both locally and beyond. The identification with place and the symbolic upgrading of the local is contrasted with what the activists perceive as not being recognised and the limited scope for action in other arenas and on other scales. Thus, in relation to society or the city in general, the suburb is constructed as a material reality with a particular significance when it comes to the social, practical and political. Rather than being isolated strategies of 'neighbourhood nationalism', the movements are constructed around the periphery as a lived and imagined identity.

This kind of knowledge production, and the search for a position from which local activists can influence their life conditions on their own terms, brings what Megafonen has been part of creating close to the Gramscian idea of the war of position, as discussed by Burawoy (2003) in his reflection on contemporary social movements. Even if the position of the broader Swedish urban justice movement, and especially that of Megafonen as an organisation, is marginal in the context of urban politics, and prospects for the future are still unclear, the stability and expansion of the local activism is already grounded through solidary networks, interconnecting local struggles and their shared fundamental values. This may be a promising point of departure for the future, although the need for a longer-term perspective is still a project to be realised.

NOTES

1. This work was supported by the Swedish research council for environment, agricultural sciences and spatial planning (FORMAS), grant number 250-2013-1547.
2. A slogan which has connotations of past Latin American anti-imperialist struggles.
3. 'Harakat' means movement in Arabic.

REFERENCES

Allmendinger, P. and Tewdwr-Jones, M. 2002. 'The Communicative Turn in Urban Planning: Unravelling Paradigmatic, Imperialistic and Moralistic Dimensions'. *Space and Polity* 6(1): 5–24.

Ålund, A. et al. 2013. 'Framing the Mobilization of Migrants in Sweden'. *Migration Letters* 10(3): 277–87.

Ålund, A. and Reichel, I. 2007. 'Civic Agency, Market and Social Inclusion: The Emergence of Informal Economy in the Context of Swedish Associations Established on Ethnic Grounds'. In B. Berggren, B. Likic-Brboric, G. Toksöz and N. Trimikliniotis (eds). *International Migration, Informal Labour and Community: A Challenge for Europe*. Maastricht: Shaker Publishing.

Burawoy, M. 1979. *Manufacturing Consent: Changes in the Labour Process under Monopoly Capitalism*. Chicago: University of Chicago Press.

—— 2003. 'For a Sociological Marxism: The Complementary Convergence of Antonio Gramsci and Karl Polanyi'. *Politics and Society* 31(2): 193–261.

—— 2012. 'The Roots of Domination: Beyond Bourdieu and Gramsci'. *Sociology* 42(2): 187–206.

Castells, M. 1983. *The City and the Grassroots: A Cross-Cultural Theory of Urban Social Movements*. Berkeley: University of California Press.

—— 1996. 'The Reconstruction of Social Meaning in the Space of Flows'. In R.T. LeGates and F. Stout (eds). *The City Reader*. London: Routledge.

Dahlstedt, M. 2009. *Aktiveringens politik: Demokrati och medborgarskap för ett nytt millennium*. Malmö: Liber.

Davis, J.S. 2007. 'The Limits of Partnership: An Exit-Action Strategy for Local Democratic Inclusion'. *Political Studies* 55(4): 779–800.

Ekers, M., et al. 2013. *Gramsci: Space, Nature, Politics*. Chichester: John Wiley.

Elander, I. 2002. 'Partnerships and Urban Governance', *International Social Science Journal* 54(172): 191–204.

Gramsci, A. 1971. *Selections from the Prison Notebooks*, ed. and trans. Q. Hoare and G. Nowell-Smith. London: Lawrence and Wishart.

Hall, S. 1986. 'Gramsci's Relevance for the Study of Race and Ethnicity'. *Journal of Communication Inquiry* 10(2): 5–27.

Harvey, D. 1989. 'From Managerialism to Entrepreneurialism: The Transformation in Urban Governance in Late Capitalism'. *Geografiska Annaler* 71(1): 3–17.

—— 2001. *Spaces of Capital: Towards a Critical Geography*. New York: Routledge.

Kings, L. 2011. *Till det lokalas försvar: Civilsamhället i den urbana periferin*. Lund: Arkiv.

Laclau, E. and Mouffe, C. 1985. *Hegemony and Socialist Strategy: Towards a Radical Democratic Politics*. London: Verso.

Leitner et al. 2007. 'Contesting Urban Futures: Decentering Neoliberalism'. In H. Leitner, J. Peck and E.S. Sheppard (eds). *Contesting Neoliberalism: Urban Frontiers*. New York: Guilford Press.

Massey, D.B. 2005. *For Space*. London: SAGE Publications.

Mayo, P. 2007. 'Gramsci, the Southern Question and the Mediterranean'. *Mediterranean Journal of Educational Studies* 12: 1–17.

Megafonen. 2010. *Att vara ung i Husby*. www.jarvadialogen.se/sites/default/files/documents/Megafonen-rapport-21sep-110.pdf.

—— 2013. *Megafonens politiska program*. http://megafonen.com/om/politiskt-program/.

Nordström Skans, O. and Åslund, O. 2009. *Segregationen i storstäderna*. Stockholm: SNS förlag.

Pickvance, C. 2003. 'From Urban Social Movements to Urban Movements: A Review and Introduction to a Symposium on Urban Movements', *International Journal of Urban and Regional Research* 27(1): 102–9.

Regeringskansliet. 2008. *Överenskommelsen mellan regeringen, idéburna organisationer inom det sociala området och Sveriges Kommuner och Landsting*. Stockholm: Integrations- och jämställdhetsdepartementet.

Schierup, C.-U., Ålund, A. and Kings, L. 2014. 'Reading the Stockholm Riots: A Moment for Social Justice?'. *Race and Class* 55(3): 1–21.

Stockholms stads kommunfullmäktige. 2007. *Utlåtande: Inriktning Järvalyftet*. Dnr 314-1325/2007.

—— 2009. *Utlåtande: Vision Järva 2030*. Dnr 319-2070/2008, 336-2252/2004.

Tahvilzadeh, N. 2015. 'Understanding Participatory Governance Arrangements in Urban Politics: Idealist and Cynical Perspectives on the Politics of Citizen Dialogues in Göteborg, Sweden'. *Urban Research and Practice* 8(2): 238–54.

—— and Kings, L. 2015. 'Under Pressure: The New Politics of Invited Participation amidst Urban Planning Conflicts'. In E. Gualini, J.M. Mourato and M. Allegra (eds). *Conflict in the City: Contested Urban Spaces and Local Democracy*. Berlin: Jovis.

Wijkström, F. 2012. 'Mellan omvandling och omförhandling: civilsamhället i samhällskontraktet'. In F. Wijkström (ed.). *Civilsamhället i samhällskontraktet: En antologi om vad som står på spel*. Stockholm: European Civil Society Press.

—— and Lundström, T. 2002. *Den ideella sektorn: Organisationerna i det civila samhället*. Stockholm: Sober.

12

Spaces of Resistance and Re-Actuality of Gramsci in Refugees' Struggles for Rights? The 'Lampedusa in Hamburg' between Exit and Voice

Susi Meret and Elisabetta Della Corte

BORDERING LIVES, SHAPING RESISTANCE

Restrictive asylum and immigration policies implemented by virtually all European countries and aimed at setting common standards and regulations at EU level (Ette and Faist 2007; Geddes 2000) increasingly prioritise securitisation, control and policing, particularly at Europe's external borders (Betts 2013). Recent developments highlight the fact that Europe's borders stretch to shores across the Mediterranean as control and policing are 'outsourced' to other countries (Betts and Milner 2007). While politicians publicly mourn the hundreds who have drowned in the Mediterranean Sea, as happened on Lampedusa in October 2013, their words and public grief rapidly vanish, giving space to policies that bring more of the same: increased securitisation, surveillance, military patrolling and externalisation of border controls, and a pharisaic humanitarian approach.

The heterogeneity and ubiquity of borderscapes (Balibar 2002; Mezzadra and Nielson 2013) restrain movements and deprive people of their basic rights, but have over the past decade triggered reactions, protests, resistance and militant activism among migrants at local, national and European levels (see for instance Monforte and Dufour 2013; Monforte 2014; Lentin and Moreo 2012). Since at least 2010, collective acts of protest, dissent and civil disobedience by migrants have proliferated across Europe. An array of collective acts, protests and rebellions has surfaced and developed in many spaces: hunger strikes in asylum centres, sit-ins, demonstrations and protest camps at borders, mouth sewing in migrant detention centres, local riots, strikes, walking caravans, etc.

In this chapter we discuss how asylum seekers and refugees organise and voice their claims, and observe how their political struggles for recognition and emancipation create new geographies of resistance. Their episodic, spontaneous, fragmented nature can potentially develop into socially and politically coherent projects and organised acts of dissent. We are also interested in the ways in which processes of collective mobilisation and struggle are perceived and counteracted by the establishment. In particular, we find it helpful to explore alliance formation that can influence the potential for transformation and consolidation within migrants' struggles.

Our empirical observations and reflections started several years ago with a field study on migrants' working conditions and refugee settlements in South Italy, particularly in Calabria. Our observations and reflections in this chapter focus on 'Lampedusa in Hamburg' (LiHH), a group of refugees who passed through Italy to the German city in 2013, giving rise to a social movement that embodies the migrants' international and transnational movements and their fight for rights, organised resistance and struggle to stay. We argue that LiHH's indomitable fight for rights and recognition (Meret and Rasmussen 2014) can be best understood in relation to a Gramscian framework that stems from concepts such as hegemony, dominant relationships of (economic, social, political) power and subalternity. In this framework, contesting practices and forms of rebellion and resistance that Antonio Gramsci saw historically generated by 'subaltern groups' are engendered by and within a context of domination, discipline and submission. This structure is produced and reproduced by the hegemonic powers in our societies. Such power relations existed in Gramsci's time and still do today, as exemplified by LiHH. For us, re-actualising Gramsci means being inspired by his reflections, but also being aware of the limits of his analyses by taking into account similarities and differences between the subalterns' past and contemporary conditions and struggles. We do not entertain any illusion about an imminent migrant-led revolutionary momentum knocking at our doors, ready to radically transform society. Our purpose is rather to observe antagonist forces at play in society: where and how transformative efforts arise, develop, and often also fail in the permanent struggle for economic, social and political hegemony.

GRAMSCI AND THE IMMINENT
POLITICAL PROMISE OF THE SUBALTERN

Gramsci defines subalternity as a condition relating to experiences and positions of subordination and marginalisation in a context of capitalist domination and capitalist power relationships. In this sense, subalternity can exist in different degrees, forms and phases. Thus, the experience of subalternity is primarily a result of our subjective position and existence in and under the capitalist system (see Modonesi 2014: 9–36). Several of Gramsci's reflections on subalternity and the role of the subalterns were developed in close connection with his analyses of hegemony as explaining the underlying socio-economic, cultural and political logics controlling capital production and accumulation. Capitalist hegemony builds on a mix of power, coercive methods and construction of consent. According to Gramsci, power does not only derive from the economic structure and its inner relationships of power; if economy creates the underlying form giving shape to capitalist social relationships, the reproduction of social and political control is guaranteed by the integral function and role played by actors other than the dominant economic class. For example, intellectuals play a significant role in providing, via their authority and activity, non-coercive forms of consent that allow the system to maintain and reproduce the existing economic and socio-political structures (Gramsci 1975: 1930–2, Q4§49), thus reinforcing the dominant classes' power, authority and control over subaltern groups in society (ibid.: 1932, Q12§1). Within this framework, economic, political and civil society do not act separately and autonomously, but rather constitute an organic unity, a 'historic bloc' in society, where the values, ideas and ideology of the dominant class become hegemonic (ibid.: 1931–2, Q8§182). Subaltern groups attempt to challenge these mutually sustaining power structures through their activity and opposition.

Subalternity needs to be understood as a dynamic process of political subjectivation; lived and shared experiences and narratives of subordination can lead to the configuration of autonomous initiatives, potentially featuring counter-hegemonic opportunities. In this framework, power is not an equivalent to the state system and institutional authorities; it can best be understood as a system of relations. Hence, power is dynamic, open to radical transformations and liable to change, and a theory of praxis requires awareness of a situation and a comprehensive understanding of its inherent power relations. It follows that the limits and a radical transformation of capitalism are not – exclusively – intrinsic to the way the capitalist system works, produces and accumulates. This creates the conditions in which a direct intervention from active and organised subjects aiming to transform society must push and make pressure. The faults of capitalist production and accumulation and the periodic and recurrent capitalist crises undermine the system, but do not necessarily defeat the social relationships that keep it alive. A transformation of the power relations needs to arise from the objective conditions of production, but if parochial corporate interests prevail over revolutionary potential, all transformative intents are doomed to failure. It can be argued that this was what Gramsci had directly and personally experienced during the so-called Biennio Rosso (Two Red Years) of 1919–1920 in Turin, characterised by workers' demonstrations, strikes, factory occupations and the workers' self-organisation into factory committees (Gramsci 2013; Spriano 1973).

In this struggle for power, the concepts of hegemony and of the hegemonic bloc represent perhaps Gramsci's most original and central contribution to the political theory of praxis. In particular, Gramsci sees the cultural sphere as an important domain of 'struggle' for the reproduction of the status quo as well as for a new politics and praxis. From this perspective, forms of power and control emanate from the cultural hegemony that the ruling classes exert on the dominated; examples include the educational system, mainstream media and the Church. Through these institutions and influences, subordinated groups learn how to passively accept their condition of subalternity. Within this framework, Gramsci's approach to subalternity is a valid contribution to interpretations of how alternative and antagonist voices can articulate and unfold in present-day neoliberal capitalist societies, motivating self-empowerment, self-organisation strategies and mobilisation among, for instance, asylum seekers, refugees, migrants, unemployed, precariats and other social groups. It also prompts observations of how space, place and society become involved in these transformative and politicising processes (Morton 2007; 2012). In this respect, Gramsci still validly explores the 'imminent potential of the subalterns', while also highlighting the many and manifest difficulties and constraints that can obstruct and restrain these emancipatory projects and concrete transformative initiatives directed at the capitalist system and its ruler(s). Gramsci hints at what we believe can best be termed 'misplaced alliances' (see Mayo in this volume): alliances that subaltern groups may create with dominant groups and elites along the way. These alliances disrupt processes that otherwise might help to configure new collective political identities, featuring antagonist political consciousness, eventually creating new forms of solidarity and cooperation among subalterns, dispossessed and precariats in society. In Gramsci's time, the urbanised industrial working class in Northern Italy seemed to embody the real vanguard of the political and social transformation of society. However, Gramsci also realised that this process would not succeed without alliances with and support from other groups, such as the peasants in the Italian South. Some of his early articles in the journal *Ordine Nuovo* noted his reflections about the need to connect the activities and struggles of the communist workers in Turin with other subalterns in the South (Gramsci 2013: 76–80). Gramsci wanted to reconnect through the struggle the cleavage between city and countryside, between subalterns of the North and the South, between peasants in the South and industrial workers in the North, whom he undoubtedly saw as the 'battering ram' in this process for emancipation. The workers, many having originally emigrated from the South, would free the peasants of the South. Later, Gramsci would credit the Southern peasants with a more active and dynamic role in the struggle for emancipation and social justice.

Gramsci's political militancy matured in the industrialising Turin, where he was in direct contact with the workers and with many immigrants from the Italian South, among them many Sardinians like himself. Here, in the Turin years, Gramsci started to give form and content to his ideas about the close relationship between theory and praxis: for example the struggle between proletariat and industrialists, the soviet, self-organisation and autonomy of the workers in the factories (Gramsci 2013). He also addressed the building of alliances and support, which he linked closely to his reflections on hegemony. The theme of alliances appears several times in Gramsci's writings: alliances between states, between social classes, subaltern groups, intellectuals. In these alliances Gramsci also sees the potential energy that would give shape to a common resistance against the hegemonic order, through pressure generated from the margins, as in the October revolution. Gramsci reminds us of the importance of knowing and understanding the complexities of history and the socio-political settings and opportunities, but also about the difference between beneficial alliances and alliances that are best avoided. History is full of examples of good and bad alliances, e.g., the Ciompi revolt, the Paris Commune, the Turin Biennio Rosso. Thus, the subject of alliances becomes central in Gramsci's analysis of and reflections on political theory and praxis, particularly after the failures of the Biennio Rosso, followed by the quick rise and consolidation of fascism.

Subaltern groups consist of large bodies of marginalised people at the periphery of society who are denied access to rights and to positions of power. Gramsci's approach is perhaps best expressed as a reconnection of philosophy and experience, and a re-evaluation of how and what ordinary men and women think, feel, and endure, and how their everyday lives can give rise to collective efforts that can erode the boundaries of power. The marginalised are deprived of voice in socially available hegemonic narratives and discourses; the majority is excluded from actively participating in dominant positions in institutions, society, politics, culture and media. Because of their exclusion and marginalisation they are disadvantaged if they want to develop a critical understanding of the nature of power relations that create and reproduce their subalternity. Achieving political awareness and agency therefore takes a central place in the development of what Gramsci refers to as the subalterns' integral 'autonomy' (Gramsci 1975: 1934, Q25§4). The 'dispossessed', the *lumpenproletariat* at the very margins of history, often 'constitute one of the most spontaneously and radically revolutionary forces' (Fanon 1967: 103). In his writings, Gramsci developed ideas for a method of studying the history and development of the subalterns, emphasising the importance of mapping their undertakings, developments and 'reactions' (Gramsci 1975: 1931–2, Q8§195; 1975: 1934, Q25§2; §4; §5). An aspect to consider is that Gramsci's context was represented by pre- and post-unity Italian society that for him was defined by the historical dynamics and social relationships that accompanied the Italian Risorgimento. The Italian national question was in this sense paradigmatic of a unification wanted and realised 'from above' and imposed on the people 'below', in which the Italian language had been declared 'national' by decree. The unification had allowed the dominant classes to consolidate their position, merging a country without the support of a mass movement and actively excluding subaltern groups from participating in developing a post-unitary society.

In 'Some Aspects of the Southern Question' (Gramsci 1966), Gramsci observes the extreme disintegration and fragmentation dividing Italian society and hindering the potential for radical socio-political transformations that would contest and challenge the status quo. In his view, this contrasted with the 'perpetual ferment' he observed among the peasants in the South, whose efforts were nevertheless incapable of achieving an organised and politically coherent expression (Gramsci 1966). Gramsci underlines the need to overcome these constraints, foreseeing the creation of an alliance between peasants and the urbanised working class in the North. At the same time, he describes the many difficulties posed by the hegemony of the ruling classes and elites, whose dominant values, positions and ideas have permeated all levels of society. Economics, politics and culture work together; it would thus be reductive to underestimate 'the function of the intellectuals in the life of the state' (Gramsci 1975: 1932, Q12§1).

> Every social group, coming into existence on the original terrain of an essential function in the world of economic production, creates together with itself, organically, one or more strata of intellectuals which give it homogeneity and an awareness of its own function not only in the economic but also in the social and political fields. (Ibid.)

This makes it even more difficult for subalterns to avoid misplaced alliances with social classes and groups whose real intent is to neutralise and contain any strong transformative energy. Within this frame, Gramsci attributed Italian intellectuals of his time a central function in the reproduction of a culture, language and politics controlled and imposed from above. Intellectuals reproduce and maintain conditions and experiences of inferiority, passivity and dependence, particularly among subalterns; Gramsci speaks about the role of 'intellectuals': '[t]hose who reproduce and maintain conditions and experiences for inferiority, passivity and dependence among subalterns' (Gramsci 1966: 45–8). Gramsci significantly emphasised the 'intellectual bloc' as one reactionary force that had contributed to blocking the realisation of the necessary social and economic transformations by reinforcing and reproducing paradigms of 'Southern backwardness' and hegemonic narratives on the 'congenital human barbarity of the Southern man' (ibid.: 39).

Intellectuals' failure to support the subalterns and engage on their behalf is one obstacle to a deeper political awareness among the latter and to progress:

> The history of the subaltern classes is necessarily fragmented and episodic; in the activity of these classes there is a tendency towards unification, albeit in provisional stages, but this is the least conspicuous aspect and it manifests only when victory is secured. (Gramsci 1975: 1934, Q25§2)

Gramsci's interest in the history and development of subaltern groups also had an analytical and methodological character. Green (2011) describes Gramsci's approach as threefold: (1) to produce a methodology of subaltern historiography; (2) to create a history of the subaltern groups that would oppose a history based upon the making of the dominant classes and elites; (3) to define a political strategy of transformation (praxis), based upon the subaltern groups' historical development, experience and initiatives. In this vein, and perhaps contrasting the role of the subaltern in postcolonial studies (Morris 2010; Srivastava and Bhattacharya 2012), subalternity is interpreted simultaneously as a condition, as an experience and as a process. Being subaltern means being 'subordinate to capital', and subalternity is therefore to varying extents 'part of our daily experience and cannot ... be simply wished out of [our] existence' (Holloway 2014, xiv). Gramsci foreshadows in the initiative and activity of the subaltern groups the presence of features of autonomy that can arise and trigger socio-political transformation through a conscious and collective political programme and action.

THE 'LAMPEDUSA IN HAMBURG': 'WE ARE HERE, WE STAY'

Background and Beginnings of a Refugee Social Movement

Both similarities and differences can be found between Gramsci's approach to subalternity and the concrete case of the refugee movement 'Lampedusa in Hamburg' (LiHH).

LiHH was formed in Hamburg at the end of March 2013 and soon became a prominent group of self-organised refugees openly and visibly fighting for their rights. LiHH asked for a political group solution, for support for their right to stay in Hamburg and for freedom of movement in Europe. For more than two years now, and with shifting phases of activity, they have struggled hard to mobilise support and to inform public opinion about the conditions asylum seekers, refugees and migrants face in Europe. Their struggle for rights addresses issues of denied rights, equal treatment, freedom of movement, and claims for decent living and working conditions in Germany and Europe. Their mobilisation must be seen in the context of increasingly restrictive asylum and immigration laws and regulations in Europe that first attempt to stop people from arriving by militarising and policing Europe's external frontiers, and then deny basic civil and human rights to those who do manage to get through.

LiHH has succeeded in creating a major, well-organised, politically motivated refugee movement of historically unprecedented dimensions, with a sizeable impact on Hamburg society and an appeal that manifested itself in broad civil society support, solidarity and direct engagement in the struggle for rights (interviews with Karawane activists 2013 and 2014; migration lawyer Björn Stehn 2014, Hamburg Ver.di leader Peter Bremme 2014). Despite this, the movement has – at least at the time of writing – not made any headway in terms of political recognition of the claims the group has advanced since its formation in early Spring 2013 (interview with Asuquo Udo 2015; Meret and Della Corte 2014; Meret and Jørgensen 2014). As emphasised by migration lawyer Björn Stehn:

> It was a difficult and big decision by the majority of the [Lampedusa] group to say we want a political decision, we want authorities here in Hamburg to take responsibility, seeing that something is wrong in the system ... and it is not by individual solutions this can be achieved, but by facing the situation of these 350 people, right here. This might very

well ... start a discussion on the Dublin situation and on how to change it fundamentally. It is great they still continue with this fight.

This translation of the local to the national and European levels suggests the opportunity struggles have to pursue, developing locally but aiming for coalitions and solidarity with other subaltern groups nationally and transnationally in order to gain strength and consolidate. Yet these efforts are continuously challenged by dominant groups, and their achievements can be demonstrated only 'once the historical circle is completed' (Gramsci 1975: 1934, Q25§2). However, as Gramsci also observed, when subaltern groups are successful, they are in a continuous 'alarmed state of defence' (Gramsci 1975: 1934, Q25§2).

Asuquo Udo (interview 2014), one of the refugees who founded the LiHH movement, recollects in two interviews how forming the group represented a political and civil refusal to comply with unjust laws and rules dictated by a system expecting subordination and passivity. Building political awareness among the members of LiHH was part of a process that, for some of them, had matured while they were asylum seekers in Italy. Most of them entered Europe in March 2011 when they were forced to flee the war in Libya. Thousands of civilians died and the war provoked the involuntary exodus of more than 50,000 Africans who had to flee to Europe for survival. The consequences of that war are still producing instability, chaos and violence in Libya, which migrants continue to escape.

In 2011, the Italian government declared (yet) another immigration emergency, the Emergency North Africa, which ended in February 2013 with general institutional and societal disinterest in Italy and abroad, and the refugees were sent to sleep on the streets. Italian authorities issued them travel papers, unofficially prompting them to leave for other countries.

Refugees from Emergency North Africa materialised in Hamburg, where they lived in shelters provided by the city winter programme until it closed in mid-April. During a rally organised by the local branch of the Karawane für die Rechte der Flütlinche und MigrantInnen (Caravan for the Rights of Refugees and Migrants), refugees and demonstrators met, in what turned out to be a crucial encounter. The group describes itself as a 'network of individuals, groups and organisations of refugees, migrants and Germans based on anti-imperialism and antiracism, ... engaged in the struggle for socio-political justice, equality and respect for the fundamental human rights of everyone' (Karawane 2011). In LiHH's start-up and subsequent phases, Karawane was a principal supporter and a key provider of knowledge about the socio-political situation in Hamburg and Germany, with solid experience in migrants' self-organisation and self-empowerment. It was also a valuable link with The Voice Refugee Forum (www.thevoiceforum.org), a group of self-organised refugees formed in Germany during the 1990s. Unlike other groups and organisations, Karawane is committed to encouraging self-empowerment and autonomy of asylum seekers, refugees and migrants, especially at the local level, where it struggles against an increasingly discriminatory environment due to ever stricter immigration and asylum laws in Germany that limit movement and curtail basic rights.

Also the independent trade union Ver.di (about 2.1 million members) contributed actively to LiHH's political mobilisation. The Ver.di Hamburg branch registered 185 LiHH refugees as non-paying members. The aim was later to formalise and discuss at regional (*Landesbezirke*) and then national level the role of Ver.di in relation to immigrant workers arriving from outside the EU, who were not registered as unemployed but had papers issued by an EU country (interview with Bremme 2014). For Ver.di Hamburg this was in line with the ongoing work on non-unionised, paperless and highly exploited migrant work in Germany and other countries, e.g. in care and domestic migrant work. While the members of the Hamburg section supported the initiative, it was condemned by the union's national leadership, which argued that 'this was not [a Ver.di] domain'. Internal disagreements about LiHH membership were eventually resolved when the workers' council approved a motion in favour. In practice, LiHH membership of Ver.di is symbolic, although it did widen the support in the initial phase of the LiHH struggle. However, membership does not give refugees any concrete advantage in obtaining a labour permit, nor did it prompt further support from other established trade unions and labour organisations. In fact, the limited number of LiHH unionised members contributed to a differentiation between original and later members of the group, and thus to internal divisions and unfortunate hierarchisation. Still, the union and particularly its youth section remain among the few institutional actors still overtly supporting the group.

LiHH was not formed in a socio-political vacuum; the movement was supported by onsite organisations, advocacy groups and networks, all of which have a rich history in Hamburg. The city was historically a fertile location for social movements in the 1960s and 1970s, and in the 1980s and 1990s it continued as a thriving urban space for autonomous, anti-imperialist, anti-nuclear and anti-racist movements (e.g. Geronimo 2012). The Hamburg movements are also characterised by their early and local fight for the rights to the city and the struggle against municipal plans to control urban development, particularly in profitable areas for the capitalist housing market, such as the waterfront St Pauli district, historically the inner-city working-class area. During the 1980s, the squatting in houses in the Hafenstraße and other buildings in the St Pauli area became a symbol of popular resistance. Empty buildings earmarked by the municipality for demolition as part of the city's 'urban renewal' plan were occupied, and evictions were prevented via a broad mobilisation of the resident population. This historical legacy continues to influence younger generations of Hamburgers too, encouraging political activism and advocacy. Despite internal divisions and political divergences, this history has benefitted the support for and mobilisation of migrants started by LiHH.

Struggles

In May 2013, LiHH and its supporters asked for an open dialogue with the local authorities about Libyan refugees living in the streets of Hamburg. An open letter to the assembly and mayor of Hamburg drafted by the group outlined their first political statements and claims.[1] Hundreds rallied for and with LiHH from the central train station to the Hamburg Rathaus, where LiHH wanted to meet local authorities and SPD mayor Olaf Scholtz. Asuquo Udo recalls the day (interview 2014):

It was so chaotic; the policemen were looming at us coming. We were chanting ... A policeman asked where we came from and who sent us there. I said, 'We are the Lampedusa in Hamburg and we want to see the mayor ... or you can kill us.'

The refugees were intimidated and reminded that they were infringing the law by violating the City Hall space (a member of Karawane was later charged). The authorities threatened them with immediate deportation (interviews with Asuquo Udo 2014, 2015). They went away with the promise of an early meeting with the mayor, but the promised meeting never took place.

Attempts to set up three tents in a parking lot near the central train station and the SPD headquarters were brutally stopped by the police. The group was authorised to set up an information tent at Steindamm, to be used only as an information and meeting point. The tent, which is open 24 hours a day every day, has since become the main gathering place for LiHH members, activists, supporters and newcomers. Of course, this did not resolve LiHH's immediate and vital need to find shelter, support and the means to survive and remain in Hamburg.

The events outlined above show that the surprise factor – the rapid, sudden and unexpected actions of LiHH and its supporters – distinguished the initial phases of the refugee movement. This strategy provoked increasing attention and awareness in civil society. Hamburgers and Germans became interested in the history, background and claims advanced by this new group of refugees. Public opinion was outraged by the manifest law-and-order reaction of the Hamburg Senate, which refused dialogue and instructed the police to carry out racial ID profiling. On their side, LiHH refugees strived to reclaim visibility within the public space, highlighting their condition as subalterns and non-citizens in Hamburg and Europe, and refusing to comply with attempts to silence and repress their protests.

Powerful slogans and political messages distinguished the way LiHH communicated in the public sphere, like the motto 'Wir bleiben hier!' (We are here to stay!) combined with a logo featuring a clenched raised fist (symbolising the struggle) rising out of a pair of curved flukes (an anchor, symbolising LiHH's will to stay and Hamburg's admiralty coat of arms). The slogans 'Wir sind mehr' (We are more), 'We want freedom' and 'We fight for our rights' signalled the awareness that many other refugees and asylum seekers live in distress and without rights.

During the first year, LiHH opted for strong, explicit political messages, articulating their existence as subalterns deprived of rights, recognition and voice. The 'We' form often used in their slogans signals the collective, shared nature of the struggle and the need for a common fight as a group united with other subalterns fighting in similar struggles for emancipation in the rest of Germany and Europe. At the same time, LiHH's slogans and banners reminded public opinion that they are survivors of a war and thus about the responsibilities of the West to the African continent due to past and present colonialism. Some of the group's banners between May 2013 and March 2014 – 'Wir haben nicht den NATO-krieg in Libyen überlebt um auf Hamburg's Straβen zu sterben!' (We did not survive the NATO war in Libya to die on the streets of Hamburg) and 'We are here because you destroy our countries' – express the highly politicised space and a strong and developing political awareness; this also contributed to defining a clear-cut strategy, with claims supported collectively and in solidarity with other groups and networks.

The Church Enters the Scene

The St Pauli Church opened its doors to about 70 or 80 LiHH refugees at the beginning of June 2013, many of whom were sleeping in the streets.

The church got considerable press coverage, although Erlöserkirche and the St Georg's mosque also took about 30 refugees, and Hamburgers in St Pauli and other neighbourhoods privately housed many more.

The church's involvement was crucial at a time of urgent need for shelter and sustenance. Furthermore, the St Pauli Church played an important role in mobilising the St Pauli community and many of the churchgoers who otherwise would not have taken action for LiHH. However, the way the alliance with the church developed raises questions about the efficacy and consequences of alliances more generally and about the way these, as Gramsci argues, can eventually evolve into misplaced alliances. The partnership with the church became a misplaced alliance when church authorities realised that helping the group implied supporting their voice and their political fight and claim for rights. This inevitably required backing up demands for a concrete political transformation of asylum and immigration policies and for a critical stand against dominant power relationships and dominant elites. Historically, however, the role of the Church has been to preserve rather than to subvert the status quo, and in the struggle against hegemonic powers it is unlikely that church authorities and elites will commit themselves to profound political and societal transformations.

The proposal of the Federal Senate of Hamburg in late October concerning LiHH's requests exemplifies the point. The Hamburg Senate proposed that the refugees accept the status of *Duldung* (toleration status). This is an asylum application made on an individual basis and the applicants often spend years waiting for a residence permit, with restrictions on freedom of movement, work and living conditions. For the LiHH refugees, the *Duldung* means restarting the asylum procedure and renouncing the papers issued by Italy. In the probable case that the German authorities will refuse asylum, a deportation procedure to the country of origin is begun. But even more obviously, the Senate's 'offer' declined any recognition of LiHH as a group and featured a motivation to split the group up. The majority of LiHH members declined it, suggesting alternative approaches and reiterating their desire to open a dialogue.[2] The Hamburg Senate and the bishopric entered political negotiations and reached an agreement after a huge demonstration on 2 November 2013 that gathered between 10,000 and 20,000 protesters on the streets of Hamburg, undoubtedly one of the biggest mobilisations in the city. This worried local and national authorities, who were urged to act against the increasing and broadening support for the group and did so by directly approaching the Church authorities, side-stepping the refugees. LiHH replied with an open letter:

[I]t's about all of us, it is about a group recognition ... The proposals of the Senate result in more months and years of uncertainty for us. They want us to go through individual residence procedures. We do not see this as a constructive solution, but as a game on time to later get rid of us individually ... At the same time the leaders of the Nordkirche have accepted the Senate's proposal over our heads and advertised it to the public ... The Nordkirche may have its reasons ... [b]ut then it would be fair and decent to say this as well ... The former speaker of the refugees sleeping in the church of St Pauli ... accepted the offer, because the pressure was too large. Some others ... because they were told there was no alternative. (www.thevoiceforum.org/node/3396)

A St Pauli Church activist explained that it was a question of pragmatism versus utopianism: 'One thing is to intervene when the situation shows that certain policies do not work, another is to claim a radical change of asylum policies'; he observed that 'the humanitarian act is also a political act' (interview with St Pauli Church activist, 2013). However, he admitted that the nature of the power relationship between Church and institutional powers also dictates political and economic constraints. The Church's action works mainly within a humanitarian framework, driven by the logic of individualisation rather than that of politicisation within the asylum issue (see also Monforte 2014: 9). The alliance with the Church lasted until it became clear during the November public demonstration that it was virtually impossible to keep the two approaches separate, and events were unescapably developing towards a politicisation of the issue and direct confrontation with the authorities. Asuquo Udo claims that the Church acted in accordance with a deep-seated colonial mentality, 'dictating people what to do and how to do it ... and this divided the group' (interview with Udo, 2015). Several of the LiHH members who refused the *Duldung* expressed regret and resentment towards the way Church elites took things into their own hands without consulting LiHH. Besides, several other serious logistic and material problems affected events: Church representatives continued to comment on LiHH refugees in the mainstream press, giving their own version of the facts[3] and accepting economic donations to LiHH by 'school groups, restaurateurs, the supporters of FC St Pauli football club, doctors, entrepreneurs, clubs, artists, theatre people ... A total of 250000 euros were donated'.[4] Despite a huge mobilisation of resources, volunteers and goodwill, LiHH's main political claims and collective demands were disclaimed, and decisions were made on its behalf. LiHH's potential and collective resistance and dissent against hegemonic practices were destabilised; the Church ultimately performed its organic role within the bloc of hegemonic powers (Gramsci 1975: 1930–2, Q5§7; Q20; 1975: 1934–5, Q5§3).

LiHH Today: From a Political Framing to an Uncertain Framing?

The people who came from Libya were forced to leave, they were pushed out and they did not have a chance. This became clear to Hamburgers and Germans only with the LiHH. Until then for the German way of thinking this was not a point to be considered: 'Why did you leave your own country ... ?' This question is something the majority of Germans simply do not wish to ask nor think about asking. A question which they think it does not make sense to pose. (Interview with Stehn, 2014)

The power, strength and unambiguousness of LiHH's political messages contributed to the group's organisation, mobilisation and cohesiveness. While great efforts were made to inform public opinion about the refugees' history and the complex reasons behind their migration, the group coherently and soundly kept asking for a group solution. This stance has from the start challenged the practice of tackling asylum normatively, primarily from an individual basis. Also, LiHH introduced a new set of questions to the asylum debate: how should the movements of people with papers from a European country in crisis that cannot grant their rights be dealt with? As formulated in one LiHH document:

to be constructive ... would mean to accept that we are not guaranteed the appropriate refugee protection in Italy, as a result of the failure of the Dublin II-system and that in Hamburg the refugees ... should not be made to pay for this failure ... we call §23 of the Resident Act, which ... offers a solution to our existential crisis.

Paragraph 23 of the Foreign Law Resident Act was for a relatively long period the concrete path for a political group solution. The feasibility of this proposal is endorsed by previous cases, e.g. the 1980s case of the Roma minority from former Yugoslavia, Bulgaria and Rumania, who had lived in Germany under a status of 'toleration' (*geduldet*) and achieved residence permits via a political decision. For LiHH this would require defining the group based on its members' status as refugees of the war in Libya with a humanitarian permit from Italy and a subsequent arrival date in Hamburg within a specific period. In this approach, the issue of 'one group, one solution' would automatically generate a discussion about this group in relation to a broader dialogue surrounding the Dublin regulations. Within this framework, the initiative to mobilise locally opens windows of opportunity and visibility, thus endorsing what Gramsci suggested as the need to unite struggles in order to overcome fragmentation by strengthening broader forms of solidarity among subalterns.

Today, LiHH's struggle seems positional rather than a struggle of movement and cohesiveness. As observed by Asuquo Udo, '[M]ost people are not ready for a long-term political movement and to fight back. They get tired to be waiting for decisions from political parties and some of the supporters were weak and unused to long-term solutions' (interview 2015). The question remains: to what extent it is still feasible to wait for political and institutional solutions, particularly in light of past experiences? Also, recent developments in Hamburg and Berlin suggest that the voice of the people is being drowned out by more vocal but less united advocacy and support groups: the potent 'We' used by LiHH in the early days is now often mediated by 'They'. These developments also seem to have strongly depoliticised LiHH in the public sphere, as reflected in the virtual replacement of most of the group's political slogans with slogans prompting 'Never mind the papers', 'Paper to all, or papers to none', which arguably decontextualise and decontentualise LiHH's spaces of struggle and resistance, electing more abstract rights to the city as core emancipating factors.

SOME FINAL REFLECTIONS

In this chapter we have mapped some of the elements defining contemporary migrants' struggles for rights, their attempt to organise, mobilise and emancipate within the Gramscian frame of hegemonic power relationships, subalternity and domination. The case of LiHH is in our view significant since it indicates how struggles emerge and move geographically and physically from the outside to the core of Europe, to our cities and neighbourhoods. Contemporary migration flows are unique mainly in the sense that they are triggered by an accelerating process of globalisation and capitalist accumulation that has reached the limits of the world market. The consequences and effects of forced migrations are long-term and permanent, and thus the attempts to multiply and fortify borders are doomed to failure. Migration flows are signs of the capitalist system's weakness and fragility, not of its supremacy.

Gramsci would probably have suggested that dissent and rebellion against the hegemony of the capitalist power can today be found among the migrants who made it into Europe, particularly after their arrival, when they discover the real face of capitalism. Among these migrants we find architects of new political subjectivities and collective identities. These collective acts emerge in those spaces where migrants live or to which they are often confined to (transit spaces, detention and deportation camps, borders, urban spaces). In these spaces, migrants start to organise, mobilise and verbalise the rights to which the majority of the population is entitled – to live, work, move freely and stay. The rise of this migrant organic intellectuality finds allies and solidarity not just among advocacy groups, but also in civil society, which understands the common sense of their claims.

Gramsci's reflections on good and bad alliances are in this context useful for mapping the opportunities and limits in realising change. It is by knowing who we are fighting for and who we are fighting against that we can make progress in the struggle.

NOTES

1. http://lampedusa-hamburg.info//page/21/
2. http://yorkshirestpauli.com/2013/10/31/statement-from-lampedusa-in-hamburg/
3. www.eimsbuetteler-nachrichten.de/ehrung-fuer-st-pauli-pastoren/; http://st.pauli-news.de/lampedusa-fluechtlinge-andreas-darf-endlich-arbeiten/
4. www.neues-deutschland.de/artikel/934379.gotteserfahrung-hilfe.html

REFERENCES

Balibar, E. 2002. 'What Is a Border?' In *Politics and the Other*. London: Verso.
Betts, A. 2013. *Survival Migration: Failed Governance and the Crisis of Displacement*. New York: Cornell University Press.
—— and Milner, J. 2007. 'The Externalisation of EU Asylum Policy: The Position of African States'. DIIS Brief. Danish Institute for International Studies. December.
Ette, A. and Faist, T. (eds). 2007. *The Europeanization of National Policies and Politics of Immigration*. London: Palgrave Macmillan: 3–31.
Fanon, F. 1967. *The Wretched of the Earth*. Harmondsworth: Penguin.
Geddes, A. 2000. *Immigration and European Integration: Towards Fortress Europe?* Manchester: Manchester University Press.
Geronimo. 2012. *Fire and Flames: A History of the German Autonomist Movement*. Oakland, CA: PM Press.
Gramsci, A. 1966. *La questione meridionale*, Rome: EditoriRiuniti.
—— (2013 [1964]). *Nel tempo della lotta e lettere (1929–1937)*. Milano: ilSaggiatore.
—— (2014 [1975]). *Quaderni del Carcere: Edizione Critica dell'Instituto Gramsci*, ed. V. Gerratana (4 vols). Turin: Einaudi.
Green, M.E. 2011. 'Gramsci Cannot Speak'. In M.E. Green (ed.). *Rethinking Gramsci*. Abingdon: Routledge.
Holloway, J. 2014. 'Foreword: Sounds in the Undergrowth'. In M. Modonesi. *Subalternity, Antagonism, Autonomy*. London: Pluto Press.

Karawane [Karawane Für die Rechte der Flüchtninge und MigrantInnen]. 2011. *Contribution to the Second Assembly of the International Migrants Alliance.* http://thecaravan.org/ima2011

Lentin, R. and Moreo, E. (eds). 2012. *Migrant Activism and Integration from Below in Ireland.* New York: Palgrave.

Meret, S. and Della Corte, E. 2014. 'Between Exit and Voice: Refugees' Stories from Lampedusa to Hamburg'. *Open Democracy.* www.opendemocracy.net/can-europe-make-it/susi-meret-elisabetta-della-corte/between-exit-and-voice-refugees-stories-from-la

—— and Jørgensen, M.B. 2014. 'From Lampedusa to Hamburg: Time to Open the Gates!' *ROAR Magazine.* http://roarmag.org/2014/07/lampedusa-hamburg-europe-refugees/).

—— and Rasmussen, J.B. 2014. "We are here to stay and we won't shut up': Lampedusa in Hamburg's indomitable fight for rights'. *Open Democracy.* https://www.opendemocracy.net/can-europe-make-it/susi-meret-jeppe-blumensaat-rasmussen/

Mezzadra, S. and Nielson, N. 2013. *Border as Method, or, the Multiplication of Labor.* Durham, NC, and London: Duke University Press.

Modonesi, M. 2014. *Subalternity, Antagonism, Autonomy.* London: Pluto Press.

Monforte, P. 2014. *Europeanizing Contention.* New York and Oxford: Berghahn Books.

—— and Dufour, P. 2013. 'Comparing the Protests of Undocumented Migrants beyond Contexts: Collective Actions as Acts of Emancipation'. *European Political Science Review* 1(1): 83–104.

Morris, R.C. (ed.). 2010. *Can the Subaltern Speak?* New York: Columbia University Press.

Morton, A.D. 2007. *Unravelling Gramsci.* London: Pluto Press.

—— 2012. 'Traveling with Gramsci'. In M. Ekers et al. (eds). *Gramsci: Space, Nature, Politics.* Oxford: Wiley-Blackwell.

Spriano, P. 1973. *L'ordine Nuovo e i consigli di fabbrica.* Turin: PBE Einaudi.

Srivastava, N. and Bhattacharya, B. (eds). 2012. *The Postcolonial Gramsci.* New York: Routledge.

Interviews

St Pauli Church activist: 18 November 2013.

Karawane activists: 19 November 2013 and 1 February 2014.

Asuquo Udo: 1 February 2014 and 11 April 2015 (by Waldemar Diener).

Björn Stehn: 3 March 2014.

Peter Bremme: 6 October 2014.

Conclusion

13

Against Pessimism:
A Time and Space for Solidarity

Óscar García Agustín and Martin Bak Jørgensen

What does Antonio Gramsci (or a Gramscian perspective) have to say about immigration? How would such a perspective analyse the protests and struggles taking place in civil society? And what is the potential for emerging alliances and forms of solidarity for social and political transformation? These questions have guided this entire volume and our attempts to explain the relevance of thinking migration and civil society alliances from a Gramscian perspective. Before highlighting some of these aspects, we would like to reflect on the need to rethink Gramsci, and particularly 'Some Aspects of the Southern Question', and why this need has emerged. Briefly, we can summarise it in terms of two dichotomies: optimism versus pessimism, and solidarity (or alliances) versus borders.

BEYOND PESSIMISM AND BORDERS

From a nation state perspective the current situation in Europe does not inspire optimism. The response of European countries to the financial and economic crisis has not led to a new deal but to a hard readjustment of capitalism, increasing the precarisation of society and the dismantling of welfare systems. The few political options (such as Syriza in Greece or Podemos in Spain) that have emerged with the aim of directly contesting the politics of austerity are facing enormous difficulties when they take on power – as seen in the asymmetrical negotiations between the Greek government and the Troika. Furthermore, far right-wing populist parties are gaining space in the political and public debate and are assuming roles as main opponents of the threat of globalisation (or Europeanisation) to national sovereignty.

European migration policies are not faring much better. They are being tightened on all dimensions: control of undocumented immigrants and refugees, quotas for asylum seekers, and discrimination against second- and even third-generation immigrants. Until very recently it was difficult to find exceptions to these policies in the political spectrum in Europe (particularly among parties with government responsibility); such policies and the hegemonic discourse on migration are hardly challenged at all.

Let us take the example of the 'Five years strategy for asylum and immigration', presented by the British government in 2005 and significantly entitled 'Controlling our Borders: Making Migration Work for Britain'. In its foreword the then prime minister Tony Blair stated the intention of controlling immigrants both beyond the borders (preventing their 'illegal' entry) and within them (detecting those who abuse the system). The control measures were not aimed at everyone but targeted a select group (people without the skills needed by the British economy). The objective consisted in reinforcing the neoliberal system and reducing migrants to mere commodities:

> We will replace out-dated and confusing rules with a clear and modern points system so we only allow into Britain the people and skills our economy needs. Those who want to settle permanently in the United Kingdom will have to show they bring long-term benefits to our country. (Blair 2005)

The financial and economic crisis has only worsened the situation, bringing more unemployment among national workers and increasing immigration from East and South European countries.

So there is no reason for optimism? This is where Gramsci's warning about the fatal consequences of pessimism becomes essential. At the fifth anniversary of the Communist International, Gramsci considered the pessimism that was spreading among the most able and responsible militants to be a great danger, because it implied political passivity, intellectual slumber and scepticism about the future. He wondered how the Communist Party's project would differ from that of the Socialist Party 'if we also knew how to work and were only actively optimistic in periods when the cows were plump, when the situation was favourable?' (Gramsci 1924). Gramsci strongly emphasises the risks of pessimism and the importance of reclaiming optimism in times when not everything is working out well. Note that Gramsci refers to 'active' optimism and not to a facile or naive optimism that progress will happen or every change is possible. We see this active optimism as being rather close to the sociology of emergence, which focuses on possibility. Boaventura de Sousa Santos, who identified the sociology of emergence, claims that 'the Not Yet [the future] has meaning (as possibility), but no direction, for it can end either in hope or disaster' (de Sousa Santos 2004: 241).

All the chapters in this book share the same impetus to identify existing experiences within civil society that challenge the current hegemonic order and can be seen as signs of future experiences. Pessimism due to neoliberal policies in Europe must not lead us to refuse active optimism and ignore what is already happening in civil society and how it can influence the future. Since the chapters of this book were written, further examples have arisen of popular mobilisation against the hegemonic system. The chapters included here themselves show glimpses of developments to come.

The second argument highlighted above relates to Gramsci's reflections about social alliances among different classes with the purpose of challenging hegemony and the reproduction of the system of exploitation. This implies that solidarity becomes a key for this process, which must be understood as mutually constitutive for the actors involved. This is important, first, because alliances are not only tactical and temporary: they also shape common interests, demands and identities; and second, because solidarity acquires a political dimension among equal actors rather than reflecting an asymmetry between those who 'possess' the ability to be solidary and those who need their solidarity. In the case of migration, solidarity is a political relation which strongly opposes the imposition of borders.

Étienne Balibar (2006) shows that borders are not geographical, but historical institutions, established politically and legally. The function attributed to the state, as reflected above in Blair's words, of controlling citizens' movements and activities is due to the 'right of ownership' of territory and the fixation of its borders. The challenge is thus to democratise the borders which define who is a citizen (whether he or she is a political subject with corresponding rights). The transnational scale is denied (or reduced to its economic dimension) and the national one, through the state, maintains its power to decide. This is what Saskia Sassen (1996) explains when she claims that economic globalisation denationalises the national economy while immigration renationalises politics, meaning political borders.

In addition to their historical dimension, borders are subjective, since the idea of a border is interiorised and internalised so that individuals represent 'their place in the world to themselves ... by tracing in their imagination impenetrable borders between groups to which they belong or by subjectively appropriating borders assigned to them from on high, peacefully or otherwise' (Balibar 2004: 8). Borders reproduce divisions – majority versus minority, native versus foreigner – usually stigmatising the minority and the foreigner. However, their institutionalisation as social or subjective processes always reflects the confrontation of two notions of people: as *ethos* (an imagined community of membership and affiliation) and as *demos* (a collective subject of representation, decision making and rights). This opposition, which can also be understood as the tension between the democratic universality of human rights and the particular national belonging, shows the importance of challenging borders (and their function of constituting exclusionary communities) through solidarity (and its capacity to shape a larger political community).

We focus on alliances between civil society and immigration because this is not only a matter of questioning discriminatory or racist practices but above all about transforming democracy. It implies an understanding of citizenship not as a right derived from belonging to a community fixed by borders, but as a democratic practice derived from participating in the community's decision making which is not reducible to borders. Solidarity is essential in this expansion of community as it deepens democracy.

Furthermore, as pointed out by Andy Robinson (2011), migrant struggles 'prefigure the struggles of the precariat, firstly because migration tests the limits of capitalist control, and secondly because the precariousness of migrant labour threatens to spread to the entire workforce'. As we claimed in the introductory chapter, the way in which a social and political system treats immigrants and refugees also sets the standard for the rest of society. This adds an important dimension: the sense of class, or of *class-in-the-making* as Guy Standing (2011) characterises the precariat. Migrants are dirctly exposed to the control of borders and economic precariousness and they suffer like all workers, although more, because labour conditions are deteriorating. There is no need to create another border which separates workers from migrant workers based on an imagined community. Also here alliances prove relevant for sharing experiences of exploitation and resistance. Solidarities become essential in constituting a broader political community (by contesting the culturalisation of politics based on essentialised identities) and a new emerging class (by sharing struggles and experiences of exploitation due to the intensification of neoliberal policies and the politics of austerity). Shaping alliances on this basis allows us to appreciate, with active optimism, the ongoing struggles and to prefigure the possibilities they open up for the future.

ALLIANCES BETWEEN CIVIL SOCIETY AND IMMIGRANTS

The chapters of this volume present a variety of dimensions which we find useful in considering the question of social alliances. While Gramsci's Southern question concerned the alliance between proletariat and peasants, we now have to consider which actors might play similar roles, from which economic and social positions and with what aim. We have identified different fields of political action which share the possibility of developing alliances between civil society and immigrants based on a continuous process of precarisation, social control and repression that affects wider social segments.

The key point, present throughout the book, is that we place the immigrant in a broader context of spaces and acts of resistance. As argued above, migrant struggles can be said to prefigure the struggles of the 'precariat' (see also Mezzadra 2007). The Italian Frassanito Network, which was among the first precarity movements to organise transnationally, made a similar diagnosis of migrants sharing all the forms of precarisation and depreciation:

> To talk about migrants' labor means to talk about a general tendency of labor to mobility, to diversity, to deep changes, which is already affecting although with different degrees of intensity all workers. Because of the possible extension of these conditions we speak of a political centrality of migrants' work. (2005: IV)

This points to the centrality of migrants not only in the analysis of neoliberal globalisation, but also for political strategies to create a more just and inclusive society. The conditions of migrant workers show us what might become conditions for all workers, in terms of both labour-market rights and social rights. The retrenchment of the existing social rights in the European welfare states shows that exclusion may not be steered by categories of citizenship alone. Migration trajectories take many forms, but irregular migrants arriving legally by air who end up overstaying their visas and enter the clandestine labour market, irregular migrants arriving in Europe via transit hubs in Northern Africa, Turkey and Eastern Europe, and Eastern European labour migrants, each in their different way shows how immigrant struggles are fought in arenas beyond the immigration system.

Their conditions differ of course. It is difficult to compare the living conditions of the Lampedusa group in Hamburg discussed in Meret and Della Corte's chapter with the Eastern European labour migrants discussed by Agustín and Jørgensen. Nevertheless, both analyses emphasise the role of the immigrant as a political actor in relation to the labour market and beyond. Immigrant struggles become connected to the restructuring of and exclusion from the labour market and the welfare state as well as to the struggle against the European asylum system and in support of human rights (see chapters by Apitzsch and Cox).

Most of the struggles analysed in this volume are in essence about the 'rights to have rights' and how to claim these rights. We can also claim – following Balibar and others – that the transformation of citizenship and precarisation have created social and political stratification which leaves migrants in what Balibar (2004) termed a 'new Apartheid in Europe' that entails a broader erosion of social and work rights and institutionalises precarity (Schierup, Hansen and Castles 2006). Not much has changed over the decade since Balibar wrote these words. The continuing economic crisis in Europe has caused a massive and devastating development of austerity policies, which have deepened inequalities, and a political crisis, which has resulted in political disillusion all across Europe.

Whereas much of the literature on the precariat (not least in Standing's popular conception of the term; Standing 2011) tends to victimise immigrants and downplay their capacity for social change and for acting on their own behalf, the contributions in this volume have, in different ways, done the opposite. Our point of departure comes closer to Michael Hardt and Antonio Negri, who characterised migrants as 'a special category within the multitude that embodies revolutionary potential' (2004). The contributions in this book reflect on this potential and on the circumstances under which it can be released and show how migrants in some situations can be the decisive factor in the development of social struggle (as in the case of the Gezi uprising; see Şenses and Özcan, this volume).

Gramsci took a similar position decades ago. His work centred on the characteristics and potential of the subalterns. He sought to understand and outline the autonomy of the subaltern, which could potentially trigger social and political transformation through collective political action. Being subaltern not only implies resistance against restrictive immigration and integration regimes; on a more fundamental level it means being 'subordinate to capital' (Modonesi 2014). Understanding the potential of the subaltern thereby offers an entrance point for understanding the contestation against global neoliberalism.

Another important aspect is that the focus on alliances offers a much-needed research perspective on how they are constitutive not only for subjectivities but also for processes of becoming common. Immigrants are often deprived of agency and placed 'outside' the mobilisations taking place across Europe. This book has demonstrated how immigrants are included in these alliances and how the alliances may construct a new common ground for struggle and for developing political alternatives. As already emphasised, we have discussed immigrants as political actors with the capacity to enter and influence struggles for social change and equality. The contributions have also emphasised how immigrants constitute subaltern groups engaged in struggles in different social spaces (especially Mellino; Featherstone; Kings, Ålund and Tahvilzadeh; Meret and Della Corte). It has been important for this book to broaden the perspective of the struggles and investigate how immigrants collectively unite with other groups in civil society. Connecting immigrants with the precariat opens up the scope of the analysis and the potential of the struggles.

The social, political and economic forces driving neoliberal capitalism are global (Sklair 2002), and therefore the spatial organisation of the struggle needs to be expanded. The category of the subaltern in its essence disturbs methodological nationalism, since subalterns cannot be constrained to any particular national context. Immigrants are characterised by transnationalism and by contesting national borders – sometimes on an everyday basis. Alliances not only strengthen the basis for making claims, they also expand the limits of the political analysis. As shown here (Hyland and Munck; Agustín and Jørgensen), alliances between immigrants and civil society organisations (in these two chapters, trade unions) have produced a joint diagnosis of the problem at stake: austerity policies, not immigrants, are responsible for the decline of welfare state models. Alliance building between natives and immigrants is one of the few possible steps to take to avoid the formation of national blocs which impede solidarity beyond borders. Gramsci's writings, as shown throughout the volume, offer tools to analyse alliance building that go beyond the national–popular. Just as importantly, he also offers reflections on misplaced alliances (see the chapters by Boothman; Mayo; Agustín and Jørgensen; Meret and Della Corte), meaning alliances which impede social and political transformation or are directly detrimental to equality and should be avoided.

This last issue leads us to a third significant aspect: understanding that social struggles on different scales are important in terms of enhancing new forms of solidarity and avoiding misplaced alliances. Cooperation between civil society and immigrants strengthens social bonds and allows for the constitution of new subjectivities, as processes of precarisation are constructed and shared at different levels. To contest neoliberal globalisation satisfactorily, the different scales of resistance must be interconnected through an identification of the mechanisms both of exclusion and of the constitution of internal and external borders. Internationalisation entails a more efficient approach to migration policies and prevents mystification of national communities that defend welfare against the arrival of (worker) migrants.

All in all the Gramscian approach to rethinking solidarity beyond borders and the emergent alliances between civil society and immigrants allow us not only to understand the current situation better but also to conceive alternative scenarios. The Gramscian re-reading is also a political project of exploring the possibilities of resisting and constituting alliances which are capable of questioning the dominant neoliberal system and moving beyond it. The contributions in this book represent another step in this direction.

A PATH FORWARD: LOOKING BACK TO FIND THE STEPS TOWARDS FUTURE ACTION

Social struggles to democratise political borders or simply to democratise democracy can only succeed if they organise against the hegemonic order. When Gramsci witnessed the development of the workers' struggles in the FIAT factories during the Biennio Rosso (the two red years), he addressed the workshop delegates through the journal *L'Ordine Nuovo*. He believed in self-organisation, in the capacity of the working class to educate itself, and in the possibility of achieving socialist democracy through factory councils. These would end domination by showing that workers are capable of *doing things themselves* without management by the owners. Self-organisation becomes a mode of emancipation against capitalist slavery:

The more the productive human forces acquire consciousness, liberate themselves and freely organise themselves by emancipating themselves from the slavery to which capitalism would have liked to condemn them forever, the better does their mode of utilisation become – a man will always work better than a slave. (Gramsci 2000: 90)

The delegates play a fundamental role because there are so many unorganised elements; they would show these (unorganised) people 'that a worker's strength lives wholly in union and solidarity' (ibid. 2000: 91). Now it is clear that the factory is not the only place of production, but the strength of union and solidarity is still the same and emancipation can only come from human awareness of its productive force. Daouda Thiam, an immigrant living in Madrid and member of an association of undocumented immigrants, shows how the conflict goes beyond that between workers and owners and indeed takes place between people and politicians: 'Unity of people scares them [politicians], solidarity scares them, and companionship among citizens scares them. Why? They should be pleased! Because if we all want democracy, facing together problems and supporting each other, they should like unity but it does not happen' (in Fuhem 2013).

That unity, the alliance between civil society and immigrants, still needs to be built. So far, we have seen only the contours of this unity. Its potential to challenge the political borders and expand democracy is huge. Thus, our proposal is to rethink Gramsci, or rethink, with him, solidarity without borders, as a first indispensable step towards emancipation and a fairer world. The need for rethinking politics and social relations in terms of solidarity remains even clearer in the light of the lessons taught by the refugee crisis in Europe.

THE EUROPE OF SOLIDARITY
OR THE EUROPE OF AUSTERITY?

We used the example of the refugee crisis in Europe to introduce the importance of solidarity beyond borders at the beginning of the book. Solidarity has become the core for reviving a declining European project. However, we identify three different processes which show the complexity of the situation and how there is a need for articulating emerging solidarities in order to offer a genuine alternative. These three processes are social solidarity, institutional solidarity and anti-solidarity. The first two imply actions beyond national borders, whilst the last consists in the reinforcement of national borders.

Social solidarity, as already presented in the introductory chapter, refers to the practices by civil societies (from rallies to the creation of communicative spaces with refugees) which are struggling for fair policies of admission and integration of refugees. This movement has been supported by the majority of the population both in countries such as Germany which have adopted a more favourable approach to refugees (despite increasing numbers) and in countries which follow more antagonistic politics, such as Denmark. The lack of a common European policy in this area and the defensive attitude taken by most of the EU member states have been strongly contested by questioning the arbitrariness of national borders and their unjust exclusionary role.

Institutional solidarity refers mainly to the way in which EU institutions react to strengthened cooperation between member states. The EU commissioner of migration and home affairs, Dimitris Avramopoulos, announced that the EU was finally able to develop solidarity in practice. He added that this will stop solidarity being used merely as a slogan and that instead it will become a reality. Herein lies a recognition of the absence of any real solidarity within European practices, as well as the need for solidarity as the basis of the EU. This statement entails several contradictions since it is mostly understood in terms of the relocation of refugees by the member states and it contradicts the strategy of border control which had characterised EU policies so far. In presenting a more humanitarian approach (sometimes in conflict with the positions held by nation states opposed to the relocation of refugees), the European Commission can absorb the critique made by the grassroots solidarity movement and neutralise the movement by integrating its proposals into the EU migration framework. In a similar way to transformism, as defined by Gramsci, institutional solidarity as formulated by the EU might find a way of increasing its hegemony by appropriating and dismantling the solidarity movement.

Anti-solidarity is an evident risk which entails the reinforcement of exclusionary national identities opposed to any form of migration or subjectivity perceived as the 'other'. It opens up the possibility of an increasing space for xenophobia and racism. This can be seen not only in the strength of extreme right movements, such as Pegida, but also in the positions assumed by some political leaders. The Hungarian prime minister, Viktor Orban, declared his rejection of European 'invitations' to migrants on the grounds of defending Christian culture against Muslims. Besides the conflicts between states, this kind of reaction makes any practice of solidarity and positive change in the politics of migration and refugees difficult.

The challenges of combating anti-solidarity movements and governments and of avoiding a redefinition of the hegemonic system are huge. However, solidarities are being developed in multiple places and the consciousness of moving beyond borders becomes clearer than ever. The financial and economic crisis is now followed by a refugee crisis. This requires that the crisis must be rethought in economic terms too, and not just in isolation as the EU seems to think. In the end it comes down to a choice between the Europe of solidarity and the Europe of austerity. Opting for the latter would disguise the political crisis Europe is facing and take attention away from how a fair and just Europe can be developed.

REFERENCES

Balibar, É. 2004. *We, the People of Europe? Reflections on Transnational Citizenship.* Princeton: Princeton University Press.

—— 2006. 'Fronteras del mundo, fronteras de la política'. *Alteridades* 15(30): 87–96.

Blair, T. 2005. 'Foreword by Prime Minister'. In 'Controlling our Borders: Making Migration Work for Britain'. Five year strategy for asylum and immigration. London: TSO.

Frassanito Network 2005. *Precarious, Precarization, Precariat?* Original link is defunct – the text can now be found at: http://05.diskursfestival.de/pdf/symposium_4.en.pdf

Fuhem, E. 2013. 'Entrevista a Daouda Thiam, miembro de la Asociación de Sin Papeles de Madrid'. *Boletín Ecos* 24: 1–7.

Gramsci, A. 1924. *Against Pessimism*. www.marxists.org/archive/gramsci/1924/03/pessimism.htm

—— 2000. *The Antonio Gramsci Reader: Selected Writings, 1916–1935*, ed. D. Forgacs. New York: New York University Press.

Hardt, M. and Negri, A. 2004. *Multitude: War and Democracy in the Age of Empire*. Penguin Books.

Mezzadra, S. 2007. 'Living in Transition: Toward a Heterolingual Theory of the Multitude'. http://roundtable.kein.org/node/653

Modonesi, M. 2014. *Subalternity, Antagonism, Autonomy*. London: Pluto Press.

Robinson, A. 2011. 'The Precariat and the Cuts: Reconstructing Autonomy'. *Rebel*. www.rebelnet.gr/articles/view/The-Precariat-and-the-Cuts--Reconstructing-Autonom/original

Sousa Santos, B. de 2004. 'The World Social Forum: Toward a Counter-Hegemonic Globalisation (Part 1)'. In Jaid Sen, Anita Anand, Arturo Escobar and Peter Waterman (eds). *World Social Forum: Challenging Empires*. New Delhi: Viveka: 235–45.

Sassen, S. 1996. *Losing Control? Sovereignty in an Age of Globalization*. New York: Columbia University Press.

Schierup, C.-U., Hansen, P. and Castles, S. 2006. *Migration, Citizenship, and the European Welfare State: A European Dilemma*. Oxford: Oxford University Press.

Sklair, L. 2002. 'Democracy and the Transnational Capitalist Class', *The Annals* 581 (May), American Academy of Political and Social Science.

Standing, G. 2011. *The Precariat: The New Dangerous Class*. London: Bloomsbury.

Contributors

Óscar García Agustín is associate professor at the Department of Culture and Global Studies at Aalborg University, Denmark. With Christian Ydesen he has co-edited the book *Post-Crisis Perspectives: The Common and its Powers* (Peter Lang, 2013). He is author of *Discurso y autonomía zapatista* (Peter Lang, 2013) and *Sociology of Discourse: From Institutions to Social Change* (John Benjamins, 2015).

Aleksandra Ålund is professor at REMESO, the Institute for Research on Migration, Ethnicity and Society at Linköping University. She has published widely in Swedish, English and other languages on international migration and ethnicity, identity, culture, gender, and youth and social movements.

Ursula Apitzsch is professor of political science and sociology in the field of culture and development at the Goethe University of Frankfurt am Main. She has published broadly in the fields of the history of ideas and of migration and ethnicity, with special regard to the analysis of gender and biography. She is the editor (together with Peter Kammerer and Aldo Natoli) of the German critical edition of the correspondence of Antonio Gramsci during his prison years. The most recent volume of this edition appeared under the title *Antonio Gramsci Briefe III: Briefwechsel mit Tatjana Schucht 1931–1935* (Argument-Verlag, 2014).

Derek Boothman has published widely on Gramsci and edited and translated *Further Selections from the Prison Notebooks of Antonio Gramsci* (reprinted Delhi, 2014) and a wide selection of Gramsci's pre-prison letters (*A Great and Terrible World*, London and Chicago 2014). He is working on an English language edition of his Italian book on Gramsci and translatability and, with Adam D. Morton, on a full English version of the Italian Communist Party's important 'Lyon theses' of 1926. He is a member of Rome's Gramsci Seminar, having contributed to their volumes, and currently edits the online International Gramsci Journal.

Laurence Cox is director of the MA in Community Education, Equality and Social Activism at the National University of Ireland Maynooth and co-editor of the open-access social movements journal *Interface*. He is co-author of *We Make Our Own History: Marxism and Social Movements in the Twilight of Neoliberalism* (Pluto Press, 2014) and co-editor of *Understanding European Movements, Marxism and Social Movements* (Routledge, 2013) and *Silence Would Be Treason: Last Writings of Ken Saro-Wiwa* (CODESRIA, 2013). He has been involved in a wide range of social movements for over a quarter of a century.

Elisabetta Della Corte is a researcher and lecturer at the Department of Social and Political Sciences at the University of Calabria. Her research involves two key areas: labour mobility and the discipline of the industrial labour force, and the relationship between science, technology and society. Her qualitative research on migrants and on automobile and dock workers' labour conditions has been conducted in South Italy, England and Argentina. Her recent publications include 'Gramsci: migración, ejército industrial de reserva y valorización del capital en los países del sur', *Taller* (second series), vol.3, no.4, 2014.

David Featherstone is senior lecturer in human geography at the University of Glasgow. He has a long-standing interest in Gramsci's political thought, particularly in relation to solidarity and uneven geographies. He is the author of *Resistance, Space and Political Identities: The Making of Counter-Global Networks* (Wiley, 2011), *Solidarity: Hidden Histories and Geographies of Internationalism* (Zed Books, 2012) and co-editor (with Joe Painter) of *Spatial Politics: Essays for Doreen Massey* (Wiley, 2013). He is on the editorial board of the journal *Soundings*.

Mary Hyland is a senior researcher in the Office of Civic Engagement at Dublin City University. Her research is in the interconnected areas of industrial relations and labour migration. She has previously worked in public policy and political communications consultancy. Among her most recent publications are 'Trade Unions and Migration: A Case for New Organisational Approaches', in Schierup et al. (eds) *Migration, Precarity and Global Governance: Challenges and Opportunities for Labour* (Oxford University Press, 2014) and 'Migration, Regional Integration and Social Transformation: A North–South Comparative Approach' (with R. Munck), *Global Social Policy Journal*, vol.13, no.3, 2013.

Martin Bak Jørgensen is associate professor at CoMID at the Department for Culture and Global Studies, Aalborg University, Denmark. He works within the fields of sociology, political sociology and political science. He has co-edited the special issue 'Civil Society and Immigration: New Ways of Democratic Transformation' (*Migration Letters*, 2013) and co-edited the book *Politics of Dissent* (Peter Lang, 2015). He has published articles in journals such as *Internal Migration Review*, *Critical Sociology*, *Journal of International Migration and Integration* and *British Journal of International Politics*. He is currently working on a special issue of *Critical Sociology* on migration and precarity.

Lisa Kings received her Ph.D. in sociology from Stockholm University in collaboration with Södertörn University in 2011, with a thesis on civil mobilisation in the Swedish urban periphery. She is currently a senior lecturer in social work at Södertörn University. Her research interests include urban theory, civil society and social movements, and studies of everyday life.

Peter Mayo is professor and head of the Department of Arts, Open Communities and Adult Education, University of Malta. His *Gramsci, Freire and Adult Education* (Zed Books, 1999) was republished in seven languages. His latest books include *Hegemony and Education under Neoliberalism: Insights from Gramsci* (Routledge, 2015), *Lorenzo Milani, the School of Barbiana and the Struggle for Social Justice* (co-authored, Peter Lang, 2014) and *International Critical Pedagogy Reader* (co-edited, Routledge, 2015). He edits a book series, 'International Issues in Adult Education', for Sense Publishers and co-edits another, 'Postcolonial Studies in Education', for Palgrave–Macmillan. He also co-edits the journal, *Postcolonial Directions in Education*.

Miguel Mellino is lecturer in postcolonial studies and interethnic relationships at the University of Naples 'L'Orientale'. He is the author of *Stuart Hall: Cultura, razza e potere* (Ombre Corte, 2015), *Cittadinanze Postcoloniali: Appartenenze, razza e razzismo in Italia e in Europa* (Carocci, 2012), *La Cultura e il Potere: Conversazione sui Cultural Studies* (2006, with Stuart Hall). He is the editor of the Italian translations of Frantz Fanon's *Pour la Révolution Africaine: Ecrit Politiques* (2006) and *L'an V de la révolution algérienne* (2006), and Césaire's *Discours sur le colonialisme* (2010).

Susi Meret is an activist and an associate professor at the Department of Culture and Global Studies, Aalborg University, Denmark. She is affiliated with the Centre for the Study of Migration and Diversity (CoMID). Her main areas of research are radical right-wing populism and extremism, migrant struggles and social movements.

Ronaldo Munck has developed a broad set of overlapping interests under the general rubric of political sociology and more recently the globalisation problematic. His work on Latin America culminated in *Rethinking Latin America: Development, Hegemony and Social Transformation* (2013), which brought a Gramscian perspective to bear on current politics. Another constant theme is the sociology of work and labour movements from a broad comparative orientation, culminating in the widely cited *Labour and Globalisation: The New 'Great Transformation'* (2002). His studies of globalisation include *Globalisation and Social Exclusion: A Transformationalist Perspective* (2005) and *Globalisation and Contestation: The Great Counter-Movement* (2006).

Kıvanç Özcan is a Ph.D. candidate in the Department of International Relations at Middle East Technical University. His research interests are Turkish foreign policy, social movements and Middle East studies. In his graduate study he focused on the Islamic Movement in Israel. He has published in *Haaretz, Turkish Policy Quarterly, Radikal2, Doğudan, Altyazı* and *GWU-International Affairs Review*.

Nazlı Şenses is an assistant professor at the Department of Political Science and International Relations at Başkent University, Turkey. Her research interests are comparative politics, politics of civil society, international migration, and politics of irregular migration. Her Ph.D. dissertation analysed the irregular migration policies of Greece, Spain and Turkey from a comparative perspective with a specific focus on the role of civil society actors. She has co-authored publications on the Europeanisation of irregular migration polices of Turkey and the role of civil society organisations in the field of migration in Turkey.

Nazem Tahvilzadeh holds a Ph.D. in public administration and is a research fellow at the Multicultural Centre in Botkyrka. He is affiliated to REMESO, Department of Social and Welfare Studies, Linköping University. He conducts research on urban politics and governance, political participation and social movements.

Index

methodological nationalism 152, 229
Mezzadra, Sandro 157
middle/working class alliances 47–50,
    52, 53–4, 81–3
Miglioli, Guido 84
migrants
  as activists 104–5, 182–3
    in Germany 204, 210–19
    in Ireland 121, 123–9
    in Sweden 186–7
    in Turkey 50–2
  alliances with civil society 226–30
    anti-austerity 11, 16–17, 169,
      181–3
    anti-development 45, 47, 49–52,
      186–7
    refugee rights 37–8, 211–13, 215
  Gramsci on culturalist view of 23–9
  misplaced alliances 214–17
  neoliberalism, role of in 139–41,
    224
  refugee crisis 3–4, 37–8, 136–9,
    204, 210–19
  resistance to 150–64, 176–9
  unions and 98–110, 157–64, 176–9,
    212
misplaced alliances 12–14, 31–2,
    177–8, 194–5, 206, 209, 214–17
  nationalism and 120–1, 122–3,
    135–6, 150–64
modernity, differences in degrees of
    25–7
Morton, Adam David 15, 17
Mouffe, Chantal 8, 188
MRCI (Migrant Rights' Centre
    Ireland) 103–4, 105–6, 107
mushroom pickers' rights campaign
    103–4, 105
mystification 164n2, 189–90

narratives. See framing and ideology
National Union of Seamen (UK) 177,
    178–9
nationalism and hegemony 135–6,
    140–1, 152–6, 229
  in Denmark 156–62

to divide working class 152–6,
    176–9
  in Ireland 115–16, 120–4
Negri, Antonio 228
neoliberalism
  austerity and 179–81, 223–5
  authoritarian, in Turkey 41, 42–5,
    47
  impact of 151
  migrants, role of in 139–41, 224
  nationalism and 121
  as postcolonial capitalism 71–3
  see also austerity; capitalism;
    financial crisis
Nielson, Brett 157
Norway 158

Occupy movement 8, 182–3
O'Connor, Jack 103, 108
Okmeydanı (Istanbul) 50–1, 52
Öktem, Kerem 43
Ong, Ahiwa 72
Orban, Viktor 232
Ordine Nuovo Group (Turin group)
    30, 31, 32, 34–5, 85

Palestine 138
Pavee Point (Ireland) 126
PCI (Communist Party of Italy) 84,
    170–2, 174
peasants
  alliances with proletariat 7–11,
    80–1, 96, 116–18, 141–3, 154–6
  cohesion, lack of 14, 80–1, 83–4,
    208
  peasant parties 85
Perri, Francesco 24
pessimism and passivity 224
Pickvance, Chris 200
Pisani, Maria 147n10
place, and urban justice 187, 200
political discourse. See framing and
    ideology
postcolonial Gramsci 58–73
precarity class 16, 42–3, 153, 228
  see also low-pay workers